PRAISE FOR *THE MESSY MIDDLE*

"This is required reading for founders. Experienced entrepreneurs all know this period Scott refers to as 'the messy middle' and a few of us have worked our way out of it, but this is the first time I've seen an expert—both as a founder and as an investor—break down in such detail just how to endure, optimize, and make it through."

—ALEXIS OHANIAN, cofounder of Initialized Capital and Reddit

"Scott Belsky is a master of generous work worth doing. *The Messy Middle* will help you see that you have more control than you dare to admit, and the ability to make a difference if you care enough."

—SETH GODIN, author of *Linchpin*

"Building a lasting business is 1 percent idea and 99 percent resilience. *The Messy Middle* details the unglamorous but essential lessons every founder needs to learn."

—JENNIFER HYMAN, cofounder and CEO, Rent The Runway

"Starting a new venture is like jumping off a cliff and sewing a parachute on the way down. This book is the parachute."

—JOE GEBBIA, cofounder and chief product officer, Airbnb

"Having been through the ups and downs of the messy middle many times, it's critical to understand the challenges ahead. This insightful book empowers you to approach them head-on. Belsky's powerful tool kit, based on hard-earned experiences, is an essential guide to building a compelling product, revolutionizing an organization, or growing your leadership abilities."

—TONY FADELL, inventor of the iPod, coinventor of the iPhone,
founder and former CEO of Nest, principal at Future Shape

THE MESSY MIDDLE

THE MESSY MIDDLE

Finding Your Way Through the Hardest and

Most Crucial Part of Any Bold Venture

•••••

SCOTT BELSKY

PORTFOLIO • PENGUIN

Portfolio/Penguin
An imprint of Penguin Random House LLC
375 Hudson Street
New York, New York 10014

Most Portfolio books are available at a discount when purchased in quantity for sales promotions or corporate use. Special editions, which include personalized covers, excerpts, and corporate imprints, can be created when purchased in large quantities. For more information, please call (212) 572-2232 or email specialmarkets @penguinrandomhouse.com. Your local bookstore can also assist with discounted bulk purchases using the Penguin Random House corporate Business-to-Business program. For assistance in locating a participating retailer, email B2B@penguinrandomhouse.com.

ISBN: 9780735218079 (hardcover)
ISBN: 9780735218086 (ebook)
ISBN: 9780525540380 (international edition)

Printed in the United States of America
1   3   5   7   9   10   8   6   4   2

BOOK DESIGN BY AMANDA DEWEY. COVER DESIGN BY RAEWYN BRANDON.

With gratitude to Erica, Chloe, and Miles
for helping me make the most of my middle.

CONTENTS

•••••

ENDURE

THE MESSY MIDDLE

THE MESSY MIDDLE

The journey of creating something from nothing is a volatile one. While we love talking about starts and finishes, the middle miles are more important, seldom discussed, and wildly misunderstood.

You survive the middle by enduring the valleys, and you thrive by optimizing the peaks. You will find your way only by reconciling what you learn from others with what you discover on your own. You'll get lost. At times, you'll lose hope. But if you stay curious and self-aware, your intuition and conviction will be your compass.

While difficult to withstand and tempting to rush, the middle contains all the discoveries that build your capacity. The middle is messy, but it yields the unexpected bounty that makes all the difference.

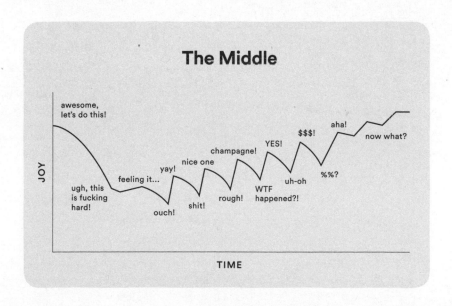

INTRODUCTION

When I set off to write a book about the middle of bold projects and entrepreneurial journeys, you might expect that I started with my own. Having endured five years "bootstrapping" my own business and facing my fair share of challenges as an entrepreneur, this was my chance to share everything I learned. But I couldn't remember anything. It wasn't memory loss—it was just all a big blur.

So I turned to the common source of answers to random ponderings these days: my phone. I flicked through years of random photos taken, back to the middle years of building Behance, my first company, hoping to jog my memory. I founded Behance in August 2006 and signed the documents to be acquired by Adobe in December 2012, so I made my way to 2009 on my phone, the absolute middle of my middle. Thousands of thumbnail images showed screenshots taken on my phone of website errors, bad copy, social media mentions of us and competitors, and various product ideas and changes. These screenshots spanned years and, in some months, outnumbered my photos. The sheer volume of them reminded me of falling asleep every night scrutinizing our product, anxiously looking for something but never knowing exactly what.

I also found another type of screenshot—customer messages and feedback. I remember capturing these insights to share with my team, but also I needed them. I wanted to hold on to and extend some early semblance of reward and significance at a time when nobody seemed to care.

Scrolling a little farther, I saw a reunion with college friends and then a special moment from my honeymoon during which my wife and I encountered elephants in Thailand. I was surprised to see how strained my smile looked. The memory rushed back, and I recalled the tension of wanting to relish this once-in-a-lifetime moment while realizing I had a team at home running on fumes and I was just a few months away from missing payroll. Being away from the team felt utterly irresponsible, and this burden followed me everywhere. Scrolling farther now, I stumbled on a team event at a restaurant kitchen where we all cooked a meal together—we couldn't afford it, but I knew the only thing that mattered was keeping the team together. As I scrolled through our team pics, I was struck by how close and dedicated we became despite the circumstances and our differences. When the odds are against you, without revenue or margin to protect you, teams and relationships are different. It's not work; it's survival and self-discovery.

These photos reminded me just how exhausted and uncertain I had been—fueled by my relentless determination to make something awesome. Perhaps, in such periods of struggle, our preoccupations and emotions take up so much mind share that the events themselves become a blur? Or perhaps we don't remember the middle because we don't want to?

· · · · ·

You're probably reading this book because you're about to embark on a massive journey— or are already trekking through the middle of one. Whether you're a writer, start-up entrepreneur, big-company innovator, or an artist, you share many of the same hopes and fears.

You might be working within a multinational company, a small nonprofit, a new creative studio, or on your own. No matter what it is you're trying to create or transform, the myth of a successful journey is that it starts with the excitement of an idea, followed by a ton of hardship, and then a gradual and linear rise to the finish line.

But no extraordinary journey is linear. The notion of having a bold idea and making consistent incremental progress is impossible. Those seeking a linear journey with less instability can still be successful, but they often struggle to create anything new.

In reality, the middle is extraordinarily volatile—a continual sequence of ups and downs, expansions and contractions. Once the honeymoon period of starting a new journey dissipates, reality hits you. Hard. You feel lost and then you find a new direction; you make progress and then you stumble.

Every advance reveals a new shortcoming. Major upsets give rise to new realizations

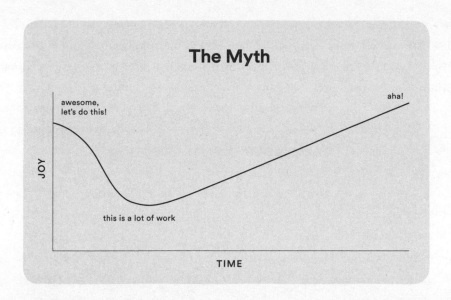

that lead to breakthroughs in progress. At best, you move two steps forward, one step back—at worst, you realize you've been walking the wrong path entirely for months. This is what that journey actually looks like.

I've come to call the journey of creation one of "relative joy." Your job is to endure the lows and optimize the highs in order to achieve a positive slope within the jaggedness of real

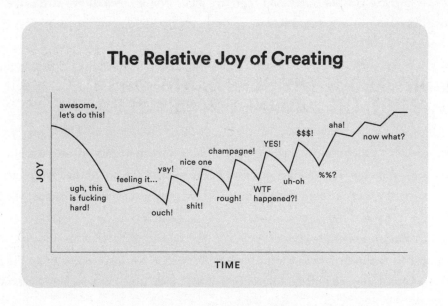

life—where, on average, every low is less low than the one before it, and every subsequent high is a little higher. In the moment, you can see only the uphill or downhill in front of your nose, but over time, you come to recognize that there is a median that keeps you moving forward in the right direction.

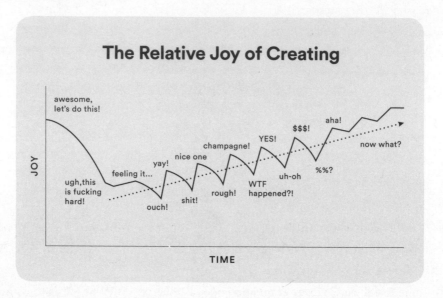

The volatility of this tug-of-war is hard to stomach. You must pay less attention to the day-to-day incremental advances and more on achieving an overall positive slope. And that's entirely determined by how you navigate the messy middle.

IT'S NOT ABOUT THE START AND FINISH, IT'S ABOUT THE JOURNEY IN BETWEEN.

There are just a handful of thrilling and treacherous moments as an entrepreneur. Most of them happen at the start or finish of the journey (or one of the restarts or false finishes along the way). They're all we talk about, but they reveal very little about the journey itself.

We love talking about the starts.

The start is romantic. We love talking about it because it is inspiring without the complication of substance and strife. Conception is an adrenaline rush fueled by grandiose visions paired with naivety. You're inspired by a destination and have no idea how you'll get there. The solution in your mind's eye is rose colored. You don't yet know how the cards are stacked against you.

In this case, ignorance is not only bliss but also enables you to dream up solutions at the edge of reason. You're untethered.

We also love talking about finishes.

We imagine the rush, the exhaustion, and the pride of finally making it. This is what we dream of throughout the struggle of creating, isn't it? How relieved we'll be when the workout is finally over. A "finish" can happen at different parts of a journey: Launching a product. Publishing a book. Raising money. Reaching a key milestone. Being acquired. Shutting down. Going public. Closing the quarter. The press likes to write these headlines and we like to read them. But the superlatives obscure the fact that they are simply abstract mile markers. We learn very little from these moments despite their gravity.

One of the strangest parts of being an entrepreneur is being part of a community obsessed with starts and finishes. Investors tend to be interested only in starts (when they're able to invest) and finishes (when they get a return). Similarly, stories tend to be written only about public inflections. Even between entrepreneurs or big company CEOs, what is intended as a network of support becomes an echo chamber. Nobody wants to talk about their self-doubts and the insecurities that fuel them. Every business is "going great" until it fails. The bumps along the road are endured in isolation. The majority of the journey itself is unchronicled because it is unappealing and too revealing.

As a young entrepreneur, the focus on starts and finishes always bothered me. As a manager, I sought to hire people who were seeking a journey rather than a particular outcome. The more immersed I became in the start-up world, the more I wanted to operate without sensationalism. When the journey feels gritty and real, your potential becomes more tangible.

Then I went to work as an investor with dozens of entrepreneurs at all different stages of company building, where it became clear how destructive the spotlight on starts and finishes really is. As we celebrate the success of others, we're liable to draw lessons from a drastically edited story that excludes the middle. What's in the middle? Nothing headline-worthy yet everything important. Your war with self-doubt, a roller coaster of incremental successes and failures, bouts of the mundane, and sheer anonymity.

The middle is seldom recounted and all blends together in a blur of exhaustion. We're left with shallow versions of the truth, edited for egos and sound bites. Success is misattributed to the moments we wish to remember rather than those we choose to forget. Worst of all, when everyone else around us perpetuates the myth of a straightforward progression from start to finish, we come to expect that our journey is meant to look the same. We're left with the misconception that a successful journey is logical. But it never is. Don't let others' stories pervert your understanding of the journey. Emulating someone else's story is following a playbook without all the pages in the middle.

We don't talk about the messy middle because we're not proud of the turbulence of our own making and the actions we took out of despair. Sharing our challenges shakes our egos. And finally, the middle of a journey doesn't make for good headlines.

The middle isn't pretty, but it is illuminating and full of essential realizations to finish whatever it is you set out to start. It's time we start talking about it.

$$\bullet\bullet\bullet\bullet\bullet$$

The journey to create a product or service is reflected in the outcome in ways you may not even expect. It matters, tremendously.

Consider a product you use in your everyday life—is it simple or complicated? Too many features or just the functionality you need? Is it enjoyable or is it a chore? The experience of using someone else's creation comes from the path the creator took to make it. It is not the plastic, metal, or pixels that make a successful product or service. Rather, it is the thoughtfulness and tough choices made by the makers—the team dynamic, the perseverance, the organizational design (and redesigns), the constraints, the battles fought, and the values that governed the path taken.

This book is about mining every insight from the volatility and the depths of despair to improve your team, product, and self. This book is also intended to help you survive the creative process when you lack any sense of traction, recognition, or significance.

A few years ago I set out to understand what founders and other leaders of bold new projects do throughout their journeys that they don't talk about. I sought to chronicle the pain-management techniques, the tactics for optimizing, and the instincts that not only help their teams survive the journey from start to finish but also thrive.

This book is the culmination of seven years' worth of scribbled notes, mobile memos captured on the run, and one-liners committed to memory. It covers insights witnessed and realized in boardrooms, on midnight calls with teams solving a crisis, during sleepless nights fretting difficult decisions, in brainstorming sessions with entrepreneurs, and often in the reflective haze of long-haul plane flights. The perspectives in this book are derived from experiences with many different people and teams, from entrepreneurs to writers from small agencies and start-ups to billion-dollar companies transforming their industries. When a tactic or tenet fascinated me, I'd capture it and share it with others for feedback or better ideas, and the ones that made the cut are in this book. The following pages cover insights garnered from interviews, from my own struggles and relative triumphs, and from working alongside the many entrepreneurs I have advised over the years. While the insights are organized into sections, the book is intended to be more of a buffet than a plated six-course meal. I encourage you to navigate to whatever parts of the journey resonate most at the moment, using the table of contents.

As they have for me, I hope these insights bolster your confidence, fortify your plans, and make you question your assumptions. As you seek to make an impact in what matters most to you, this book will help illuminate your path from start to finish.

THE STORIES FALL SHORT.

In 2006, I founded Behance, a company devoted to connecting and empowering creative professionals. The problem my team and I set out to solve was a simple one: The creative world was one of the most disorganized communities on the planet—there was no way to track a photographer's work, find out who designed a particular product, or track down the motion graphics artist or creative director behind a particular campaign. We wanted to help organize creative people, teams, and the community at large.

The problem was simple, but the solution was anything but. After several fits and starts, lessons learned the hard way, and five years of bootstrapping (building a business that relied on revenue rather than venture capital), we built a multifaceted business. The Behance Network grew to enable more than twelve million creative professionals to showcase their work, connect and collaborate with one another, and get jobs. Over the years, Behance became the leading online platform for creative careers and provided me with the opportunity to grow a large design and technology team. We then expanded Behance by offering content and events for the creative community, online and off-, by creating a think tank, website, and annual conference called 99U in 2007. Influenced by the famous Thomas

Edison quote, "Genius is 1 percent inspiration and 99 percent perspiration," 99U is dedicated to the execution of ideas rather than the ideas themselves.

In late 2012, Behance was acquired by Adobe, one of the world's largest technology companies responsible for products like Photoshop, Illustrator, and the PDF (Portable Document Format), among many other products for the creative world. It was an incredible and unexpected outcome for the entire team—certainly not the one I imagined for myself when I started designing paper products and running seminars for freelance designers to pay the bills. I joined Adobe as a vice president of products, leading an overhaul of the company's mobile and cloud asset strategies. The three years that followed were enlightening in ways I didn't expect. I had to wind down old products, help launch new ones, and lead teams through a great deal of uncertainty and change. I left this role with an appreciation for the frictions in a big company—how they hurt, how they help, and how to keep the ship moving forward, inch by inch.

Being an entrepreneur working at the intersection of design and technology brought all sorts of opportunities as an investor and adviser to help fellow entrepreneurs build their teams, brands, and products. Some of these companies, like Pinterest, Uber, Warby Parker, sweetgreen, and Periscope, are now successful operations that have, at least to some degree, accomplished what they set out to do. Others are still meandering mid-journey, enduring their rough patches and optimizing on the upswings in every way they can. But regardless of the stage, change is the only constant. After successfully seeing my own business over the finish line, and three years at Adobe, I spent a couple of years as a full-time investor, adviser, and occasional cofounder, working shoulder to shoulder with entrepreneurs and helping them navigate their own journeys. And then, at the end of 2017, I jumped back into the fray, building products and services for creative people as Adobe's chief product officer.

When sharing my story of Behance, I normally skip over the years of challenge and personal growth that existed in between the start and finish. The story I normally tell goes something like this:

> We bootstrapped the business for five years before one of our products, the Behance Network, eventually started to gain traction. This allowed us to raise some funding from a top-tier VC [venture capitalist] firm, which gave us the chance to build a dream team that turned our product into a ubiquitous global creative platform. When Adobe

turned Photoshop and the rest of their software into a subscription service, they needed a network like ours. The timing and opportunity was great, so Adobe acquired us. It was a great outcome for the entire team, and we happily continued working together for years afterward.

And boom, an entire decade of work tied with a bow.

My tale sounds a lot like other pithy stories of humble beginnings, progress, and an ultimately successful outcome. But there were years at Behance when nobody beyond our team seemed to understand or care about our work. There were moments when it all seemed on the brink of falling apart. In fact, in the early days, antinausea medication was my only way to keep an appetite. Everyone doubted us—if they ever cared—and I endured bouts of self-doubt as well. Persevering long enough to transform vision into reality was harder than I ever thought it would be; anything that challenged the status quo was an uphill battle, and the natural forces of rejection that kill new ideas didn't discriminate between the good and the bad. Innovation has a nasty headwind, rarely a tailwind.

In our first year it was just four of us. We were completely unqualified for the journey ahead, but our lack of experience didn't shake our confidence and determination, which came from our love of an idea—and the sheer ignorance for what would be required to make it happen.

Matias Corea had recently arrived in New York City from Barcelona and had practiced graphic design only for a few years. When we first met, he showed me a small brochure he had designed for a saxophone manufacturer. Matias loved jazz and typography, but he had never designed a website. Dave Stein joined us straight out of college. He had studied psychology and had covered his tuition by building simple websites out of his dorm room. The showcase website on his résumé was for an erotic lingerie shop in upstate New York. Our third hire, Chris Henry, had built a few websites in the year or two since he'd graduated from college, but he had never built search applications or databases. And me? My day job was working as an associate at Goldman Sachs. I had taken some design classes in college, but I was not an engineer, and I had never led a company. I had meandered through the worlds of finance and organizational development, but my real aspiration was to create digital products and work in the creative industry.

I had assembled this team of newbies to explore an idea that would connect the creative industry. The odds were most certainly against us. We didn't know it yet, but we were embarking on a decade-long journey that would shape both us and the global creative community in unimaginable ways.

So let's get real: The pithy success stories we hear are missing something. My short story of Behance is equally puzzling. How does a team stay together for five years with no traction, barely making payroll? How do you stomach years of anonymity and blank stares when you tell others what you're doing? How does an unqualified team recruit, manage, and retain very qualified people—often more qualified than ourselves? How do you survive long enough in an industry you know nothing about to become an expert? How do you keep changing (and often killing) parts of your business without destroying morale? And how does a team with no experience pull off something like this?

The volatile terrain of the messy middle of a journey is the real story nobody talks about. Left to hack the middle of the journey on our own, we quietly endure the downs and optimize the ups as best we can. We experiment with ways to motivate our teams when problems feel insurmountable. We agonize over conflict and try to manage drama. We act as magicians, helping our coworkers feel incremental progress when there is none.

The dirty little secret that entrepreneurs hate to admit is just how fine the line is between their success and failure. The middle makes and breaks you, and ending up on the right side of this line depends on how you manage everything in between. It requires immense perseverance, self-awareness, craftsmanship, and strategy. It also requires luck, harvested whenever you encounter it.

As we struggle, we gain insights. Hardship forces us to optimize. Our instincts are honed and our intuitions sharpen. These gems from the journey make you more capable for whatever comes next, and in my own life, they have made all the difference.

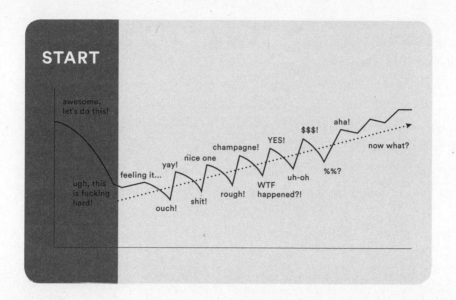

START, ENDURE, OPTIMIZE, FINISH, THEN REPEAT.

The Start

The start is pure joy because you're unaware of what you don't know and the painful obstacles ahead. Wearing the start-up world's equivalent of beer goggles is important at the start, because very few would ever have the tenacity to begin their journey otherwise.

But after the excitement of a new idea dissipates, reality sets in. You'll become mired in logistics and daunted by the unknown. You'll frantically attempt to level out your overworked synapses. You'll be in a freefall without knowing how far away the bottom is—and that's when the headwinds kick in. Everyone will doubt you. You will struggle to see your own progress. You'll realize that your industry, your team, and your competitors don't like change—and society doesn't, either. Not even your customers.

And then finally: The bottom arrives, and you hit hard. After scrambling to get your bearings and not lose too much time, money, or face, you'll look back up to see a monstrous peak in front of you.

This is where the journey truly begins.

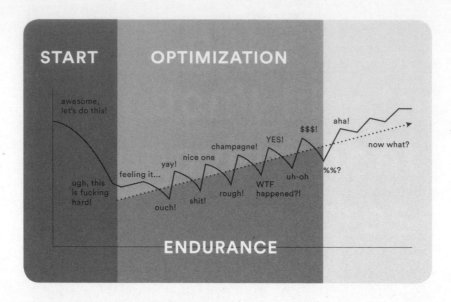

The Middle: Enduring and Optimizing

The middle of the journey is all about enduring the valleys and optimizing the peaks. After the joy of conception subsides, your objective is to make every setback less difficult than the one before it—and make every recovery hoist you slightly higher than where you were before.

To achieve the elusive positive slope, you must endure the downs (the incremental setbacks and struggles) and optimize the ups (everything and anything that seems to be working). Your progress will feel rewarding, but only relative to your most recent struggle. The best you can do is harvest and integrate the insights you need to keep moving in the right direction up the slope.

Volatility is good for velocity. The faster you move and the more mistakes you make, the better your chances of learning and gaining the momentum you need to soar above competitors. Moving fast means conducting lots of experiments—many of which will fail—and making quick turns that are liable to leave you and your team dizzy. This volatility can hurt morale and cause anxiety, but you have a better chance of extraordinary results.

The middle of the journey is an excruciating struggle. But there are momentary recoveries throughout the journey that keep you going, like the sensation of seeing your team's DNA in your product, meeting a customer who sincerely thanks you, watching a culture take shape and the people you hired evolve to become entirely different leaders... there are so many moments along the way that keep you going. You just need to endure the lows and optimize everything that works.

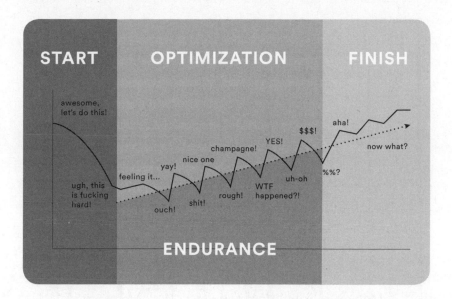

The Finish

Your "finish" is the final mile of your journey and the recovery time between one project and the next. It's hard to know when you're finished, because every project has a piece of you in it that never goes away. In this way, the finish is more a state of mind.

However, there are inflections in every project where everything changes: You debut your creation to the world, you sell your company, or you publish your book. Even though the race continues, it feels like a finish because you're no longer racing against the clock. Either the volatility subsides or your interest ceases—or both. Your pace changes, and you finally allow yourself to take a break and make a change.

Finishes come in all shapes and sizes and are never as certain (or desirable) as they seem. In fact, finishing should never be the end goal, and you shouldn't aspire to ever feel truly "finished"; life loses value when challenge dissipates.

In my own experience at Behance, our founding team didn't have a particular finish in mind when we started. Sure, I imagined a day in the distant future when we might be profitable, have an amazing team, make a profound impact, and be running a brand and company we were proud of. But getting acquired was not even a subconscious thought within that early narrative.

In the end, Behance's acquisition provided a natural punctuation mark for the end of a chapter. Journeys have all kinds of finishes along the way, and in many respects, you're never finished. You can always write another chapter.

● ● ● ● ●

Part of my motivation to write this book was to "out" a bold creative project or new venture for what it really is: endless endurance and optimization.

I have organized the insights ahead into a section on *endurance* and a section on *optimization*—the two complementary forces that help you conquer the middle of any bold project. Fair warning, the "Endure" section will be uncomfortable and, at times, frustrating to read. Rather than sugarcoat the hurt, anguish, and doubt, I have worked to bring these emotions and painful moments to the forefront. It's important to become familiar with these inevitable hardships and how others worked through them. When you make your way through "Endure," you'll be greeted by a more optimistic and actionable "Optimize" section that is all about capitalizing on your strengths and improving every aspect of your team, product, and self. Enduring and optimizing is the *rhythm of making*—the pattern of ups and downs that every journey takes you through. It is certainly true for your professional aspirations, but this rhythm also applies to all of life.

One realization I hope you have from this book is the relationship between volatility and preparedness. The lengthy distance between where you are and where you wish to be—with all of its difficulties—is there for a reason, and the ups and downs feed each other in valuable ways. In Zen, the Buddha says *you cannot travel the path until you have become the path yourself.* Only by embracing the middle will you find your way through.

The easiest route to take is to glide in the direction of wherever fate pushes. But living at the mercy of circumstance makes you a passive participant in your own story. Without a fight against fate (aka the status quo), you'll never venture beyond the expected. You can stretch your potential only by enduring the volatility of the journey, by getting curious about the bumps, and by optimizing every aspect of your product, team, and self.

the path is the goal
You cannot travel the path until
    you have become the path yourself
embrace the middle in order
    to find your way through

ENDURE

Three years in. Or maybe it was two, or four. I have no idea. The middle years all blend together. I call them the "lost years," because Behance's progress felt excruciatingly slow, and we learned everything the hard way. I'm surprised we survived.

Our team was our own little world. We manufactured our goals and self-esteem in the same way we made our product: with imagination and poetic license. The fights and fun were all part of the drama that kept our made-up world intact. We barely had a business, and most of our customers were doing us a favor. Our relationships with one another and our sense of hope were the only things we were building with undeniable value.

Nevertheless, I felt so small whenever I walked out of our office, which was a cordoned-off part of my apartment a few blocks away from Union Square. New York City was always bustling. The guy selling fruit on the sidewalk had more customers than we did. Out at night I cringed when the "what do you do?" conversation came up. I knew my answer—building a company to help organize the creative world—would get a blank stare. Would people think I got fired from my real job? If I told people my vision, would I lose respect if I failed? My family and friends always offered to help me, but there was nothing they could do. I felt the weight of every decision, and the careers of those who quit their jobs to join me, on my shoulders. My shoulders alone.

When I think back to those lost years, I recall a constant somber loneliness, a suffering from the feeling that nobody else could relate. The struggle was further compounded by the optimism I had to exude to my team and potential customers and partners. My hope had to be mined deep beneath the surface of fear and reality. The juxtaposition of the intensity of a start-up and feeling invisible and despondent was soul crushing. Staying positive was exhausting, and there were times when I felt depressed.

Aside from the psychological struggles, these years felt lost because we ran in circles. We had to rebuild the Behance Network's core technology three times. We switched vendors, hired some of the wrong people, and made countless bad decisions. Keeping our product functional was a game of Whac-A-Mole: Every fix seemed to break something else. But we were determined to get it right. We didn't make rapid progress with our product, but the hardship strengthened our resolve. As a team, and as individuals, we found a way to endure every valley we faced.

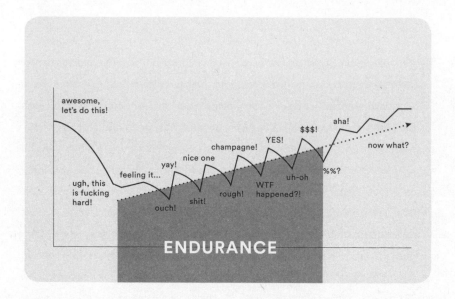

The middle miles of a venture are full of ambiguity, uncertainty, fear, runarounds, crises, disagreements, and endless bouts of the mundane. Every time you untangle yourself and find your way out of a jam, you'll fall into another one sooner than you think. These are the inevitable and seemingly endless dips of the middle that we must endure.

Endurance is about much more than surviving late nights and laboring without reward. It's about developing a source of renewable energy and tolerance that is not innate. Without any customers or evidence of progress, the continuous validation and encouragement that motivates teams will be absent. Without a steady stream of rewards, you will feel empty. You must supplement this void with manufactured optimism. You will have to endure anonymity and a persistent state of frustration. You'll have to generate a unique and intrinsic sense of belief in yourself as you manage the blows to your plan and ego. Sure, your passion for the problem you're solving will help. But running a marathon while hungry requires supernatural sustenance in the form of some key insights and convictions that we will discuss in this section.

The line between a big win and failure is thin. You can get the important stuff right and still lose by not enduring long enough. When I recall our years of bootstrapping at Behance, I cringe thinking about just how close we came to falling apart—several times. We survived these troughs in our journey as a team. We relied on one another, managed to find levity in even the darkest moments, and hacked our own reality to endure years of struggle.

The insights in the section ahead will equip you for the middle-journey turbulence. They will also remind you that you're not alone. But we need to face the mess head-on and learn how to endure and mine the volatility. Exploring the trenches of lost hope, uncertainty, and exhaustion help make such conditions more familiar—and therefore bearable, maybe even manageable.

LEADING THROUGH THE ANGUISH AND THE UNKNOWN

Short-circuit your reward system.

One of the greatest motivators is a sign of progress. Hardship is easier to tolerate when your work is being recognized (either through external validation or financial rewards), but long journeys don't show progress in the traditional sense. When you have no customers, no audience, and nobody knows or cares to know about what you're making, the greatest motivators have to be manufactured.

I would characterize much of my first few years leading my team at Behance as an adventure in manufacturing motivation. In 2007, and for a few years thereafter, we had very little traction, revenue, press, or any other traditional form of progress to celebrate. We had launched a blog and simple network for creative professionals… that nobody knew about or cared about. When you did a web search for Behance, the first result was *Did you mean: enhance?* Even Google thought we were a mistake.

The traditional measures of an internet business—page views, customers, subscribers, revenue—didn't do much for us because we were starting from nothing and struggling to exist. As the team's leader, I tried all sorts of ways to keep the team engaged. We would make bets for when we would achieve certain milestones based on our priorities. As a life-long vegetarian, I would commit to trying certain kinds of meat if we reached certain milestones (which the team found, strangely, motivating). We would celebrate any new customers, even if the overall numbers were tiny. We would celebrate completing a page of tasks on the wall or bashing a particularly elusive bug in the software with cheap champagne. Whatever we could repurpose as a milestone, we would.

One of my favorite early manufactured milestones was overcoming Google's Behance/enhance error message. We longed to be considered a legitimate search result. To achieve this, we needed to game the spread of "back links" to influence Google's search algorithm. We knew that the more blog posts we wrote and the more portfolios our customers uploaded, the closer we would get to internet recognition, not by our customers, but by Google's digital gatekeepers. The goal was short term, and the tasks to achieve it were all actionable. It would just take time and effort. "Someday," I assured the team, "we will no longer be a mistake."

Then one day, someone on the team went to Google and gave it another go and, lo and behold, Behance came up as the first result without any prompt to correct the search query. We had won—we finally existed! It was a small win manufactured as a way to help us feel a semblance of progress, but it felt great.

And then, I kid you not, in 2008, Beyoncé became popular. And we were a mistake again. *Did you mean: Beyoncé?* Google asked. But we were undeterred, and it was only a matter of weeks until we were, once again, a legitimate search result.

It is hard to summon a sense of hope and self-worth when you're on your own. So you squeeze out any semblance of progress you can find, and then you celebrate it.

The great void of feedback and reward that early-stage start-ups must endure cannot be overstated. It is especially apparent when I attend start-up conferences like Web Summit, an annual gathering of start-ups from Europe, the Middle East, and Asia. While the United States has an established ecosystem of start-ups, incubators, venture capital firms, and angel investors, the rest of the world benefits from megaconferences like Web Summit to bring entrepreneurs and investors together. Strolling around the start-up pavilion at Web Summit, I always take heart in the literally thousands of start-ups that have a three-foot-long space to engage anyone willing to hear their pitch.

It's fun to see so many ideas in the early stages, but with all the energy I also feel the pain and despair. When you're putting everything on the line, your business and art becomes intertwined with your identity and self-esteem. Nothing is more humbling than everyone passing by your three-foot cube that represents your future without even taking a second look.

Anonymity means you can make mistakes and drastic changes to your product without disappointing anyone, but only because nobody cares. Breaking through anonymity is a game of endurance, so you have to hack your reward system so that the absent short-term rewards you typically rely on, like revenue or new customer goals, are replaced by something else.

Starting at a very young age, we are trained to be governed by a powerful short-term reward system. As toddlers, we behave in ways that yield affection and instant gratification from our parents. In school, our learning is rewarded with good grades. And grades, we soon learn, yield the reward of approval from parents, teachers, and peers. When we enter the job market, we receive a monthly salary and bonuses. And as legendary venture capitalist (VC) Fred Wilson paraphrased at the 99U conference: "The two greatest addictions in life are heroin and a weekly salary."

Monica Mehta, author of *The Entrepreneurial Instinct*, studies the role of brain chemistry in entrepreneurship. She explains in *Entrepreneur*, "With each success, our brain releases a chemical called dopamine. When dopamine flows into the brain's reward pathway (the part responsible for pleasure, learning and motivation), we not only feel greater concentration but are inspired to re-experience the activity that caused the chemical release in the first place." This guaranteed dopamine rush and the self-confidence it provides makes short-term rewards addicting. Alternatively, "Each time we fail, the brain is drained of dopamine, making it not only hard to concentrate but also difficult to learn from what went wrong." Thus, physiologically, we're hardwired to have a strong preference for actions, decisions, and projects likely to yield quick wins, because delayed gratification causes anxiety and discomfort.

If you consider how short life expectancy was in the dawn of humanity, it's no surprise that we're naturally biased toward short-term rewards. Even as late as the seventeenth century, average life expectancy in New England was twenty-five years of age, and 40 percent of people died before reaching adulthood. For early humanity, the prospect of spending five or ten years working toward an eventual outcome, however great it might be, was just not rational. No wonder it is so difficult to stay engaged with a long-term goal—we are biologically wired to abandon such efforts in exchange for shorter-term rewards.

Our addiction to short-term validation is so engrained that trying to defy it is hopeless. Accept this fact. While many people paint an incredible long-term vision for their teams, the prospect of long-term rewards is insufficient for long-term motivation. It is virtuous to aspire to these goals, but a noble venture is not exempt from the need to feel incremental progress and be rewarded for it. Rather than fight the need for short-term rewards, you must hack your reward system to provide them.

As you craft your team's culture, lower the bar for how you define a "win." Celebrate anything you can, from gaining a new customer to solving a particularly vexing problem. The problem with traditional rewards like money, which can be counted and accumulated, is that they require the least imagination. Make the most of the period in your journey when you must create your own rewards out of necessity. By doing so, you are engaging your team more dynamically than a raise or bonus ever will. Milestones that are directly correlated with progress are more effective motivators than anything else.

Don't seek positive feedback or celebrate fake wins at the expense of hard truths.

While important to celebrate and manufacture wins early on, make sure they're not fake wins. It's understandable to seek validation, but actively searching for positive feedback provides false positives. If you keep searching for something positive, you'll find it—but often at the expense of more important truths.

In the early days of founding Behance and helping start other companies like Prefer, a referral network for independent professionals, I found myself looking at our product analytics every day. Did more people sign up today than yesterday? Did engagement go up this week versus last week? How many more followers did we gain on Twitter? These are important metrics to track, but I was looking only for the positive trends rather than objectively reviewing all the trends. More than anything else, I wanted validation.

Upon reflection from several start-up experiences, product manager and technology entrepreneur Ben Erez talked about the perils of being encouraged by positive feedback.

When you're starting a company, anything resembling positive feedback looks like a delicious steak. I've never enjoyed hearing how awesome my idea was than I did during the process of starting my company. I've never had a baby, but to me having a start-up felt a lot like showing off my new baby. You tell everyone about it like an excited parent and every single person congratulates you for the news and tells you it's flawless. In hindsight, seeking positive feedback was toxic, because it was giving us the impression we were on the right track.

To objectively observe the performance of your new creation or product, put yourself in others' shoes. You can piece together something resembling the truth only from many different perspectives. How would a skeptical investor look at your numbers? How would an impatient new customer attempt to navigate your product? What are competitors saying about your product? Actively seek out the negative trends as well as the positive, as your longevity over time will be determined by your awareness of weaknesses as much as your strengths.

It's all too tempting to sugarcoat a bitter pill. Momentum is an especially effective distractor, as are press accolades. But finding a positive metric or getting glowing press coverage does not make a hard truth go away. Our thirst for good news means we focus on it, or worse, manufacture it. Sometimes when leaders are trying to rally confidence and support, they are actually blunting a blow that must be felt in order to feel the reality and make difficult decisions.

I often see leaders circulate positive articles to their teams to overshadow larger problems facing the company. As an investor, I see this in shareholder updates from entrepreneurs running businesses I've supported. These updates almost always start with "Things are going really well!!" and then, buried on page 5 of the update, is the news that the team has been pared down to two people, they've had to move out of their coworking space, and they have five months of funding left before they stop paying salaries. "But *Forbes* gave us a great write-up last month!" It's the business equivalent of the grimacing emoji.

As Ben Horowitz, founder and general partner of venture capital firm Andreessen Horowitz, once explained in a blog on the topic, "The truth about telling the truth is that it does not come easy for anyone. It's not natural or organic. The natural thing to do is tell people what they want to hear. That's what makes everybody feel good . . . at least for the moment. Telling the truth, on the other hand, is hard work and requires skill." He goes on to cite the kinds of messages that are painful to deliver, like executives quitting, a plan for massive layoffs, sales declining, and other perilous situations. "You must tell the truth without destroying the company. To do this, you must accept that you cannot change the truth. You cannot change it, but you can assign meaning to it." Ben suggests three methods for assigning meaning to hard truths:

> State the facts clearly and honestly—Don't try to say that you needed to clean up performance issues or that the company is better off without the people that you so painstakingly hired. It is what it is and it's important that everyone knows you know that.

> If you caused it, explain how such a bad thing could occur—What was the decision process that you used to expand the company faster than you should have? What did you learn that will prevent it from happening again?

> Explain why taking the action is essential to the larger mission and how important that mission is—A layoff, if done properly, is a new lease on life for the company and an action that was necessary to fulfill the prime directive and mission that everyone signed up for. As the leader, it's your job to make sure that the company does not let those people lose their jobs for nothing. Something good needs to come out of it.

Despite the temptation, don't focus on "good news" at the expense of what's going south and how to deliver bad news. In a journey that is so reliant on positive energy and hope, it is vitally important to make consistent time and space where people can focus on what isn't working. Perhaps it is a regularly scheduled monthly meeting, or a period during an off-site meeting when the team is encouraged to share their doubts. Some teams do anonymous surveys of the team's gravest concerns and then share the results. Whatever your method, don't gloss over the news your team needs to hear. Be up front, and then share a plan. You cannot win unless you know how you're most likely to lose.

And when you find something worth celebrating, only applaud the progress and actions you want your team to repeat. It's dangerous to celebrate accolades or circumstances that are not linked with productivity, like getting "press" that you paid for or winning awards that are not representative of your impact. After all, the most exciting pursuits don't yet fit in a reporter's beat or an award category! Another example of a dangerous fake win is raising capital. Funding shouldn't be celebrated. If anything, raising money should make you nervous: It means you have more to lose and more people you are responsible to. For strong companies, financing is a tactic. For weak companies, financing is a goal.

When you use smoke and mirrors to help boost self-esteem and help your team endure hardship, you're perverting your values. Fake wins are the reward equivalent of cocaine: They will artificially inflate morale but then take you down, perhaps lower than where you started.

What should you celebrate? Progress and impact. As your team takes action and works their way down the list of things to do, it is often hard for them to feel the granularity of their progress and you need to compensate. Celebrate the moments when aggressive deadlines are met or beaten. Pop champagne when the work you've done makes a real impact. Even if it's just a few customers that make use of a new product or feature, these are the real milestones you want to celebrate.

Accept the burden of processing uncertainty.

We crave certainty but must learn to function without it. We want to be told that a glass of wine a day is definitely good for us, but life isn't that simple. While searching for a definitive answer, we often cherry-pick insights from experts or studies that support the view we already hold. By avoiding uncertainty and desperately seeking a quick answer, we're liable to embrace premature or incorrect solutions. Only by learning to tolerate uncertainty can we allow processes to play out and experiments to unfold.

Emre Soyer, a behavioral scientist and assistant professor of business at Ozyegin University in Istanbul, Turkey, has studied leaders navigating uncertainty and decision making: "A leader that embraces uncertainty would be open to experiment with different ideas and let others experiment, too, rather than claiming to know the correct answer all the time." When searching for stability, we'll often cut corners or ignore real issues in order to stem our fear of the unknown. "We often desire that experts absorb uncertainties for us, make consistently accurate predictions and tell us what we need to do," Soyer says. "Yet this would lead to a false sense of certainty and an illusion of control, ultimately causing us to invest in some particular strategies or treatments that may prove useless or even harmful." Instead, we should train our brains to embrace the gray area and not be too solution driven. "One of the main responsibilities of a leader or an executive is to make good decisions," Soyer adds. "Yet, uncertainty makes this task difficult. Claiming an unwarranted degree of control on uncertain situations can harm the reputation of the leader in the long run. Whereas a leader who is behaving in harmony with the uncertain nature of a situation would be judged as fair and competent even if sometimes the outcomes are unsatisfactory due to bad luck."

The necessary but difficult task of embracing the gray area means willingly wrestling with uncertainty on a daily basis. I struggled with this in my early years spent bootstrapping Behance, with no end in sight and no sure sense of traction. I remember many occasions when I valiantly fought to disconnect: Christmas, the week of my wedding, and even the birth of my daughter. And while I was "there" for all of these moments, 20 percent of my mind's processing power was preoccupied. It wasn't any specific deal or issue that stuck with me. On the contrary, it was the stuff I didn't know that ate away at me—the "unknown unknowns." The lack of a map for the voyage ahead caused an existential angst that meant I felt the need to live and sleep with one eye on the compass.

As Ben Erez recalls from his experience, "I thought at the time that my personal life was separate from my work life, but that's not true in entrepreneurship. When you're building a company, the various parts of your life have a way of all meshing together into a think blend that doesn't let you tell one part from the other. I had heard starting a company is all-consuming but the magnitude of overlap was something I was not prepared to handle." This "think blend" is the continual processing of open questions without absolute solutions. In many ways, the continual processing of uncertainty is the one part of your "work life" you can't turn off. There's no shortcut to deep thinking and crunching through scenarios in the basement of your brain.

So you must practice and learn to master the art of *parallel processing*, when you can focus on a specific problem while also churning through the omnipresent anxiety. You can quiet it down, but you can't turn it off (and you don't want to—you're slow cooking your intuition). Some people I know practice meditation, and some pride themselves on being able to ruthlessly compartmentalize. What I try to do is remind myself that I need to be present with my team, focused on the problem, yet keep a pulse on the big picture. Despite what may be processing in the back of your mind, try to get curious with whatever problem or person is in front of you. Distract yourself from your own preoccupations by finding things to learn and solve.

No matter what your creative endeavor is, uncertainty will be lingering around every corner. There is simply no way around uncertainty and the angst it will cause for you and your team. Strive to continually process it rather than let it cripple you, to accept the burden without surrendering your attention.

Fight resistance with a commitment to suffering.

Society has a grand immune system designed to suppress new ideas. To keep the water running and sustain life's other necessities, society's natural resistance to ingenuity surfaces in the form of doubt, cynicism, and pressure to conform. It takes tremendous endurance to survive such resistance.

In order to fight against the resistance, you'll need more than passion and empathy. You'll need to commit to suffering for the years required to push your idea to fruition. Not just a willingness to suffer, but a commitment. Loup Ventures investor Doug Clinton makes the case that founders must commit to suffering for at least five years. "This might sound more extreme than necessary," he writes, "but starting a company is a roller coaster of suffering. You need to be comfortable with hearing 'no' over and over and not let that destroy your will. You need to be able to withstand low periods that are inevitable—unexpected customer or employee losses, investor rejections, tax bills, fights with cofounders. Entrepreneurs don't necessarily need to revel in difficulty, but it helps.... It usually takes at least two years before you have any reasonable traction to show that your business might be working, then another few years of driving growth to create something that looks like a moat. Then you can afford to breathe. A little."

With a commitment to suffering, teams are able to tolerate struggle and overcome major psychological challenges like, for example, throwing everything away and trying again. When a start-up or product team realizes they're headed nowhere and decides to change everything, the loss of years of work combined with the feeling of starting all over again is soul crushing. And yet, some of the greatest modern companies we know and love today were second incarnations of completely different ideas. YouTube was originally a dating site that never took off, despite relentless efforts to get people to sign up. Twitter started as a podcasting network called "Odeo" that was going nowhere, and Instagram's team started with a hard-to-use check-in game called "Burbn." Instagram as we know it today was an attempt to salvage the situation, designed with such extreme simplicity as a reaction to what they had learned the hard way with Burbn. In each of these cases, we tend to celebrate the breakthrough products without fathoming how hard it must have been to keep the faith and start from scratch. I've heard cofounder Kevin Systrom discuss how difficult the decision was, even though Burbn was going nowhere. Such bold moves are psychologically toiling, and while common sense may suggest otherwise, you must be committed to the suffering.

Despite whatever hacks and strategies you employ, you will get burned repeatedly. Society's immune system is powerful and indiscriminate. Suffering is inevitable, but by expecting it, you can manage your expectations and those of your team. You can build a culture that is as much about the experience building the product together as it is about the product itself. By doing so, at least you're in your own little world suffering among friends! As you hire people to join you, you can evaluate not only their skills and interests but also their tolerance and commitment to enduring the fight against the self-doubt and gut-wrenching hardships that real life and society will throw at you.

Friction brings us closer.

Our aversion to obstacles, setbacks, disagreements, and other forms of resistance is a bit ironic, because this friction is what builds our tolerance for future friction. We expend so much energy avoiding friction rather than inviting and leveraging it.

The old adage "Friction polishes stones" is true: Friction not only reveals character, it creates it. By avoiding conflict, we don't smooth out the rough edges of our ideas and plans. In *Quartz*, Hugo Macdonald, the former design editor of *Monocle* magazine, made the case for friction:

> The thought of friction may make us bristle, but it's not synonymous with difficulty. The standard linguistic definition recognizes this: Friction is derived from the Latin word ***fricare***, meaning "to rub," and ... generally means *a force that opposes relative motion between two objects*. Rubbing in opposition to something instinctively sounds like an undesirable experience—a disagreement, a struggle, a fight—and so over time, we've come to connote friction with negativity.

But on the whole, rubbing things together creates, not destroys. Friction gives us heat and fire. It quite literally moves mountains. Rubbing two people together may cause arguments—but it also makes babies. Friction is a positive force in all walks of life precisely because it's only when we're in opposition to something that we learn how to move forward. In order to advance both individually and societally, we need more friction in our lives, not less.

The aspiration for a "frictionless" experience is shortsighted. A truly frictionless experience, where you avoid or deny every ounce of struggle, is mindless. Friction makes you feel the texture of a process, and the texture helps you remember what you've experienced. Without friction, teams are liable to move too fast, and edges that are too smooth fail to form sustainable bonds.

Hardship brings your team together and equips you to endure for the long haul. The upheaval of ordinary life causes a group of people to overlook their differences and unite around common causes. Bonds forged through adversity are most apparent when calamity strikes. Whether in wartime or after a natural disaster, shared struggles bring people together. I remember walking through the streets of Soho during the massive New York blackout in 2003 and saw stores giving away drinks, random civilians helping direct traffic, and everyone talking with one another.

Friction unlocks the full potential of working together. When triggered, your ancestral preference for group survival through collaboration over isolation aligns interests in a powerful way.

"When staying alive is not just the responsibility of the individual, but other members of the species help the individual to survive, and vice versa, all members' chances are enhanced," explains Richard Taflinger, a professor at Washington State University. The more a group cooperates, the more resources it can accumulate, the more territory it can defend, and the more it can protect itself from predators; those who stray from cooperation threaten the majority's safety, motivating the majority to eliminate them. Cooperation is a natural instinct, and friction brings it to the surface.

The more neurally complex the animal, the more social groups are used to enhance survival. Humans band together for physical and psychological protection. "In ancient history and prehistory, tribes gave visceral comfort and pride from familiar fellowship, and a way to defend the group enthusiastically against rival groups," E. O. Wilson, a biologist, writes in *Newsweek*. "Modern groups are psychologically equivalent to the tribes of ancient history. As such, these groups are directly descended from the bands of primitive humans and pre-humans."

However complex these societal groups become, our psychology remains wired on the principle that groups equal safety. So instead of facing adversity solo, we instinctively look for groups, for comfort and restoration.

Speaking on *Harvard Business Review*'s *IdeaCast* about a book he coauthored with Sheryl Sandberg—*Option B: Facing Adversity, Building Resilience, and Finding Joy*—Adam Grant, a renowned organizational psychologist and Wharton professor, describes the business incentives of group support. Studies show that when companies provided assistance programs that offer financial support and time off when employees faced unexpected adversity (such as if their home was damaged by a natural disaster or a relative fell sick), "it actually paid dividends in that people felt like they belong now to a more caring company," Grant says. "They took pride in their employer as a really human place to work. And they were more committed as a result."

Sheryl Sandberg, Facebook COO and whose personal experience of her husband Dave Goldberg dying suddenly was the inspiration for *Option B*, recalls, "I never would have gotten through this without Mark [Zuckerberg]. Mark was at my house the day I came home from Mexico and told my children. Mark literally planned Dave's funeral. And Mark was with me every step of the way. When I came back to work and felt like I was a ghost and no one would talk to me, I took refuge in his conference room.... We think about providing that kind of emotional support to our friends.... But we can also do it at work. And it makes us closer to the people we work with. And I think it builds a much stronger organization."

Groups help us manage life's frictions, and the challenges we face bring groups together. Rather than circumventing or burying it, use the frictions you encounter to learn how to cooperate and build your team's capacity to handle adversity. Whatever you do, don't fear tension and confrontation. Passivity arrests your development as a team. The fights bring you a level deeper, they force you to cover more surface area of opinion so you can ultimately discover the best solution. And, often times, we desperately need the clarity that crisis provides. As the early Roman emperor Marcus Aurelius once quipped, "The impediment to action advances action. What stands in the way becomes the way." Indeed, the frictions we encounter help us find a better way so long as we face them.

Be the steward of perspective.

The middle of a venture is like a lengthy road trip without windows. It is psychologically torturous to travel without any sense of where you are along the way—no sense of progress or landmarks—and without a sense for how many miles remain. Your concept of time becomes warped, and impatience stews.

Teams need to be reminded where they are and what progress they are making. As a leader, you are your team's window. You need to call out and describe the landmarks that you pass along the way, constantly reinforce the terrain you have already covered, and prepare folks for the map ahead.

Reporting facts and managing expectations are only a small part of this job. More important, you are a storyteller. Your job is to make history more interesting and relevant when retold than when it happened. After all, the middle of a journey is a blurry, mundane landscape. To get through the tremendous voids of nothingness in between the milestones, provide guidance. You're the narrator of this journey.

People who worked with Apple founder Steve Jobs over the years often talked about how his "reality-distortion field" could alter his team's perspective, assumptions, and limits to allow for new ideas. Perhaps Jobs believed in his vision so much so that the reality around him was distorted by the power of his conviction? When you're articulating a vision and set of assumptions with such passion and confidence, reality starts to bend your way. You're not lying or manufacturing perspective—you're merchandising your perspective. You're not creating a story that you think others will believe—you're retelling the same story you tell yourself.

The same forces can help a team endure another form of reality: work with no end in sight. In this case, your reality-distortion field shows people hope when they can't see it for themselves. For example, you may see these tough days you're currently enduring as character building for your team and as a source of defensibility for your product—even though it currently feels anything but. Are you lamenting a lack of progress or celebrating your survival and newfound strength? Are you merchandising hard work as tiring or as achieving defensibility in your market? As you summarize your team's exhaustive work and struggles over the months or years that have passed, conjure up the perspective that excites you the most, and then share it. Storytellers make the past relevant to the future, even when it is dry and irrelevant.

Likewise, it is your responsibility to steward perspectives when you're not even sure the conversation will end in a solution. Some of the best conversations are ones that are not trying to answer a "yes or no" question. In such conversations, instead of prompting closure, your goal should be to lead your team through a process of self-discovery.

Conversations with no near-term actions or solutions reveal the surface area of the issue—blind spots, wrinkles, and unexpected edges. But, if nothing else, the ongoing discussion supplants ambiguity and any "elephants in the room" by keeping the team engaged and motivated. By participating, everyone feels more in control of their destiny.

Especially when failures or major setbacks occur, you need to carry your team through it. For example, imagine working years to launch your product to much fanfare and then suddenly having your product shut down by the government for a couple of years. That's exactly what happened to Anne Wojcicki, CEO and cofounder of genetic testing company 23andMe. Founded in 2006, 23andMe allowed customers to spit in a small tube and, within a few weeks, get access to a wealth of genetic information about their ancestors, predisposition to health issues, and other insights based on their genes. The company thrived in its early years, attracting excited customers and some of Silicon Valley's greatest investors. But then, in 2013, the U.S. Food and Drug Administration (FDA) abruptly ordered 23andMe to discontinue marketing its personal genome service, based on concerns about the potential consequences of customers receiving inaccurate medical results. For two years, the company conducted the necessary research and addressed the FDA's concerns, until October of 2015, when 23andMe announced that it would be offering a revised health component with FDA approval.

In retrospect, this major blow to the business and the team's morale may be nothing more than a blip in the company's early history. But how do you manage such a setback when it happens? As Anne recalls, the team was so bought into the mission that they were largely undeterred. "The more passionate you are about the cause, the less hard it is," she explains. "When you have so much conviction that you're doing the right thing, you see such a challenge as part of the process rather than a road block. We were used to people not understanding us or not liking us, so our attitude was always 'We need to prove it to them' versus 'What are we doing wrong?' With enough conviction, you can cut through ambiguity."

As for helping a team reach and sustain enough conviction to endure such setbacks, Anne believes it comes down to the people you hire, how you communicate, and decisiveness. "From the very beginning, we've wanted people that really believe in the mission. If you have FOMO ["fear of missing out"], go elsewhere. We are impacting lives of people and transforming health care. Everyone here knows the mission and my job is to reflect it. During regulatory challenges, we didn't lose many people. I would go around the company and remind people, 'We're on the right side of history.' This was our mantra, and we needed to take another path forward... it was a matter of our first path being wrong, never our mission being wrong. We wavered only on how we were going to get there but not the endpoint."

By luring new employees with your mission, as opposed to flashy titles or the best compensation package, you'll build a more durable team that is willing to try different paths to achieve the mission they signed up for. But still, your perspective during the most difficult times will help your team defy their own self-doubt. When distractions and drama arise, acknowledge them, and then recontextualize them so that the suffering pales in comparison to the broader opportunity before you. Remind your team why you're all there. They signed up to work with you because they believe in your vision and want to make something extraordinary. Your story has more gravity than you realize. Your job is to help your team make sense of the strategy—what they're seeing, doing, and working toward. You are the steward of your team's perspective, and there is always a way forward so long as you explain it.

Leave every conversation with energy.

Whether you're building a new business or transforming an old one, you'll face an endless battery of painfully long conversations that have no outcome. Unresolved conversations are draining. People want resolution, and they want the confidence and motivation that comes along with a clear plan.

As a leader, you can't always provide answers. And you shouldn't, as the correct solution may still be premature. But what you can do is always add energy. This ability to turn negative conversations into positive ones is a trait I've always admired.

My former colleague David Wadhwani is especially adept at this. Before he became CEO of AppDynamics, an enterprise software company in Silcon Valley, David ran the digital media portion of Adobe when I joined the team after Behance's acquisition. At the time, the company had just begun a historic transition from being a traditional software company that sold boxed software to being a services company that offered customers a series of services for a monthly fee. Adobe was one of the very first publicly traded software companies to make this transition and faced tremendous risk in doing so. David had the difficult task of leading teams of Adobe veterans, most of whom had been at Adobe more than a decade, to make the requested changes to their products. While the company had changed directions, many in the ranks were still resistant. The implications were far reaching, and some product leaders were neither prepared nor willing to rethink their products.

The teams were not equipped for the onslaught of challenges. Every Tuesday at David's staff meeting, we would untangle these problems and discuss paths to resolution. We usually realized that things would get worse before they got better. Many meetings, every option was a bad option, but we just needed to take the steps to keep pushing forward.

Despite the circumstances and solemn sense of many of these meetings, David had a way of leaving every meeting on a high note. He would acknowledge the challenges before us while reminding each team why their work was important and what success would eventually look like. Even after painful meetings that lasted multiple hours without any sense of closure, David still managed to bring it together at the end in a way where we all left with energy—something along the lines of, "Hey, I know this is rough and we've got some serious work to do, but I also know we've got a good plan and the right people," and adding something funny and uplifting at the end.

Your job is to be an energy giver rather than taker, which is common among founders and leaders I admire. Chief among them is Jon Steinberg, the former president of BuzzFeed who went on to found the news media network Cheddar. Those who know Jon will attest that he is a force of nature. Every team pep talk is an infusion of energy and insight about why the "old model" of cable news is wrong and why Cheddar is the pioneer for the future of the industry. If an idea from his team is great, he'll turn the company on a dime to make it happen. Having served on Jon's board, I have witnessed firsthand how he motivates his team, board members, and clients. The common theme across interactions with Jon is that he's *all-in, all the time.* When Dunkin' Donuts became a big Cheddar client, Jon started wearing Dunkin' apparel, catering every meeting with Dunkin' Donuts and coffee, and sharing weekend shots of his family at Dunkin' on Instagram. What better way to infuse energy into a partnership and send a clear message to current and prospective clients that Cheddar values loyalty and service? He turns every milestone into a source of energy rather than a celebration. When a record is broken, he'll follow with something like "That looks pretty fucking awesome to me. Who else is achieving these goals on average? Nobody. Look at that trend line.... I know it's a lot of stress, but it's working. Hold yourself and your colleagues and me accountable for great content AND views AND deals AND more hours of

LIVE! ... Let's push harder, fight harder, keep the trend going!" When you leave a meeting with Jon, or read an email from Jon, you have more energy than when you started.

Your team needs energy transfusions, especially in the middle miles when circumstances feel dire and there is no end in sight. Acknowledge the trials and uncertainty you're facing, followed by reiterating your plan of how to climb out, what you're aiming to achieve, reminding your team why you've come together to do that, and then add your own enthusiasm and confidence. In the final moments of every meeting and communication, you need to reiterate purpose and leave people with the energy to achieve it.

If you don't like the way government is being run, cross party lines.

For all the criticism they get, big companies have a tremendous opportunity to make a global impact. The bigger you are, the more muscle you have to force a new idea into existence. But size typically works against us. Just as weight lifters' bulging biceps make them great at lifting weights but terrible at scratching their own backs, larger companies tend to gain weight disproportionately and trip over themselves.

I have come to call it *corporate obesity*. If you've worked at a heritage corporation, you've probably witnessed the following phenomena:

- Discussions are more about who owns what and who reports to whom rather than how you are going to make something happen.
- Emails are more about who should solve problems than how to solve problems.
- Teams spend too much time figuring out how to circumvent other teams to get something done rather than getting everyone aligned.

- The BCC field gets too much action, and emails typically end with passive-aggressive (or sometimes just plain aggressive) comments or condescending questions.
- People act one way in meetings, another way out of meetings.
- When you question people, you offend them rather than engage them in a constructive debate.
- You often nod your head or stay silent when you disagree for fear of retribution.

When working in an environment filled with these behaviors and tendencies, progress slows to a painful crawl and talented people lose their energy and imagination. Not every big company suffers from corporate obesity, but they're susceptible to it unless leaders willfully seek to feed their teams a healthier diet.

After my first six months at Adobe, post-Behance's acquisition, I was asked to take over the mobile and services portion of Creative Cloud. I quickly became mired in questions around who should be in charge of what and who should and shouldn't work with whom. I faced a decision: Do I play within the entrenched politics by respecting the layers of management and the chain of command I had walked into? Or do I try to find the right people across the organizations, regardless of whom they reported to, and get them talking? At the time, it wasn't an obvious decision; the pressures of a big company are real, and it is tempting to adjust and avoid stepping on toes by not stepping across party lines and respecting an organization's existing political structure.

I decided to eschew the operating system I found myself in and created my own. After I had identified the people I thought could help us achieve our goals, I needed to work out how to break them free from hierarchy and bureaucracy. To engage key people from other parts of the organization, we invited them to our meetings, despite reporting lines. We kept all interested parties included on communication lines, regardless of whom they reported to. Rather than focus on the senior leaders of every team, we sought to engage the people who were closest to the technology and had their team's respect. Rather than have product leaders present designs, we brought in the actual designers to present their own designs. I encouraged my leadership team to speak up right away if something didn't make sense. And I pushed all of us to have in-person conversations when disagreements came up. There were fits and starts, but we ultimately grew a team of hundreds of people who were remarkably aligned and effective.

I realized that the politics of the organization encouraged people to focus on small and less disruptive wins rather than make a dent in the more controversial, and more important, problems. It was easier to let conflicts linger than wade through layers of management and follow up on communication lags. We had to break these barriers to make progress—without breaking the organization. We picked our fights carefully. Of course, much of this is easier to implement as a senior leader in an organization, but the same principles can be fostered from junior ranks as well. It starts with building your own relationships with people in different teams across your organization and proactively serving as an ambassador, connecting the right people to expedite solutions.

Just a year or so later, in 2015, a special moment happened when a senior designer on the team, Eric Snowden, was onstage demoing our new products in Apple's keynote for the launch of the first iPad Pro. Another member of my team, Govind Balakrishnan, who ran all of engineering for our group, walked over to me and commented that he still couldn't believe it had all come together. We recalled some of our most trying moments and how daunted we felt at the beginning when all of this was a sketch on a whiteboard. Sure, there were fights for head count and debates about reporting lines and priorities across different teams, but we had aligned enough people to use the organization's weight in our favor. Now, with a whole new suite of applications and a clear strategy, our team was part of Apple's keynote—which carried extra significance, given Apple and Adobe's long-standing feud over Flash, which was now, finally, water under the bridge.

In a big company, change causes some degree of disarray and often requires many people and processes to shift. Given these circumstances, it's tempting to stay safe by adhering to protocol, hierarchy, and process. But by doing so, it is more difficult to get the right people talking to one another. It's more important to be collaborative than to be correct.

If an organization doesn't let politics and burdensome processes get in the way, then size becomes an advantage. If not, well… big companies become couch potatoes while the future of their industry passes them by. Of course, this all comes down to the leaders themselves and whether or not a culture supports people stepping out of their traditional roles. Fight corporate obesity by gathering the right people in a room and depoliticizing process as much as you can.

DYFJ. Do Your Fucking Job.

Every journey has heavy, all-consuming moments. Firing employees. Solving a PR crisis. Weathering legal battles. On such occasions, you'll struggle to push through the muck. You'll fret the aftermath of confrontation. You won't want to upset people, especially those who may be left without jobs because of your decisions. You'll find every reason to analyze further, delay action, and blunt the blow. But most of the time, the right answer is clear, and the next step is yours.

You need to do your fucking job.

This is what I would tell myself before going into a tough meeting, nail-biting negotiation, or making the decision to fire an employee. Whenever I needed to force myself to take action that would be painful in the short term but was for the greater good, I would whisper to myself, "Scott, do your fucking job."

Don't blame yourself for feeling skittish. Avoiding conflict and hesitating before you disappoint others is not a weakness, it is having a conscience. Relationships matter, and the cost of upheaval in any relationship or team culture is very real. But just as a common cold can become full-blown pneumonia if left unchecked, infections in a team grow when not addressed. Your job is to detect infection, determine whether it is viral, and nip it in the bud if it is.

Leading a team through enduring times requires many "rip off the Band-Aid" moments. Nobody wants to inflict pain on their team, but quick and controlled pain is better than a drawn-out infection. If the cost of waiting exceeds the benefits of acting now, you have a job to do—DYFJ!

In the middle of 2017, the cofounder and CEO of a fast-growing start-up in the social video space reached out to me for some help. We had met only once or twice and I was not an investor in his company at the time, but he asked if we could talk. We met at a small coffee shop in New York City's Soho neighborhood to discuss his dilemma. A senior member of his team had been accused of inappropriate behavior from some of his subordinates and a short investigation had confirmed it. His board members were urging him to hold off on any "rash" decisions because of an imminent round of financing and the company's recent traction. But that didn't feel right to him. He was struggling between what he knew, in his gut, he must do, and all the noise from investors and the usual anxieties that accompany decisions that cause a lot of turbulence. As we talked through the costs and benefits of waiting and how to start these conversations, it occurred to me that he didn't need any more rationale to fire the person. Rather than continue thinking about the repercussions and his discomfort with the decision he already knew was right, he had to just do it. He came to this conclusion on his own, and as we parted ways, I said, DYFJ, and he nodded. Perhaps all he needed was a reminder that some critical tasks—often the most difficult ones—will not be taken until the leader summons the courage to stop considering it and just does it.

During the most trying times, you may also struggle to remain composed and continue carrying the torch. While members of your team will express doubt and air their hopeless moments, you will need to keep the pace by keeping the faith.

One of the entrepreneurs I have admired over the years is Kegan Schouwenburg. After some time working at Shapeways, a 3D printing company, Kegan set out to found her own business designing custom orthotics. Her company, SOLS, was on a rough ride: Kegan had to fire a cofounder, shift the business's focus multiple times, and land subsequent rounds of funding at a time when it was hard to raise money for hardware start-ups. While her business was ultimately sold, which wasn't the outcome she had hoped for, I was especially struck by her persistence and positivity along the way. Reflecting on some of her most challenging periods in the business, Kegan recalled, "One of our ex-employees told me in passing recently that I used to sing under my breath, 'Just keep going.' Honestly, I think that is most of it. You just have to show up and be there because your team depends on you. When you've got your entire staff looking to you for leadership, listening to your language, and even your body language to give them a sense of confidence in what you're doing as a company, that responsibility really gives you the energy to power through the uncertainty."

"It's amazing what you can achieve if you refuse to be discouraged, refuse to let down your team, and you check your ego at the door," Kegan added. Indeed, the possibilities are endless if you just keep going and, at your most difficult and trying moments, push yourself to do your fucking job.

STRENGTHENING YOUR RESOLVE

The only "sustainable competitive advantage" in business is self-awareness.

Your sense of self shifts when you're at a peak or in a valley.

During great moments, we are liable to have an inflated sense of self. We believe we are right more often than we actually are. As both a defense mechanism and the presumption that we should just continue doing what we're doing to keep climbing, we become less open to the advice and signals around us. We start to believe the nice things people say about us and become too confident in our own abilities and less in touch with reality.

Similarly, in difficult periods when we are struggling to find the motivation and direction to move forward, we can become less aware. When we stress, we regress. As our strengths become weaknesses, our superpowers turn against us when we feel vulnerable. We blame people and forces around us as a way to maintain our confidence and the soundness of our plans.

Self-awareness starts with the realization that when you're at a peak or in a valley, you're not your greatest self. When things are going well, ego gets the best of you. When times are tough, insecurities run rampant for everyone involved. Only by recognizing these shifts in ourselves and others can we manage them and protect the integrity of our judgment and actions. We are not necessarily the cause of the situation, but we are the cause of how we see it. Our perspective is our promise or peril. With such insight, you can more carefully vet your reactions and decisions when things are going very well or poorly. Effective advisers and boards are most helpful at the extremes, when the tough questions are less apparent but critical.

Self-awareness means understanding your own feelings enough to recognize what bothers you. Whatever triggers your frustration or irritates you is rooted in a core value you have, something you vehemently stand for or against. For example, injustice really bothers me. Whenever I see unfairness, I need to right it. When I am taken advantage of, I will opt to right the wrong even if the economic cost of doing so exceeds the economic impact of letting it go. This behavior could potentially be destructive, and it is tied to one of my core values. But now that I have made myself aware of it, I can see it bubbling up in myself and learn how to mitigate it. At least I try. Being conscious of your triggers helps you take your finger off that trigger.

Self-awareness means being permeable. An undeniable theme among founders I've worked with is that the less defensive they are, the more potential they have. Those who are able to openly absorb and selectively integrate what they hear consistently outperform those who are impermeable to suggestion. I deeply admire founders and designers I have worked with who seek feedback proactively. But being open-minded while receiving constructive criticism is challenging. When you feel criticized or attacked, what happens? Do you immediately try to explain yourself? Do you go on the offensive and try to fight back? Do you become reclusive and try to avoid the conflict altogether? Do you become more steadfast in your ways, or are you too shaken and too impressionable? Self-awareness helps you achieve balance between these tendencies. If you acknowledge your behavior when it happens, and then investigate what is driving it, you will become more open to the right insights from others.

Self-awareness comes from chronicling your patterns. The insecurities, brash reactions, and self-doubts that emerge in difficult times are reflexes that started long ago. The leaders I admire most have invested a great deal of time understanding their own psychology and unpacking their past. Whether through executive coaching, psychoanalysis, or some form of group therapy, your effort to understand how your own mind works is the only path to reliable self-awareness during times of stress.

Understanding the sources of your own negative tendencies also helps you make sense of others' behavior. As psychoanalyst Carl Jung, who founded the field of analytical psychology, once said according to numerous accounts, "Knowing your own darkness is the best method for dealing with the darkness of other people." Being in touch with your own flaws helps you support others with their flaws. Discussing your flaws invites others to do the same.

Self-awareness means dispelling your sense of superiority and the myths that people believe about you. With any achievement, we're liable to overestimate the role we played in it and underestimate the role of others—and of luck. By doing so, we alienate those who did contribute and become less relatable. We obsess over ourselves a bit more and tune into others a bit less. I have watched a number of successful artists and entrepreneurs I know become more isolated and paranoid as they became well known. Perhaps they begin to question the motives of everyone around them, or perhaps they start to believe they are superior. Regardless, the result is a loss of genuine connection with the people who helped launch their careers and, with it, empathy. Without empathy for others' problems, ideas become less viable solutions.

The trick is to integrate humility in your life. It could be a sense of spirituality that keeps you open, a partner who keeps you grounded, or an insatiable sense of curiosity that keeps you inquisitive. Attribute your wins to those around you, and be the first to take responsibility for losses.

Ultimately, self-awareness is about preserving sound judgment and keeping relatable and realistic. However big your project or ambition, your journey is nothing more than a sequence of decisions: You're probably many decisions away from success, but always one decision away from failure. Clarity matters. The more aware you are of yourself and your surroundings, the more data you have to inform your decisions, and the more competitive you will be.

Nobody remembers, or is inspired by, anything that fits in.

If you're building a new business, you'll be tempted to describe what you're making in the context of what already exists as a shortcut to relatability, like the "Uber for massage" or the "Apple of razors." The pressure to conform stems from the natural desire to be understood. But what you gain in relatability by latching onto an existing model, you lose in free-range innovation.

One of my favorite thinkers on this topic is James Victore, a widely respected designer who has committed a part of his life to educating the next generation of designers. I've attended workshops that James puts on for his students, and a theme throughout is resisting the urge to fit in. I asked James to explain why he seeks work that, at first, strikes others as strange, and how he handles it:

> I do the work I do because I have to. I can't help it. I was born this way—I can't be false to any man. I know what the current trends and moods are, but I can't concern myself with them. I also can't force myself (as many do) to make work

that fits within the going commercial style. Trends change, and I believe that is why my work is still relevant today, because I am the only one making work like mine.

The idea of being born "weird" means you have a gift—like being born a star athlete. It would be a sin to deny my gift. My "weird" is powerful. It stands out. I know that it attracts some individuals and clients, and repels others. I have to be cool with that. I am not for everyone—just the sexy people. Like you.

When you pursue something on the fringe that uniquely fascinates you, you'll repel those who just don't relate. You may be shunned. And most people won't understand. But the future always starts as fringe. When front-running the future, the trick is to aspire for a small audience that loves your product rather than aim to please the masses.

James wants us to find peace with our "weird." Embrace the stuff you're most proud of that others don't understand because this is your proverbial ticket. But more important, James is pushing us to use weirdness and the rejection that comes along with it as a barometer for our originality. Are you seeking acceptance too early in your project? Are you too deterred by being misunderstood? Are you trying to normalize what you're making and, in the process, regressing to the mean?

Don't succumb to society's gravitational force toward what is common and familiar. One of the worst tendencies of the messy middle is pulling wildly fresh insights back toward the mean of normalcy. Don't let this happen to you. While society wants you to conform, it needs you to break the mold to help us see differently and make life better for the rest of us. And as American artist Sol LeWitt once advised, "Learn to say 'fuck you' to the world once in a while." Do your thing.

Take a dose of OBECALP and suspend your disbeliefs in yourself.

My father, who began his medical career as a surgical intern in New York City's Bellevue hospital, has experienced many intense nights in the emergency room, where patients have come in suffering from drug overdoses and other dire situations.

During his time in the ER, he told me about the administration of a particular dosage of "OBECALP," which was either administered intravenously or as a pill for patients suffering from the anxiety that accompanied their physical or mental afflictions. After a dose of OBECALP, most people would calm down and engage in conversation with the medical staff.

OBECALP is, of course, *placebo* spelled backward.

Over the past two decades, many clinical trials have shown that the strange effects of placebo sugar pills are getting stronger. In a 2015 study, published in the journal *Pain*, researchers found that in 1996 drugs relieved pain 27 percent more than a placebo. But in 2013 that gap had fallen to 9 percent. Stranger still, this effect has been observed only in the U.S., which is one reason why pharmaceutical companies are struggling to get new painkillers through trials. Nevertheless, placebos are powerful. Sometimes patients need the hope that a placebo provides to recover.

In tough moments when your prospects feel grim and hope is fading, your mind will only make it worse. You'll begin to question your ideas and tell yourself that you're not qualified and that your team isn't good enough. You'll become your own worst enemy and you'll stop believing in your own plan and abilities. When this happens, what you need is 20 milligrams of OBECALP. Stat.

Imagine, for a moment, that all your self-doubts are simply a function of society's immune system, designed to extinguish nonconforming actions. You're questioning yourself because you're doing something different and society is trying to stop you—your body is trying to reject the thing that is taking it out of its comfy homeostasis. There can be only so much innovation and change in a world that runs on consistency and people falling in line. Remind yourself that progress is vision paired with initiative. The hopelessness you're feeling is a common phase that precedes progress; we often feel the weakest just before our immune response kicks in. Sometimes you need to make yourself swallow a big OBECALP to get through that time. A big part of overcoming doubt is suspending your disbelief. You want to stay grounded as you make decisions, but sometimes you need to escape the gravity of reality to imagine the possibilities.

A friend who worked for Google cofounder and CEO Larry Page told me that when teams presented product and business goals to Larry, he would often reply, "What would it take to achieve 100x of what you're proposing?" This was totally unrealistic, of course. Such questions would throw teams off their tracks, but the notion of aspiring for an entirely different magnitude of impact had some important side effects. First, whatever doubts teams came in with suddenly paled in comparison to the new concern. Second, teams were forced to question their core assumptions and untether themselves from reality's gravity. In some ways, Larry was administering a dose of OBECALP to suspend his team's disbelief and recalibrate their ambitions.

Your challenge is to work out how to administer your own placebo. Perhaps it is a bold narrative your team replays about what it will look and feel like to see your future product out in the wild? Perhaps it is your efforts to merchandise contingency plans so people can move forward with less fear? When you envision what is possible in a state of suspended disbelief, you free yourself from your previous petty problems. Once you have that goal in mind, you then should attempt to execute it as practically as you can.

You don't know what you're capable of. Whether it is navigating your career, starting a new business, or overcoming an illness, giving yourself a placebo of sorts that suspends your doubt is one of the greatest factors in making progress.

Attempt a new perspective of it before you quit it.

When times are truly rough, when should you stick with it, and when should you quit it?

In her late twenties, Angela Duckworth quit her job as a management consultant to teach middle school math in New York City. She observed that students' success was determined by their effort more than anything else. Intrigued, she began studying why some people work much harder than others, and she enrolled in the University of Pennsylvania's psychology PhD program. In 2016, she wrote *Grit: The Power of Passion and Perseverance* about her findings. Duckworth explains that what determines whether you succeed or fail is grit, a special blend of passion and perseverance directed at accomplishing long-term goals.

"Grit is having stamina. Grit is sticking with your future, day in, day out, not just for the week, not just for the month, but for years, and working really hard to make that future a reality. Grit is living life like it's a marathon, not a sprint," Duckworth said in her 2013 TED talk.

But working hard doesn't mean showing no pain or pretending all is well. Duckworth clarifies in a *New York Times* interview that "when you look at healthy and successful and giving people, they are extraordinarily meta-cognitive. They're able to say things like, 'Dude, I totally lost my temper this morning.' That ability to reflect on yourself is a signature to grit."

In the middle of any journey you'll wonder if you should just give up. It can be hard to see in the moment, but your struggle may mean you're onto something new that is defensible from competitors and copycats. The question is whether you're close to the tipping point of the project working and the difficulties you're experiencing are just wearing you down, or if they're rightfully making you question your true belief in the final vision.

It's extremely difficult to halt all progress and start all over again, but the boldest projects have multiple such "resets." Perhaps one of the most challenging and important consumer product creations of our lifetime was the iPod, and subsequently the iPhone. So I asked Tony Fadell—who, before creating the thermostat company Nest, was brought into Apple by Steve Jobs to lead the iPod project, and then iPhone—about how his teams worked their way around so many dead ends.

Tony explained, "I think there are two kinds of resets, one which is product spec based, not meeting the customer needs, and the other which is engineering based, not having a way to implement the plan with the current team or current technology inside or outside the company. We did a lot of resets along the path from iPod to iPhone, like going from iPod to an iPod Phone, to an iPod with a big screen, to a touch screen Mac, and then putting it all together to make iPhone—always searching for the right mix of technology and user experience." It sounds like a normal process in retrospect, but spending months if not years pursuing one path and then hitting the reset button can exhaust and demoralize a team. But Tony felt that, so long as you're gaining confidence in the opportunity and absorbing the lessons learned, you have a renewable energy source.

"In most cases, if the fundamental reasons for why the product or service should exist are still valid, then the team will always take on the challenge, assuming you didn't burn way too much time or cash and it was an intelligent—albeit sometimes crazy and unexpected— way to get to the learnings. We all, as a team, did a conscious recommit at the end of each one of these 'resets,' or what I call 'learning phases,' to describe the lessons learned, what assumptions have changed, and which ones didn't, to muster the energy to make another go at it."

The trick is to separate the hardship from what you're learning. If you're learning that your assumptions were wrong—that customers don't want your product or that you're building the wrong thing—then you should ask yourself: Knowing all that I know now, would I pursue the project all over again? Would I invest the money and energy all over again to get as far as I've come in solving this problem?

If the answer is yes, don't quit. Keep at it. Feeling impatient with progress and deflated by process is fine, so long as you still have conviction.

But if your answer is "Hell, no! If I could go back to the day before I got into this mess, I would head in a totally different direction," then ask yourself why you are still trying. Are the sunk costs keeping you from quitting? Are you still going only because of how much you've invested in it so far? Is it just ego? Try not to value the progress you've made thus far based on how hard it was and what leaving will cost you.

I've never been fond of the "winners never quit" mantra because it goes against what I've learned from many successful start-ups that pivoted from their original idea with great success. Twitter, Pinterest, Airbnb, and many other companies started with either a different approach or a vastly different product before they got it right. If you've lost conviction but refuse to change course because of what you've already invested or achieved, then you're officially doing things for the wrong reason.

As you contemplate new approaches to a problem rather than quitting altogether, it's important to let go of past conclusions proven wrong. One of my friends who worked at Apple for a number of years recalled Steve Jobs's ability to change his mind on the turn of a dime when a better solution was presented—he didn't get stuck with an operating mode just because it had been one that was working. He had famously strong opinions, but he was also able to detach from them. In this way, Steve was the embodiment of the famous advice to have "strong opinions, weakly held." Only by letting go are you able to truly attempt a new perspective of your venture before you quit.

To create what will be, you must remove yourself from the constant concern for what already is.

The spring of 2015 was one of the most exciting albeit challenging periods of Alexa von Tobel's life. Just off a $35 million financing round for LearnVest, a company she had launched exactly five years earlier to help American families with financial planning, Alexa was fielding multiple acquisition offers. She was at a critical juncture in the company's growth and has just finished overhauling her management team. She was also expecting her first baby any day. On top of it all, Alexa was still on the line to manage her team and continue her role as a very public face for the company and, increasingly, for the financial industry.

"In a weird way, the level of craziness provided an even greater sense of perspective and judgment," Alexa explained to me. "I kind of felt like I was doing an Ironman—you can't get too stressed about a few miles of swimming or the hundred miles of biking, because you've got a marathon waiting for you after that. The fact that such extreme things were happening at the same time conjured up a forced sense of perspective and calm, reminding me what really matters and preventing me from getting too consumed by any one of the challenges I was facing. If bad decisions are made when we lose perspective, then facing all of these important moments in my life—all at once—was a good thing. Paradoxically, the busier you are at any moment in time, the better your decisions may be because of the greater perspective you have. Bringing life into this world, unsurprisingly, brings perspective."

The many challenges Alexa faced kept her from becoming overwhelmed by any one of them. Alexa was able to compartmentalize and focus on each with an eye toward the future. In her decision to sell her business, she focused on the three constituencies she served—shareholders, employees, and clients—and led a process that proved successful for everyone involved. Alexa sold her company, LearnVest, to Northwestern Mutual on a Wednesday for a reported $350 million and then went into labor on Sunday.

Alexa kept a longer-term perspective and managed each challenge on its own. When viewed in context of her ultimate goals—becoming a mother, leading her team, and ensuring a good outcome for her company—the day-to-day issues were dwarfed.

As you encounter such periods in your own career, compartmentalize each drama individually and remind yourself on the horrible days that tomorrow will be better. Compartmentalizing doesn't mean burying or denying the emotional toll; it means facing one challenge at a time and using each one to provide more perspective for dealing with the others. Storms have the habit of feeling like their own little worlds, even though they're just weather patterns and they move on.

Compartmentalizing is just as hard on a daily basis as it is during a perfect storm. The more responsibility you bear, the more your collective concerns will limit your productivity. To move forward, unbounded by the anxieties and insecurities of the moment, you must apply controls to the energy you spend assuring yourself that all is OK.

TAKE NOTE OF YOUR "INSECURITY WORK"

Over the years, I have come to recognize the amount of time I spend checking things: Daily sales data, website traffic trends, what people are saying on Twitter, analytics for our customers, team progress on projects, the list goes on. For you, it might be diving into a spreadsheet to manipulate budget numbers or scanning through your unanswered emails again and again. When you're anxious about your business, there is no easier quick-relief antidote than checking things. The problem is that you could spend all day checking things and fail to do anything to change things.

I call it *insecurity work*—stuff that you do that has

1. no intended outcome,
2. does not move the ball forward in any way, and
3. is quick enough that you can do it unconsciously multiple times a day.

Insecurity work puts you at ease, but it doesn't actually get anything done.

The antidote is a combination of awareness, self-discipline, and delegation. Whether it is Googling the same search terms again and again or constantly checking your in-box as if it were a boiling pot of water, you need to identify these behaviors to then change them. When you spend 30 minutes going down a rabbit hole to answer a particular question, be sure to ask yourself, "Why is this question important and how is the answer actionable?" If the answer is just self-assuring but not actionable, it is likely insecurity work.

Once you've identified your insecurity work, establish some guidelines and rituals for yourself. For example, you could allow yourself a period at the end of every day, say 30 minutes, where you let yourself go through the list of things you're curious about. Put all of your mosquito bites in one place and allow yourself the pleasure of scratching them all at once.

The purpose of reducing the hours you spend on insecurity work is to free up your mind, energy, and time for generating and taking action on new ideas instead of checking in on old ones.

KEEP YOUR STARE AHEAD

Whether managing one of the most difficult periods of your life or just the everyday ups and downs, you can make progress only by focusing forward and removing yourself from the constant concern for what has already happened.

During one of my recent trips to Japan, I spent some time at a Buddhist temple learning about rock gardens and the design practices behind them. In these gardens, small, finely washed rocks are immaculately raked into lines and curves that create remarkable designs around larger boulders that serve as the rock garden's anchors. One Zen principle lies in the process of raking lines in the rock garden. If you focus on each line as you make it, it isn't straight. Instead, you must focus ahead to keep the line straight as you rake.

I was struck by how this Zen principle relates to leading a team through daily challenges while staying true to a long-term vision. If we rake with heads down, always concerned about the lines of stones beneath our feet, our lines run amok. The *insecurity work* we do every day is the equivalent of leading a journey focused only on what is immediately concerning us—beneath our feet—rather than focusing on where we want to be. But if you compartmentalize your ideas and look ahead, and worry less about day-to-day concerns, you'll eventually look behind yourself to see the line you drew was much straighter. You will arrive much closer to your vision.

Prompt clarity with questions.

Most of your experience enduring the middle miles will be couched with uncertainty. You'll feel like you're wading through an ocean of unknown depths and inhabitants—in the dark. But every now and then, a light goes on. Not a floodlight that illuminates the horizon but rather a spotlight that provides some context and comfort. In these rare moments, you suddenly get a sense of where you are, what is behind you, and what comes next.

The teams I have led and advised over the years make a ton of progress in these moments of clarity. It is during such moments that they settle on the perfect brand, devise a truly differentiating feature, or make a crucial decision that completely changes the course of the project. But how do you find the light switch and not get temporarily blinded by the glare of opportunity? What prompts these moments of clarity, and how do you capitalize on them?

I remember one such moment with the Periscope team in early 2014 before the launch of their first live-video product. This glimpse of light ultimately led to some drastic changes in their product, and ultimately their much celebrated acquisition by Twitter.

When I first met Kayvon Beykpour and Joe Bernstein, Periscope's founders, they were building a different product, Bounty. The original idea for Bounty was to allow anyone around the world to request a photo of a particular place or event and have someone close by capture the photo for a fee. The idea had potential, but a series of brainstorms within the team about the broader state of social media and the emerging field of live video transformed the entire premise of the company in just a matter of days.

At the time, social media was mostly photos and prerecorded video. Whether you were using Facebook, Twitter, or Snapchat, the photos and videos you saw had already happened. As a result, it was hard to feel like you were actually there. When you witness an event in person, you connect and empathize with those around you. But watching a prerecorded video—or even live television that you cannot interact with—depersonalizes the experience.

The Periscope team and I discussed the idea, coupled with the emergence of better bandwidth for mobile devices, and wondered, "As live video becomes more feasible, what kind of social experience would foster truth and empathy?" This crucial question prompted the vision of "teleportation," where anyone could witness an experience through someone else's eyes and interact with the broadcaster to influence what they were watching. The notion of teleportation was the moment of clarity that changed the course of the company. Within days, Kayvon and Joe had built a new deck and recruited a video engineer. The team raised a round of funding with this new vision—and the rest is history.

For Periscope, their epiphany came from analyzing the market, which led to the right question. As I look back, the ambiguity prior to the team's pivot was a clue that more discussion and circumspection was needed. When the right question was finally asked, everything became illuminated.

Whenever I meet with a team that lacks clarity or feels stuck, their breakthrough often comes from a new question or problem to solve rather than a better answer to the original question. When making a decision with limited time and resources (and stress), we're liable to accept the original premise and charge ahead to create new products or features without even asking questions—or questioning the problem we're trying to solve in the first place.

Whether you're an author suffering from writer's block or a start-up team struggling to satisfy its customers, *the solution is to change the question you're asking.* If the original question plaguing you is "Why aren't people signing up for our product?" maybe the better question is "What kinds of people would benefit most from our product?" When you feel lost in ambiguity, ask a different question.

A question informs the answer more than we realize. Watch any great journalist at work—like Tom Brokaw or Katie Couric—and you'll realize that asking great questions is an art in itself. Avoid questions that already include a possible answer to avoid biasing the discussion. If a question is accusatory, it will trigger defensiveness. A rhetorical question won't get alternative answers. A yes or no question won't spark discussion beyond its answer.

The perfect question is a key to clarity. It unlocks truth and opens minds. It is distilled by having empathy for your customers' struggles and ignoring sunk costs and past assumptions to get at the root of a problem. When you're building something new, focus on asking the right questions instead of having the right answers.

Sometimes a reset is the only way forward.

When all has gone to shit and morale has suffered, how do you recover? Or if your project has failed or you've been fired, how do you turn a new leaf?

Before cofounding The Muse, a popular New York–based career website, Kathryn Minshew was fired from another company she had founded previously, Pretty Young Professionals.

Working at McKinsey in 2010, Minshew and three colleagues, all young women, cofounded Pretty Young Professionals (PYP), a pink, stiletto-clad women's networking site. In December 2010, Minshew became the first to quit McKinsey, agreeing to run PYP full-time as an unpaid CEO and editor in chief. Describing this decision in 2010, she told *Forbes*'s Peter Cohen, "There is huge potential in providing useful, empowering content to young professional women. Smart women have a dearth of smart content choices." This mission acutely foreshadows The Muse, which now serves fifty million users, more than 65 percent of whom are women.

But the path to building PYP was fraught with fits and starts and disputes between its cofounders. The multiple redesigns and disagreements about how to run the company left Minshew with a tough choice less than a year after the company's founding. As she explained in an interview in *Entrepreneur* magazine: "I spent three weeks alternating between the fetal position and the whiteboard trying to figure out how strongly I wanted to fight for the existing company versus how prepared I was to strike out and do it over." Ultimately, the two cofounders with the least equity managed to boot Minshew as CEO, using legal threats. "I was blindsided; it came as a total shock," Minshew recalled. Then, behind Minshew's back, they relaunched PYP under a new (and still running) label: Levo League.

Minshew could've wallowed in self-pity and ditched her dream. Instead, she reset: Just months after being nixed, Minshew launched The Daily Muse (now The Muse), a career website run her way. The PYP staff (most of which Minshew hired) joined her, along with one PYP cofounder. The site drew more visitors in its first month than PYP did at its peak. "It was painful, but being forced to start over was a unique sort of gift, because having been through a lot together, the team comes out of it with the confidence that nothing is going to stop us," Minshew told *Entrepreneur*. In November 2011, The Muse was accepted into the Y Combinator accelerator program.

Today, The Muse is among the most trusted career platforms for millennials, listing jobs and corporate profiles from hundreds of companies like Goldman Sachs, Wells Fargo, Gap, HBO, Condé Nast, and Bloomberg. "My heroes, in real life, tend to be people who either broke through barriers or overcame tremendous obstacles—not only individually, but people who opened up pathways," Minshew said in Anthropologie's "Women of Character" feature. She, undoubtedly, is one of those people.

Kathryn's story is a common one. Conflict prompts disappointment, followed by perspective and self-examination, and ultimately another attempt with a renewed sense of purpose. Leading a reset happens in six phases: feeling anger, removing yourself, dissecting the situation, acknowledging your role, drafting your narrative, and then getting back in the game.

Feel the Anger

If you're seething with anger and disappointment, let yourself feel it. The emotion is real, and denying it keeps you angry or, even worse, leaks into other parts of your life.

Remove Yourself

The second phase is giving yourself space to get some perspective. Something went wrong, you're angry and upset—but you also have one life to live. While you may feel the urge to jump back in and vindicate yourself, your brain—and judgment—will benefit from a context switch first. It can be hard to remove yourself from the situation you're in, but when you take a time-out—perhaps a week abroad or simply a trip to the beach—you'll wonder how you could have recovered without it. You're free and you're alive—don't forget it.

Dissect the Situation

After the anger has subsided and you've put some distance between you and the instigating incident, it is time to dissect the situation with a sound mind and some perspective. What went down? Did you see it coming? Why or why not? Play back lines in your head: Who said what, and why? What other external factors were at play? Also ask your partner, spouse, or close friends for their perspective. Were they surprised? What do they think happened? This is the learning phase. You're not trying to assign blame: You're just trying to understand what happened. Think of yourself as an impartial detective pulling apart a crime scene to gather as much data as possible without coming to a conclusion too quickly.

Acknowledge Your Role

Once you have a full understanding of the situation, own your role in it. What decisions did you make that were, in retrospect, wrong? What did you fail to communicate? Who and what did you underestimate or overestimate? What would you do differently? Make sure the "if-onlys" go both ways—you should not only identify the external factors and people who would have prevented the problem, "if only they had done something different," but also apply the same scrutiny to yourself: "If only I had…" As you absorb the lessons, you optimize your future potential. It is also healthy to close the loop with people you may have wronged. Reach out to colleagues, clients, or investors you may have wounded and share your perspective. If necessary, apologize. This closure is as much for you as it is for them. You can wipe your slate clean only when you've been held accountable and address loose ends. Without such closure, you will continue to use your psychic energy to process the guilt or anger.

Draft Your Narrative

Now it's time to connect your experience with your plans for the future. Start by writing out what happened and what you learned. This narrative is less about crafting your story and more about spending the time to synthesize what happened, what you've learned from it, and what you hope to do next. This story line is what you will tell yourself as the next project begins. You'll also end up sharing a rendition of it with others for years to come as you put your past into context with your future endeavors. Sharing your recovery and the lessons you learned turns failures into opportunities and inspires others while gaining their trust and respect. I always encourage people who are switching careers or dealing with a major setback to draft a blog post or long letter, even if they don't publish or send it.

Get Back in the Game

With hard lessons learned and a clear narrative, you need to throw yourself back into action. Remember that you'll need to take a few steps back to head in a new direction. Sometimes this means reducing the scope of your aspirations, but it is progress nonetheless. So long as you are advancing your genuine interests and feeling utilized, you're headed in the right direction. When you find your mind drifting to the past and questioning yourself, focus on the fact that you are now more qualified to weather what's ahead. Every storm better prepares us for the next. Trying again after getting beaten down is never easy—but the important things never are.

You will recover and thrive. Do it one step at a time.

EMBRACING THE
LONG GAME

Playing the long game requires moves that don't map to traditional measures of productivity.

The human mind is remarkably shortsighted. We're very good at recognizing cause and effect and projecting the short-term implications of our actions. But we struggle when it comes to chain reactions and laying the groundwork for future opportunities. It takes an entirely different set of measures to engage and endure the long game.

The long game requires us to sometimes break the rules of productivity. For instance, do you take meetings that could only yield a possible transaction in the near term, or are you seeking to build relationships that may yield collaborations many years from now? Are you willing to spend time just brainstorming for the sake of brainstorming, even when you're busy? Do you make time investments only with people who can give you something you want right now, or are you willing to invest in people in whom you believe, even if you think their next project is more likely to succeed than their current one? While many people claim to value long-term moves, few people have the patience.

Curiosity is the fuel you need to play the long game. When you're genuinely curious about something, you're less likely to measure productivity in traditional ways. Instead, you're content being in the muck and gain satisfaction from learning something new, not just ticking off to-do items. Rather than seeking a positive outcome, you're exploring all options to satiate your own interests.

The greatest venture investors I know are insanely curious. For instance, over the years that I have known Bill Gurley, the famed investor behind OpenTable, Stitch Fix, Zillow, and Uber, I have always been struck by how deep he'll explore an interest despite a packed schedule. Whether learning about the transportation industry or oncology and urgent health care, Bill will explore an interest for many months or years without concern for when—or even if—the right investment opportunity will present itself. He's not racing toward a transaction against a clock; he's digging to learn.

The long game gets even harder when others get involved. If you're *really* playing the long game and turning down immediate opportunities, people will probably start scratching their heads. The seeds you're planting—long-term relationships, curiosity-driven explorations, thought experiments—are less likely to be supported by others both socially and financially.

In a talk he gave at the Aspen Institute in 2009, Amazon founder Jeff Bezos, legendary for his long-term vision, reiterated this point. "Invention requires a long-term willingness to be misunderstood," he said. "When you do something that you genuinely believe in, that you have conviction about, for a long period of time, well-meaning people may criticize that effort." To sustain yourself over this time, you can't look for accolades, and you can't rely on being understood. Playing the long game is a test of your fortitude, your ability to persevere, and just how genuine your interests are.

Strategy is nourished by patience.

There are so many people in the world with ideas to transform industries and build iconic brands. But very few people can stay loyal to a strategy long enough for their vision to materialize. While a great strategy can be conceived quite quickly in a vacuum void of time and reality, it can be executed only over a long period of iteration, agony, and harsh reality (the messy middle!). To allow strategy to unfold, you need to refactor your own expectations and measures of progress while developing a culture and structure that ensures your team has the patience to stick it out with you.

Companies are as impatient as people, if not more so. If your project is under the gaze of a large organization, often measured by its quarterly results, it is often exceptionally hard to get the necessary time and space for your bold strategy to materialize. Teams must therefore build systems to nourish patience, culturally or structurally, and you must be willing to defend your long game.

CULTURAL SYSTEMS FOR PATIENCE

During Amazon's first year as a public company in 1997, Jeff Bezos sent a now famous letter to his investors. He started it by outlining his strategy to become a market leader. "Because of our emphasis on the long term," he wrote, "we may make decisions and weigh tradeoffs differently than some companies. Accordingly, we want to share with you our fundamental management and decision-making approach so that you, our shareholders, may confirm that it is consistent with your investment philosophy." Bezos then proceeded to outline for his investors and, more important, for his team exactly what this meant. This is a helpful reminder of how a company culture can be crafted to nourish patience with strategy.

We will continue to focus relentlessly on our customers.

We will continue to make investment decisions in light of long-term market leadership considerations rather than short-term profitability considerations or short-term Wall Street reactions.

We will continue to measure our programs and the effectiveness of our investments analytically, to jettison those that do not provide acceptable returns, and to step up our investment in those that work best. We will continue to learn from both our successes and our failures.

We will make bold rather than timid investment decisions where we see a sufficient probability of gaining market leadership advantages. Some of these investments will pay off, others will not, and we will have learned another valuable lesson in either case.

When forced to choose between optimizing the appearance of our GAAP accounting and maximizing the present value of future cash flows, we'll take the cash flows.

We will share our strategic thought processes with you when we make bold choices (to the extent competitive pressures allow), so that you may evaluate for yourselves whether we are making rational long-term leadership investments.

We will work hard to spend wisely and maintain our lean culture. We understand the importance of continually reinforcing a cost-conscious culture, particularly in a business incurring net losses.

We will balance our focus on growth with emphasis on long-term profitability and capital management. At this stage, we choose to prioritize growth because we believe that scale is central to achieving the potential of our business model.

We will continue to focus on hiring and retaining versatile and talented employees, and continue to weight their compensation to stock options rather than cash. We know our success will be largely affected by our ability to attract and retain a motivated employee base, each of whom must think like, and therefore must actually be, an owner.

We aren't so bold as to claim that the above is the "right" investment philosophy, but it's ours, and we would be remiss if we weren't clear in the approach we have taken and will continue to take.

Bezos has included this letter as an appendix to every Amazon shareholder letter he has published since. He clearly wants to reiterate these principles to every investor and employee every chance he can.

Another story about Bezos addressing his team in the early Amazon days, following an incredible quarter of performance, sticks with me. Bezos congratulated his team but then reminded them, "If we have a good quarter, it is because of the work we did three, four, five years ago, not the work we did this quarter." There is a huge lag between great innovations and results. A new program takes a ton of refinement and optimization, as well as the natural passage of time, to spread and perform.

Amazon is perhaps the greatest corporate example of patiently executing a strategy over time. My friends at Amazon talk about how Bezos's external emphasis on long-term thinking constantly reinforces the value of taking risk and pursuing a long-term strategy within the company. When something fails, like Amazon's phone that barely lasted a year, Bezos makes it clear that he anticipates even more—and greater—failures ahead if the company is innovating enough. And when a new technology emerges, like Alexa, the company's voice-driven user interface, it is allowed to evolve without being immediately subjected to measures of profit or utilization. So long as the team has conviction for the long-term strategy, judgment is kept in check. By nourishing strategy and patience throughout Amazon's culture, Bezos has overhauled the natural human desires for immediate returns and near-term measures of progress.

STRUCTURAL SYSTEMS FOR PATIENCE

Some companies, like Google, nourish patience with strategy structurally. As a large company generating more than 90 percent of its revenue from advertising, the company has taken drastic steps to separate bold new initiatives from the gravity of its core business. The historic decision in 2015 to rename the entire company "Alphabet" and treat Google itself as just one of many companies in the holding company was an effort to structurally protect new projects with longtime horizons as independent companies outside of Google's operating business.

As a result, you get companies like Waymo pursuing autonomous-vehicle technology. These portfolio companies are liberated from the need to add near-term value and rationalize their existence on a quarterly basis. On a smaller scale, some companies will separate certain teams in terms of who they report to, where they are physically located, and how they are measured to provide protection against the quarterly drive for profits and shorter-term impact.

Designing the structure of a project or company to foster patience is ultimately an effort to limit our natural tendency to obsess over measuring progress with traditional near-term measures. Patience doesn't mean tolerating inaction or slower progress: It means allowing alternative forms of measuring the impact of action. Aaron Levie, founder and CEO of enterprise cloud-storage provider Box, said it best on Twitter: "Startups win by being impatient *over a long period of time.*"

Success stories downplay the role of patience. They artificially depict the speed of progress, and believing them makes you liable to give up sooner. For instance, many people look at online streaming service Netflix as an obvious replacement to Blockbuster's video and DVD rentals, but this seemingly simple process of moving from one trend to the other spanned a decade of persistent execution of a simple strategy: Move the video rental experience online and out of physical stores.

The first part of this strategy was to move customers from in-store rentals to DVD-by-mail rentals. After all, in the late 1990s, streaming two-hour-long videos online was a technical nightmare for both providers and consumers. Only with the advent of faster and cheaper broadband did Netflix's digital subscription service become a viable option on a mass scale.

For many years, Netflix was questioned and even mocked by industry analysts. Netflix

CEO Reed Hastings even approached Blockbuster CEO John Antioco in 2000, when the company was still focused on DVDs by mail, and reportedly offered to sell him the company for $50 million. According to *Variety*, Antioco thought Netflix was "a very small niche business" and declined the opportunity. Blockbuster went bankrupt in 2010 and, as I write this, Netflix is now a $150 billion market-cap company. It took nearly two decades for Netflix's strategy to play out and the tide to turn.

Seemingly quick wins have deep roots. You need to set up and provide measures for your team to help them endure long periods of doubt, ambiguity, and being misunderstood. Being able to extend your team's hunger and drive over a long period of time is the ultimate form of patience.

What you give up in near-term measures of productivity must be made up for with an increased near-term focus. Patty Jenkins, director of the recent reboot of *Wonder Woman*, remarked in a *Business Insider* interview on the necessity of a tight focus over a multiyear project. "Longevity of focus is, I think, the hardest part," she said. "To have a vision and then try to hold that vision and not have it change when a million elements around it change every day—like what a shot turned out like… or how the story changes subtly—the challenge is trying to hold on to the center." However you decide to hack the structure of your team to allow for a long-term execution of strategy, you must hold on to the key elements of your vision.

THE PERSONAL PURSUIT FOR PATIENCE

Despite how much we intellectually understand the importance of pursuing a strategy with patience, few of us are willing to pay the price of patience. In negotiations, we still seek to optimize for the fastest reward with the least near-term risk. We get impatient with an investment thesis during day-to-day market fluctuations, even if we structurally believe in it over the long term. And we'll spend a year working on a project and then begin to question it just weeks after launch rather than allow enough time to pass for an idea to become relevant or a brand to become recognizable.

Sadly, most people are not patient enough to reap the fruits of their own labor. Great teams gain their strength and resilience while toiling their way through the valleys, not just from relishing the view from the peaks. And yet start-ups lose people when the tough challenges come up. These same challenges will ultimately distinguish you and become your moat of defensibility—if and when they are conquered. Sustained patience and persistence can be such an amazing competitive advantage. Progress takes time, even when you have the very best strategy, people, and resources at your disposal.

To foster patience for yourself and those you lead, pick a speed that will get you there, and then pace yourself. Celebrate persistence over time as much as the occasional short-term wins you have along the way. Craft a culture in your project or team that values adherence to a vision and continual progress more than traditional measures of productivity. Establish a structure that allows teams to pursue long-term projects beyond the gravity of day-to-day operations. And remember just how rare it is to stick to a strategy over the long term. This competitive advantage is available to any team, big or small, that is patient enough to stay focused, stick together, and move forward.

THE EASY PATH WILL ONLY TAKE YOU TO A CROWDED PLACE

As you make decisions with long-term impact, such as selecting the technologies you will use in building your product, keep in mind that whatever is easily accessible to you is just as accessible to others. When I find myself debating a road map with a product team at Adobe, or making decisions about the technical architecture of a product, there is often an "easy option" that provides *most* of the desired functionality and a "best option" that is inevitably a step function more difficult and costly to achieve. I always prompt the questions: If we take the easy option, how quickly will our competitors be able to catch up? Is this an opportunity for us to make an investment that others cannot make to truly separate ourselves from the rest? If you want to be the industry leader, sometimes you need to take the difficult path. Be wary of the path of least resistance. It may look compelling in the short term but often proves less differentiating and defensible in the long term. Shortcuts tend to be less gratifying over time. The long game is the most difficult one to play and the most bountiful one to win.

Break the long game down into chapters.

Most teams just focus on shipping a minimum viable product (MVP). But cofounder and CEO of Pinterest Ben Silberman has been comfortable being underestimated and flying under the radar in an industry where most people judge companies by their latest headlines, flashy keynotes, and the flaunting of their progress. When it came to activating the revenue-generating parts of his business, Ben was also exceptionally (and, for some investors, excruciatingly) patient in waiting for his product and team to be ready. Ben's patience and discipline come from adopting an atypical timescale compared to the rest of the industry.

"Silicon Valley—and the technology industry as a whole—has such a compressed time-scale relative to what I grew up with," Ben explained to me. "I grew up in a family of doctors where you take seven to twelve years of your life to learn the craft, and then you find yourself as the most junior doctor. So I took this approach to Pinterest. Sure, we value speed, but just because an industry moves fast doesn't mean we always have to be obsessed with moving fast. I also try to remember, when it comes to best practices for technology companies, that the industry as a whole is still relatively immature. Why conform to the average practices or timescale of the industry? My timescale is longer."

Ben breaks up every period of his company into chapters, each with a beginning, goal, reflection period, and reward. For example, a few years after the business was founded—once Pinterest's website had a loyal and rapidly growing base of users—the company embarked on a new chapter to "become a mobile service." At the time, Pinterest was known mostly as a web destination, and Ben believed that the company needed to shift its mindset to being mobile first.

The next chapter at Pinterest was "to become a global service." Once again, the entire company shifted to make it happen, focusing on certain regions, doing research to develop strategies for serving users in different countries, and making the site available in different languages.

And then, a year or so later, the next chapter was "to become a cash-flow positive service," which meant developing a scalable business model that also enriched the product experience. This chapter ushered in a new set of leaders, partnerships, and changed product priorities.

What I like about Ben's "chapters" approach is that each one applies to everyone in the company and embodies a goal rather than a tactic. Each chapter requires a fresh perspective on the product, renewed empathy with the product's users, and a candid assessment of the team you have and the team you need. A chapter is a clear goal, underscored by why it is important, and then every team determines its tactics. As a chapter comes to an end, Ben believes teams must be reflective and rewarded.

Chapters help break down the long timescale it takes to build something extraordinary. While he doesn't claim to be an expert, Ben aspires to provide a narrative. "It's the dream, the drama, the ups and downs—these are the moments and stories that keep us all engaged," he explained to me. "But you need a mission that can generate the many mini narratives required to carry you through a chapter." Without a clear mission we're all liable to get lost.

Just stay alive long enough to become an expert.

The established paths, tactics, and assumptions relied upon by experts become antiquated. And the more expertise you have, the harder it can be to deviate from established norms.

This strong sense of muscle memory held by today's industry leaders provides an opportunity for you to jump in. The best way for a start-up to "disrupt" an industry is to be a thesis-driven outsider—someone who hasn't been jaded by the industry but has a strong opinion for what should change. You then just have to stay alive long enough to become an expert so you can compete with the different skills and practices you bring. Some call this "faking it till you make it," but I think it's just burgeoning a new path to solve a problem in hopes that it becomes the preferred path.

Companies like Airbnb, Uber, and others have done just this. Their founders were outsiders but had a strong opinion or vision about what should change. They then stayed alive long enough to become experts and compete with better technology, a superior path to market, and a lower cost structure.

Joe Gebbia, cofounder of Airbnb, knew very little about the hospitality industry when he started the company. "I was so naive. On a scale from one to ten on how prepared I was… I was at a three," he recalls. Joe and his team had the gall to start, but then it took years—and multiple attempts—for them to develop the model that ended up growing into the success we know today. But staying alive isn't easy. The government's outdated regulations may try to kill you. Years of anonymity may try to kill you. Insufficient technical skills could make it an uphill battle to survive. When you're an industry outsider, resiliency is your most critical trait.

You and your team need to understand when expertise is an advantage and when it is a disadvantage. This all boils down to the industry norms you're calling into question and whether or not key dynamics have turned such norms upside down. Rather than believe you can just "do it better" than your incumbents, anchor your thesis on what you believe everyone else is wrong about. More important, your team must value the benefits from sticking together long enough to ramp up expertise, gain velocity, and allow a long-term thesis to play out.

As I think back to Behance's early days, it is striking how underqualified we were. We were all aligned when it came to a mission and what we thought should change in the creative industry, but none of us were creative-industry veterans. We also lacked experiences building online applications at scale. You could argue we succeeded in building Behance into a massive platform despite, not because of, these setbacks. But there were some common practices among the incumbents at the time that ran counter to our ill-informed thesis.

For example, most online art showcases at the time, like DeviantArt, Myspace, and Saatchi's digital community, simply offered online profiles with a collection of images. At the time, this is what the creative web was: lots of images and very little structure. The conventional wisdom was that the more images, the more page views, the more revenue.

In contrast, the first version of Behance structured an online portfolio as a series of "projects," each with its own sequence of images, text, and any other form of media and organized information that would help tell the story behind the work. While our competitors attempted to be online galleries with collections of images, we were trying to help creative professionals tell a series of individual stories about their portfolio of work. Sounds great, but the consequence of this approach was that it was more time-consuming to add an image to Behance than other online portfolio sites. As a result, our user base was low at the start before creatives recognized the benefit the extra effort would bring.

If we had known better, we probably would have played it safe. Fortunately, we didn't know any better, and Behance became known as the more professional and organized platform to showcase and discover creative work.

Our inexperienced team stuck together long enough to see our assumptions and plans materialize. In times of extreme uncertainty about the months ahead, we would only question our conviction for the problem and the desired "end state" we wanted to make happen. The long-term conviction never dissipated. We had some near-death experiences that made us smarter and, more important, brought us closer together. Of the first dozen or so people on our team, ten of us were still working together seven years later. The degree of loyalty, tolerance, patience, and shared commitment to a mission was admittedly our team's only advantage executing in a space that we knew very little about. Cofounder of project management software company Basecamp, Jason Fried, makes the point that the best start-ups are really just "stay-ups." As he explains it, "Outlasting is one of the best competitive moves you can ever make."

Do the work regardless of whose work it is.

So much of excellence is about just doing the work—even when it's not yours to do. In big companies, people have a tendency to complain about a strategy they disagree with or a product's shortcomings instead of their own. In small companies and for freelancers, the tendency is to blame clients or circumstances. So much energy goes into directing blame and expressing disappointment rather than just taking initiative to tackle what you're criticizing.

Everyone has an opinion, but few people are willing to do something about it—especially if it falls outside of their formal job description. Surprising things happen when people take steps beyond their day-to-day role on their own volition. Think your team's marketing is horrible? Then draft it out, put together a presentation, and share it yourself. Have an insight for how to improve another colleague's product? Do it yourself, even if someone else ultimately gets the credit (attribution has a way of finding its way over time).

Across so many teams I've worked with, I've marveled at just how quickly an idea takes hold when someone proactively does the underlying work no one else clearly owned. There is rarely a scarcity of process or ideas but there is often a scarcity of people willing to work outside the lines. Those who take initiative to contribute when it wasn't their job become the leadership team of the newest stuff.

There's a reason so few people do hard work beyond their job description: It's hard work. You run the risk of expending energy or falling behind in other parts of your life, but these are the costs of playing at the frontier and having the opportunity to lead something new. You're either a cog in the system or a designer of new and better systems. Of course, if you aspire to transform your industry and leave a valuable mark in your world, you'll need to challenge every system you find yourself confined by. When you see something wrong, take the initiative to fix it.

James Murphy, the founder and front man of LCD Soundsystem, said it well: "The best way to complain is to make things." When you find yourself frustrated or critical, channel that energy into persistent creation. If it's not your job, pursue it anyway. Do research, run tests, or draft white papers and presentations to prove your position, even if it's on your own time. It'll give you a sense of satisfaction that no amount of preordained tasks will.

A shared trait among entrepreneurs and innovators within big companies is defying prescribed roles. The future is drafted by people doing work they don't have to do. You need to be one of those people—and hire them, too. There is too much wondering and talking, and too little doing. So don't talk: do. Care indiscriminately. If you're willing to actually do the work, you'll have more influence than those who simply do their jobs.

OPTIMIZE

The messy middle isn't just about enduring the inevitable dips and near disasters. It's also about leveraging the "highs" of the journey to build momentum and identify and capitalize on whatever seems to be working. If you endure the harsh lessons of the valley, they will help you find the peaks. When something actually works—a new work habit improves your productivity, a key decision improves your team, or a tweak to your product delights your customers—you need to tenaciously evaluate it. Why did that work? How do you do it again? How do you spread it to your team?

These positive peaks in the middle of your journey are rarely planned. Planning happens in a vacuum, void of real-world frictions like timing and people. The more you're trailblazing, the harder it is to anticipate the impact of what you try. Inconsequential changes will prove to be profoundly important while thoroughly deliberated decisions will prove insignificant. You need to be open to surprises, insanely curious about why things happen, and optimize the hell out of everything that gets traction.

To make great work tomorrow, you need to have a persistent commitment to outperform today. Every aspect of your product should be far better. Your team should be more capable. The way you market and describe your work should be more compelling. Your work habits and processes should be more efficient. You should be proud of what you've accomplished, but never satisfied.

Optimization stems from the conviction that you can do better. It's less about fixing what's broken and more about improving what works.

Look at how Google and other modern web companies pioneered optimization of their products through A/B testing. This is a process by which any webpage or digital experience is improved by comparing the performance of a change (version B) to the

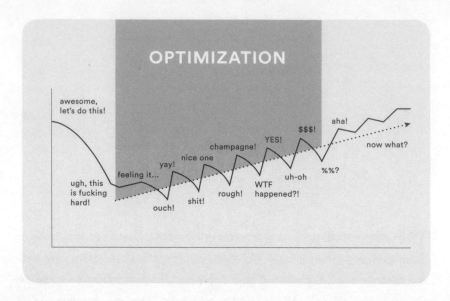

previous version (version A). For example, an ecommerce site might change the color of their Buy button for a certain percentage of their customer traffic. If the new version results in more customers making purchases, then they apply the change throughout. If it fails, they abandon the test and revert to the version without the change. So even when something appears to be working just fine, there's almost always a way to improve it.

A/B testing isn't just for digital buttons—you can use it to advance all areas of your life, from A/B testing your daily habits to how your team functions. A team might change how and when they meet, or an individual may try using a new tool for a week. If it works, the change is made permanent. If it makes things worse, you simply revert to the previous version.

The best optimizers are always trying to figure out why something works. Pinterest's Ben Silberman describes this process as "always reflecting backward and incorporating forward." As he explains it, "I actually think you learn a lot more from your successes [than your mistakes]. There are a million reasons why something can fail, but usually very few reasons why something can work. When you want to learn to be a great runner—do you study slow people or fast people? I think taking time to understand why things succeed—whether they are your successes or others—is time well spent . . . you learn the most from things that go really well by asking why. Those are the things you want to understand and do more of."

By getting curious about the things that go well, you discover the strengths that are unique to your team and product. This may sound like an obvious practice, but we rarely take the time to improve what already works. Rather than expending almost all energy on problems and putting out fires, you can increase your velocity by optimizing what is already propelling you forward.

Industry incumbents lose their position because their success limits their efforts to optimize. Big companies typically spend their time solving problems and sustaining—rather than improving—whatever it is that made them big. As a result, they enter a steady state that may please shareholders in the near term but naturally antiquates over time. "Good enough" is an open invitation for others to create something better than you've created.

Optimization is most difficult when you have a reliable route that works. Take driving, for instance: Even when you think you've worked out the fastest route from A to B, a local cabdriver will always know a way to get you there faster. When you think you already have the answer, you don't experiment with other options—if only for the sake of efficiency. The problem with large, well-resourced businesses is that they have a well-defined path for everything—and tons of people employed to keep it clear and wide. The probability of discovering a new detour therefore disintegrates with time, as the known path becomes more established.

We navigate most of our lives and businesses with cursory knowledge rather than local knowledge. Only when we stick with and deeply explore one area, whether by choice or by accident, do we learn better routes.

The section ahead is about celebrating what is working during the messy middle and then capitalizing on it. At first fixing something that isn't broken will feel uncomfortable, because doing so often requires breaking it. But optimization is the only path to excellence. A journey's positive slope, where peaks are incrementally higher, is the result of the repeat cycle of evaluating, deconstructing, and building a better team, product, and self.

OPTIMIZING YOUR TEAM

Great teams are more than the assembly of great people. On the contrary, great teams are ultimately grown, not gathered. They're made through endless iteration of roles, cultures, processes, structures, and tackling toxins whenever they emerge. The only way to build a great team is through endless optimization of how a team works together, and clearing their path to solutions.

In an entrepreneurial environment, you must prioritize your team over your goals and tend to your team before your product. If your team is not in a good place or your office culture is lacking, your most valuable resources will not be able to make great products or execute well over time. Your team genuinely needs to be as important to you as what you're making. I have met many founders who obsess over product and steamroll their team. Most of them have failed. Team comes first.

BUILDING, HIRING, AND FIRING

Resourcefulness > Resources

As your business grows and your plans become more ambitious, you will want to grow your team. When it comes to scaling, the easiest path most leaders default to is to hire. More heads, more hands, more work done. But the best managers know that growing the team is not always the answer. Too many teams hire when they should be optimizing the people they've already got. You can always get more resources, but resourcefulness is a competitive advantage. Resources become depleted. Resourcefulness does not.

I've had experiences on both ends of the spectrum. Bootstrapping a team for five years before raising capital forced me to scale by increasing productivity—even when hiring more people was the right answer. On the other hand, hiring more people was the default for scaling capacity in some of the teams I managed later on at Adobe—and it didn't always work out.

I vividly remember the pain I felt in Behance's early years when we were trying to balance the need to break even with growing the team. Our engineers had a list of people they "absolutely needed" to hire. But so did our designers and our community management and our support teams. It was a struggle to prioritize new hires (not to mention debating rank).

Our head of operations at the time, Will Allen, made a practice of pushing teams to change how they worked before resorting to hiring more people who would work the same way. "Refactor, refactor, then hire," he'd say. Teams would come into meetings with a list of positions they wanted to hire for but leave the meeting with a list of process improvements they could make with their existing team.

Before adding more people to a team, optimize how the team works together. Are there better tools that could be adopted? Can some of the work be automated or outsourced? Are there time-consuming processes that can be killed? Looking back, I am grateful for the years we didn't have resources. The human resourcefulness that resulted made our team smarter. Every time Will and I ran through this exercise with teams, we would uncover serious inefficiencies and exciting opportunities to boost productivity. We became more efficient before we became bigger. As a by-product of this smooth, satisfying work ethic, we were also able to attract and retain more qualified people. Efficient people want to work in an efficient environment.

Resourcefulness also makes you more creative. Any good designer will tell you that creative constraints help the idea-generation process. With fewer resources and options, you become more creative with what you have.

One of the best examples of this is Skybox, a company that wanted to drastically reduce the costs of global imaging and other satellite-driven services by creating a cheaper satellite. Prior to Skybox, satellites had cost hundreds of millions (if not billions) of dollars to build, launch, and manage. As a constraint, four Stanford graduate students attempted to build a satellite with off-the-shelf parts. Their first satellite, the SkySat-1, was launched in 2013 and reportedly cost between $2 to $5 million. Their success, largely a product of their self-imposed constraints, ultimately led to their acquisition by Google in 2014 for $500 million.

Nothing disrupts resourcefulness more than a sudden infusion of resources. The common debate in the early-stage investor community is how much money is too much money at each stage of a business. This is because there are some serious hidden costs that come along with raising capital.

Jessica Livingston, cofounder of Y Combinator, one of the world's most well-known incubators and start-up investors, talked about the perils of raising too much money too quickly during a talk at one of their annual summits:

> I've seen many startups shift from doing more with less to doing less with more once they've raised funding. It's easy to think money can buy your way out of problems. Don't like sales and calling users? Hire a salesperson. No one's using your product? It must be because people don't know about it—hire an expensive PR firm to get the word out. Those are both not merely lazy, but the wrong thing for a startup to do. . . .
>
> When you don't have enough money, circumstances force you to be virtuous. Once you've raised a lot, you have to force yourself to be virtuous.

The business of innovation is about a team's resourcefulness, not just resources. The media's celebration of financing obscures this fact. The constraints of early-stage business building pave the way for solid operations, healthy margins, and a self-awareness that big companies (and well-funded start-ups) often fail to achieve. These lessons are hard to gain any other way.

One of the risks of raising money too early is becoming incentivized to do something you don't love, and that you don't truly believe in. Just as you don't want to have children and commit to being parents together on your first date, wait until you're committed. Work with a project long enough to fall in love with it, constraints and all, before raising money. You must love your work to survive the journey from start to finish.

Resources come and go, but resourcefulness is a muscle that kicks in throughout the life cycle of any business. Without it, capital cannot be used efficiently. Focus on building your team's resourcefulness.

Initiative > Experience

As you assemble your team, look for people with excitement about the idea, ability to contribute right away, and the potential to learn. What your team lacks in experience they can make up for with initiative. One common principle successful founders swear by is hiring for initiative over experience. It is tempting to be a résumé snob and favor people with industry pedigree, but the unique chemistry of an early-stage venture thrives from a team with hustle and a willingness to learn anything and apply it quickly.

DOES INITIATIVE REALLY TRUMP EXPERIENCE?

Inexperienced yet smart people with initiative will almost always exceed your expectations. But when you're super experienced, it is harder to bypass assumptions and learn new things. Instead of helping reframe the question and finding new solutions, experts try to use the same answer that worked last time. But in a team that has been gathered together because of their initiative rather than experience, you are fueled by curiosity. A lack of mastery is usually accompanied by the lack of conventional wisdom, which helps you think differently. When you do hire experts, make sure their motivation is more a product of their desire to learn than their desire to provide the fastest answers.

Initiative is contagious, expertise is not. For example, one of my favorite junior hires during my days leading Behance was Malcolm Jones. At first, Malcolm became known across the team for his deep laugh, incredibly wide and constant smile, and can-do attitude. He had only a small amount of engineering experience before he joined us, but the team fell for him after his very first interview. Malcolm joined us as the third member of our dev-ops team, which is a group of engineers dedicated to the infrastructure, stability, and security of Behance's platform. The dev-ops team is at the front line of every nightmare situation: spam problems, security breaches, latency in the speed of millions of portfolios loading for millions of visitors every day, and, when the site goes down, the dev-ops team diagnoses the problem and fixes it. Putting out fires all day—and trying to make the company flame retardant—is a stressful job, compounded by the constant battery of questions and concerns coming from all corners.

On paper, Malcolm wasn't the perfect fit for the job based on his past experience. But his level of enthusiasm and willingness to take on any responsibility and master it helped him not only succeed but also elevate the dev-ops culture more broadly. Malcolm transformed the team and became a leader we all admired. Skills may be shared, but sheer initiative (and the energy and enthusiasm that comes along with it) helps the culture and spreads like wildfire—the good kind of fire.

HOW DO YOU HIRE FOR INITIATIVE?

Past initiative is the best indicator of future initiative. Look beyond the formal résumé and ask candidates about their interests and what they have done to pursue them. It doesn't matter what the interests are—bonsai cultivation, writing poetry, whatever! Instead, gauge whether the candidate has a history of being proactive in advancing their interests.

Initiative comes from obsession. The more infatuated you are with something, the more likely you are to know (or want to find out) more about it. The greatest disruptions of industries are facilitated by relative outsiders, obsessed with the industry, who find a way to survive long enough to become an expert and then leverage new techniques to change the game. While expertise qualifies you, obsession mobilizes you in a way that runs circles around the experts.

Diversity drives differentiation.

Your product's unique attributes distinguish you from the competition. These attributes are conceived through clashes of opinion and methods of thinking that diverge from the norm. As every market naturally regresses to the mean, averaging out until it becomes a set of widely established best practices, the best way to drive and sustain differentiation is to diversify your team.

The greatest teams I have met over the years are composed of extraordinarily different extraordinary people. The more different your team, the more different and innovative your product.

Rational thinking is driven by what we've seen and done before. It keeps us where we've been. But the greatest products that change our lives are made by teams willing to consider old problems in new, seemingly irrational ways. When someone on your team shares an idea or perspective that, at first, seems completely irrational but then gradually becomes the breakthrough solution, you know you've got a team of people with enough "difference."

Innovation happens at the edge of reason, and you can't reach the edge with a team of similar people.

The shortcut to differentiation of thought is diversity in the form of different personalities, genders, ethnicities, nationalities, backgrounds, and kinds of education and experience represented at the table to extend the surface area of possible solutions for every problem you face.

We spend too much time considering our own creativity and too little effort on setting up a team that allows creativity to take hold. In an interview with John Maeda on his blog, technologist Nicholas Negroponte said it best: "Where do new ideas come from? The answer is simple: differences. Creativity comes from unlikely juxtapositions."

Maeda goes on to say, "It's a simple idea really. Yet it embodies everything that I believe—that when you have people who come from different backgrounds together, then the outcome is something that is difficult to expect. By all parties involved. And an unexpected outcome lies at the basis of what creativity is all about." This is the competitive advantage of diversity.

A lack of diversity is a classic flaw of many venture capital firms. A 2015 study by venture capital firm Social Capital found that 92 percent of senior investment professionals at top firms were men, and 78 percent of senior investment professionals were white. Such homogeny, coupled with the plague of groupthink, is a major disadvantage when it comes to discovering something at the edge of reason that the world has never seen. This is the same reason I dislike angel groups, which are groups of people who come together to hear start-up pitches, discuss, and invest as a group. What a horrible model. Groups make us too rational, especially when the constituents arc too similar. Groups are even more destructive to innovation—and investing in innovation—when they require consensus to proceed.

Diversity in gender, race, sexual orientation, and political views are necessary to form a strong team that covers the maximum possible terrain of perspectives, But don't stop there; consider the other, less obvious factors—like the languages your team speaks.

Gabrielle Hogan-Brun is a research fellow in language studies at the University of Bristol and the author of *Linguanomics: What Is the Market Potential of Multilingualism?* Her main research focus is on multilingualism's effect on the brain, and a multilingual person's subsequent effect on teams. She points out how multiple studies have shown that monolingual brains are structured differently to bilingual brains. For example, bilingual brains have a denser left inferior parietal cortex, which is the part of the brain used in abstract thinking, and they also have more gray matter. Having a different lexicon to draw from can also allow your employees to approach problems in slightly different ways. In *Quartz*, Hogan-Brun provides this example:

In the German mind, the English word "put" conjures up different images: "legen" means to lie horizontally, "setzen" to make something sit, and "stellen" to stand something vertically. Each of these meanings automatically gives the German speaker access to new ways of approaching a practical problem. In this way, using different languages in collaboration may lead to new connections being made, especially when dealing with complex tasks.

And it's not all just physiological and teamwork benefits—there are obvious business benefits, too. Hogan-Brun quotes economist Larry Summers in her article in *The Conversation*, "Why Multilingualism Is Good for Economic Growth": "If your strategy is to trade only with people that speak English that's going to be a poor strategy." Hiring multilingual people also instantly opens up the potential practical reach of your organization twofold. According to research by Bern University, the economic value of Switzerland's multilingual advantage generates one-tenth of their GDP. Likewise, in another article, Hogan-Brun cites a survey by the *Economist* that surveyed 572 international company executives, two-thirds of whom said their teams' potential for innovation was increased by their multiculturalism.

Learning a second language is generally always good for your brain, but there are also different types of bilingualism. For example, growing up in a household that speaks a language different from the one you speak at school is very different from learning a second language at that same school; likewise, speaking two languages fluently from birth has a different effect on the brain than moving to a foreign country and becoming fluent in a second language later in life. But no matter the differences, seeking out people who think in different words from your own is a strength. In her essay for *Aeon*, "The Bilingual Brain: Why One Size Doesn't Fit All," Pennsylvania State University's Angela Grant argues that though some of the biological benefits of bilingualism can sometimes be overemphasized, "it's worth remembering that regardless of proclaimed cognitive or anatomical advantages, bilinguals have twice as many communities to interact with, cultures to experience, and newspapers to read. And if that isn't an advantage, what is?"

My cofounder for Behance, Matias Corea, is from Barcelona and primarily spoke Spanish until he moved to the United States as a young adult. Others on our early team were also native Spanish or French speakers, so I experienced some of these benefits firsthand. Our design aesthetic, our ability to engage international communities from the very beginning of our business—which made us look bigger than we were—as well as building a rich, multilingual culture all helped make Behance what it is.

Though it is tempting to rope in friends and "people like you" during the early stages of ventures, defy the tendency to be lazy and just hire those in your vicinity. The people who are circumstantially in your everyday life are more liable to look like you, think like you, and have similar skill sets as you. Hiring them will feel safe and easy, but it will handicap your efforts to differentiate your product. By surrounding yourself with people who are different from you, your baseline of adaptability is higher than that of teams who look and think the same. A diverse team can tolerate a greater spectrum of options and circumstances by working alongside people who have endured different conditions and experienced a wider range of challenges. How will your product be perceived by different demographics? What cultural tendencies can be leveraged—or sensitivities considered—in your marketing efforts? A diverse team is more likely to come up with the contrarian's view alongside new perspectives from different vantage points.

When you are hiring, identify your unconscious bias. Don't accept quick conclusions like "not a culture fit" without digging further to understand what, exactly, isn't a "fit." It's helpful to standardize the early part of your hiring process so it is less vulnerable to biases and more about building a pipeline of qualified candidates who deserve serious consideration despite how "familiar" they seem. Set goals and push your team to widely accept them. As you enrich your team with different kinds of people, it will become easier to do so over time. Familiarity breeds acceptance.

When you become more accustomed to working with people far younger or older than you, come from different places, speak with different accents, your mind and hiring practices become more open to the possibilities.

Hire people who have endured adversity.

Diversity includes people's past experiences, so look to build a team of people who have endured adversity and overcome substantial challenges in their own lives. This will bring strength and tolerance to the team's DNA.

In a conversation with Tristan Walker, CEO and founder of Walker & Company Brands, he talked about the role his upbringing added to the culture of his company. "Courage is our first value. The reason I have courage as a first value is because without courage, you can't practice any other value consistently. My version of courage is that I grew up in the Jamaica and Flushing, Queens, projects. I saw people get murdered, seeing people get shot. All that stuff. My worst case scenario is going back to that, and I survived it. So people are like, 'Shit—Tristan's willing to go to the depths of hell to make this thing survive.' That's an inspiring thing. I knew what it took to actually get out of that shit, and just having that context made people think about how I make my decisions differently."

When I think about what experiences have matured me the most, they are less university degrees and tenure at esteemed companies and more about the challenges I have faced in my personal life.

One of my lifelong challenges has been my relationship with my sister, Julie. She was born with a lack of oxygen reaching her brain, which resulted in severe brain damage at birth. As a child, Julie required years of special education to develop speech and basic social functioning skills. Throughout her childhood, she required a lot of support and patience throughout bouts of behavioral issues.

While Julie's life is complicated to be sure, a childhood with a disabled sibling also comes with a set of complications. On one hand, I felt immeasurable guilt. My possibilities and potential seemed endless compared to Julie's, and the opportunities and fanfare I received from family always carried a sense of sadness and inequality with it. On the other hand, while I might not like to admit it, I was angry. By no fault of her own, Julie had robbed me of normalcy. Looking back on my childhood and a lifetime of reconciling my relationship with Julie, I recognize how that combustive mixture of guilt and anger motivated me, made me self-reliant, and influenced how I work with and lead others. No doubt, adversity matures you.

Traits such as courage, a tolerance for ambiguity, self-reliance, and an urge to prove oneself are more powerful drivers of performance than a couple more years holding a particular job title. Age or accolades have never mattered to me when it comes to hiring or investing in talent: What matters to me is maturity and perspective. As you build your team, seek people who have endured adversity. Ask prospective team members about their most defining challenges. Life matures you a lot faster than time, and a lot of life can happen in a very short amount of time.

Seek people with whom discussions evolve by a step function.

In a world of pithy sound bites and smooth pitches, aim to work with people who are always building on your ideas and inviting you to build on their own.

Your second conversation with a potential hire should feel a lot more interesting than your first. First impressions count for a lot, but if you can't continually build on that energy, the relationship isn't likely to have legs beyond the initial spark. I call this kind of fire-starting ability *aligned dynamism*, which is when ideas vary but energy levels and a value for the mission align; this is the source of the embers that will keep burning long after the initial flint.

My friendship with Garrett Camp, the cofounder of StumbleUpon, Uber, and Expa, has always felt this way; same with Ben Silberman before I invested in Pinterest and Kayvon and Joe before I got involved with Periscope. In each of these cases, every conversation felt more interesting than the one before. This stands in stark contrast to most entrepreneurs I meet with, who tend to come at you in a fireball that quickly extinguishes when you meet again or present the tiniest douse of doubt. Whether you're selecting people to join your founding team or evaluating people you may want to work for or invest in, dynamism is a great litmus test.

The best team players will be the ones who are as willing to throw around their own nascent ideas as they are helping build upon others. People who shut down new notions in favor of wanting to advance their own may be heralded as creative firecrackers, but they do not make for good team players in the long term.

In the stand-up comedy world, this is known as the "Yes! And..." principle. Charlie Todd, founder of the New York improv comedy group Improv Everywhere, once explained it to me like this: "When you're vulnerable onstage and throwing out ideas, the last thing you want is to be shut down publicly. Not only does this bring a swift end to the skit, but it's also devastatingly humiliating. Instead, you should always accept whatever dilemma or circumstances an actor presents to you, and then add to it. You respond with a 'Yes! And...' rather than a no or some other form of shutting down a conversation."

Of course, to build upon ideas, everyone must understand them. Seek people who make the impossible-to-understand more accessible. One of the greater challenges leaders face on the hiring front is evaluating people with a different technical expertise. For example, how do you evaluate the skills of a cryptocurrency expert or a data scientist if you have no expertise in either one? Sure, you can get third-party opinions from others in the industry, but sometimes recruitment is confidential and your candidates have jobs elsewhere, which restricts how many people you can involve in the recruitment process. But all skills, no matter how scientific, can be explained in layman's terms—it's just extremely hard to do it. Despite appearances, simplicity takes deep understanding and synthesis. The greatest thinkers in any field can explain problems and advocate for solutions in clear and simple ways. They use analogies, teach others, and make technical concepts relatable. Genius is making the complicated simple and relatable.

Build a team of people dynamic enough to make every conversation a step function that is more interesting than the one before it, and smart enough to make the complicated simple and accessible to everyone.

If you avoid folks who are polarizing, you avoid bold outcomes.

Creating something from nothing is a contact sport. The endless debates you endure iron out your team's preconceived notions, and your vehement disagreements force you to explore unpopular options. But debates and disagreements are fruitful only if your colleagues are determined enough to ruthlessly fight it out with you, with one another, and without apathy. The more you challenge one another, the more you will uncover.

Not only does a strong culture tolerate some necessary ruckus, it gains its edge from it. People disagree and fight for their beliefs only when they are engaged enough to care. Those who are especially argumentative, opinionated, and polarizing therefore play an important role in your company, as they prevent you from settling for the familiar or easy solution and keep you questioning your norms. So long as they share your mission, these instigators are your greatest protection from groupthink and harmful compromise.

Learn to tolerate the people you struggle with. There are many people I have hired over the years whose references included some warnings. While I never compromised on ethics or integrity, I also didn't aspire to assemble a team of peacemakers. Great creative minds have their demons. After all, if creativity is born from struggle, you must be willing to tolerate the residue. In my experience, some degree of stubbornness and frustration are common attributes of technical geniuses; people who are ahead of their time are intolerant of business practices behind the times.

There are a few people I hired over the years at Behance and Adobe who were particularly difficult. But they broke through walls like nobody else. They also pissed off a lot of people, and part of my job was to blunt the pain they inflicted without blunting their impact. Fighting for bold solutions to old problems, especially within a larger company, requires a willingness to defy the typical process. In this way, being a little aggressive is a feature, not a bug.

When you find yourself working alongside polarizing people, try to appreciate the role they play and the origin of their struggle. Aspire to turn your disdain into empathy. I've always ascribed to the philosophy, often attributed to Carl Jung, that "everything that irritates us about others can lead us to an understanding of ourselves." Chances are your reaction to others is as much about you as it is about them.

The easiest way to deal with people who make you uncomfortable is to find fault with them; judging others is an easier and more cowardly path than reconciling yourself. Instead, to build your tolerance of those you struggle with, ask yourself what it is about their behavior that scares you. How might you possess or fear the same characteristics you are resenting in the other person?

If you're looking for fault or someone to blame, you're obstructing the lessons you can learn. But if you find ways to accept and empathize with difficult people, your culture will become more tolerant and your product will have more edge. As you're building or investing in teams, don't try to keep the chemistry too clean. Teach your team to value conflict and develop a tolerance for passionate and respectful disagreement. When hiring, fight the tendency of your teammates to seek people they "really get along with." A better hiring criterion is, "Will they challenge us? Are they likely to bring a different point of view?" And then, when sparks start to fly (within healthy boundaries), remind your team that they're making progress.

Cultivate your team's immune system, and occasionally suppress it.

Like the human body, every team has a natural immune system that serves multiple purposes. The most important part of a team's immune system helps quickly identify and reject infections. Without a strong response to knowing when something isn't quite right, small issues can quickly escalate into bigger ones before you have time to snuff them out. In every team I have led over the years, I have noticed that the more attuned and aligned they are, the more quickly a problem rises to the surface. Whether it was a misalignment in priorities, a bad decision, or a bad hire, I was impressed by how quickly it became clear that something was wrong and had to be addressed. But a healthy immune system can also backfire when you are, in fact, trying to change the chemistry of the team.

I recall one of the most important hires we ever made at Behance. For years, I had been trying to recruit Will Allen, who had previously run partnerships and helped develop the web offering at TED, to be our chief operating officer. Finally, in late 2011, Will agreed to join us. We were growing fast, and I desperately needed a partner to help manage the operations of our business, including financials, legal work, managing the development schedule, and keeping teams on track. I was certain that Will had the sophistication, values, and management experience to add tremendous value to the company. The team generously welcomed him and Will sprinted out of the gates, joining product reviews, engineering planning meetings, and taking over some functions that I had led for many years.

But just a few weeks in, the team's immune system started to act up.

Given his seniority and experience, Will was speaking up and making changes. He started tweaking processes that needed updating and pointing out inefficiencies in our most beloved processes. He changed a dynamic that my design team and I had been accustomed to for years.

After just a few weeks, I had a queue of employees requesting time with me to share their concerns. No doubt, Will was a new organ that was required to keep the body alive—but he was also being rejected by a strong and expedient immune system. At first, I started to worry. But as I looked beyond the inflammation Will was causing, I realized that these were merely symptoms of a new and unfamiliar leader digging in, asking questions, and influencing areas that had never been touched. I quickly got that my job was to temporarily suppress the tight-knit team's immune system. I used the one-on-ones with concerned team members to help them understand the value of the perceived interruptions and, more important, to lower their guard.

Immune systems act up in different ways. Sometimes the response is a string of complaints to management. Other times it's through active disagreement or passive resistance. Or sometimes it comes across as humor.

While I was getting my MBA at Harvard Business School, there was a long-standing tradition in every ninety-student section called "sky decks." At the end of every week, the whole group would come together for announcements, followed by a skit performed by a rotating group of students who poked fun at the week's events. The skits often involved re-enacting an altercation between one of us and a professor, a funny behavior one of us had exhibited during a case discussion, or some other quirk that stood out. It was a good way to make fun of ourselves and let off the steam from a busy week.

But a subtler and perhaps subconscious purpose of sky decks was to call out excessive behaviors, like someone talking too much during a case or raising his or her hand too frequently rather than letting other classmates chime in. Since the section had no leader, sky decks served as a natural part of the immune system to foster a healthy and balanced group dynamic. While everyone laughed, everyone also got the message. Sometimes direct confrontation with colleagues is the best path, and other times there are more subtle, comfortable mechanisms to hone a team's chemistry.

The other role of a team's immune system is to kill off foreign and risky ideas that are liable to take the team off track. Without a strong immune system, deadlines would never be met, and whatever is new and shiny would subsume attention and energy. Typically, the type A "doers" on the team are the powerful antibodies that extinguish new ideas that put time lines and budgets at risk. In contrast, the wide-eyed "dreamers" are the foreign bodies that infect a team with new ideas that challenge the status quo. Most of the time, the immune system (the doers) needs to be strong enough to hold the foreign germs (the dreamers) at bay so we can stay productive and on track. But every now and then, teams need to suppress the immune system so that the dreamers—or any new leader with new ideas—can give the team an organ transplant in the form of fresh ideas, and fundamentally change a process or a product. Much like the Behance team initially struggled with Will, the new organ.

When building a team, hire both doers and dreamers in relatively equal proportions. You also need to empower them at the right times. During day-to-day operations, doers must be positioned to question new ideas and keep creative whims in check to ensure progress on the biggest ideas that will make the greatest impact. But when a new problem emerges or a brainstorm begins, doers—and their tendencies—need to be suppressed so the dreamers can do their thing.

Of course, many of us have doer and dreamer tendencies that come to the surface at different times. The best teams optimize for a mix of both. If you're more of a dreamer, be sure to hire doers, even though they may not seem as fun and flexible as you are. They will be the core of your company's immune system, and without them, you're liable to get off track. I often see this problem in creative agencies and start-ups founded by visionary types. They seek to hire people like them and believe that a creative company is made up of creative people. On the contrary, successful creative companies have a bold vision and creative leaders who help set it, but are often managed by more pragmatic and progress-oriented doers. You need to hire and empower people who default to the opposite tendency to your own, even if it makes you feel uncomfortable.

With every new hire, and in every cycle of innovation and execution, be mindful of your team's immune system. Let it do its thing, but in times of critical change, take the necessary steps to suppress it.

Grafting talent is just as important as recruiting talent.

Strong teams tend to be effective recruiters of new talent. But the stronger the team, the more challenging it is to integrate new talent—especially great talent. Leaders spend too much time recruiting and so little time grafting.

As we just discussed, a healthy team's immune system is liable to reject new team members by default. The more senior and experienced your new team member is, the more the immune system will try to reject her. An experienced player arrives with her own playbook, but the very successes you hired her for are the very things that the team may reject her for. Having a strong will, established best practices from prior experiences, and a big mandate are all sources of friction when joining a new team. If your team is not willing to adjust and accommodate, your newest and potentially greatest hire will fail. Over time, as this keeps happening, your team will start hiring less experienced candidates in order to "solve" this problem. Your team will fail to evolve, and this is the beginning of the end.

Don't just recruit great members; graft them, too. This is about a lot more than onboarding new employees: It's about identifying with their experience, shining the spotlight on their strengths, and becoming a thought partner, coach, and advocate for them.

Setting up new talent to succeed is an active process that doesn't happen on its own. Grafting talent is about empathy, integration, psychological safety, and real-time communication.

EMPATHY

Put yourself in the shoes of your newest team members and try to imagine what they must be going through. Are they climbing a learning curve without much support? Did they just move their family from another state? Do they still have an ambiguous job description? As you become more aware of the challenges they are facing while getting acclimated, make an effort to sensitize your other colleagues, too.

Empathy is even more important when diversifying your team. Are you sitting with a group of people who are mostly the same race, gender, or age? We often seek to unify and empower a team without acknowledging the potential discomforts in the room felt by those in the minority. Simply placing everyone on an equal footing doesn't create equality: You need to empathize with the potential insecurities and concerns of everyone to help the team coalesce.

As hard as it is to be the newest member of a team, I can only imagine how much harder it is for those who are unfairly and disproportionately doubted because of their ethnic origin, age, gender, or beliefs. Being doubted for attempting something new is one thing, but bearing an additional load of skepticism based on some other signifier is something entirely different.

So many factors trigger biases. In the chaos of an early-stage project, teams are liable to just jump in and execute without taking stock of who is involved and what dynamics might be playing out beneath the surface. For example, female founders in technology, finance, and other industries face tremendous amounts of insensitive and unacceptable behavior at every stage of their venture. Underrepresented minorities and people who are especially younger or older also face biases, whether conscious or unconscious, in the process of raising money, cold-calling customers, and engaging audiences. I recall one African American entrepreneur, Jewel Burks, whose company Partpic I invested in, telling me about her meetings with various investment firms and the kinds of questions she encountered, like "Have you considered hiring someone else to be the CEO?" and "Is your team still mostly black?" My heart sank from hearing about her experience, and I realized just how much prejudice some people must endure on a daily basis. Jewel's company ultimately had a successful exit, and her success is the kind of example we need to push the industry forward and force it to change for the better.

The greatest path toward justice and equality is empathy. In my own life, I try to pause whenever I find myself in a setting where there is a gender or racial imbalance. During this moment, I listen and observe a little more carefully to see what might feel "off": Are some people cutting others off? Does anyone appear to be feeling uncomfortable? Can I step in if someone is acting inappropriately or without sensitivity? As you graft new talent to your team, do whatever you can to attempt to see the perspective of your newest members, and act accordingly.

INTEGRATION

One of the best ways to set up new talent to succeed is to align one of their specific strengths with an important task, right from the beginning. Grafting starts with new employees adding some small yet undeniable value to the team. Most often this takes the form of a specific insight, expertise, or contact from the new employee's network that can demonstrate value from the onset. Closing the confidence gap of your newest hires is more important than closing the skills gap. You can always provide more formal skills training over time, but building confidence up front is a critical ingredient in unleashing someone's potential in a new team. Having a new staff member feel like they're providing immediate value helps ease the team's immune system.

A formal onboarding process helps a new employee successfully integrate, too. Welcoming new employees with the basic requirements, rather than having them fend for themselves, goes a long way. I remember once, in the early days of Behance, walking by the desk of a new employee and seeing him just sitting there with a notebook. While saying a quick hello and asking him about his first few days, I learned that his computer had not yet arrived. We were a start-up without any HR department, and I was ashamed to realize that nobody had thought of ordering him a computer until his first day on the job. That wasn't exactly a great onboarding experience, but I learned from it.

FOSTER PSYCHOLOGICAL SAFETY

In a small team with little to lose, risks and incremental failures are tolerated well—it's the only path to success. But as companies become more structured, a tolerance for taking risk and new ways of thinking must be prioritized and built into the system, as it does not occur naturally. When people start to fear losing their bonus or getting dinged in a performance review, they stop toeing the line.

Amy Edmondson, now a Harvard Business School professor, studied medical teams at hospitals nationwide. She sought to discover what made the most successful teams so adept. To her surprise, she learned that top teams actually reported more mistakes than low-performing teams. She coined the term "psychological safety," which refers to "a shared belief that the team is safe for interpersonal risk taking," to explain this finding. It wasn't that the best teams made the most errors, she realized, but that the best teams were willing to admit and discuss their mistakes more often than other teams. Psychological safety, Edmondson wrote in a study published in 1999, is "a sense of confidence that the team will not embarrass, reject or punish someone for speaking up.... It describes a team climate characterized by interpersonal trust and mutual respect in which people are comfortable being themselves."

A widely cited *New York Times* feature by Charles Duhigg, "What Google Learned from Its Quest to Build the Perfect Team," identifies psychological safety as the defining feature of Google's most innovative, productive teams. "What Project Aristotle [the quest's internal name] has taught people within Google is that no one wants to put on a 'work face' when they get to the office. No one wants to leave part of their personality and inner life at home," Duhigg reports. "But to be fully present at work, to feel 'psychologically safe,' we must know that we can be free enough, sometimes, to share the things that scare us without fear of recriminations. We must be able to talk about what is messy or sad, to have hard conversations with colleagues who are driving us crazy. We can't be focused just on efficiency. Rather, when we start the morning by collaborating with a team of engineers and then send emails to our marketing colleagues and then jump on a conference call, we want to know that those people really hear us. We want to know that work is more than just labor."

As you seek to boost productivity and add structure and process to your team, be careful not to disincentivize the risk taking and expression of unique perspectives that got you up and running.

REAL-TIME COMMUNICATION

When it comes to sharing feedback and helping new talent immerse themselves in your culture and expectations, nothing beats real-time communication.

The challenge is that candid and constant communication is hard in new relationships. Especially in the commotion of day-to-day operations, sharing direct and timely feedback is energy consuming and uncomfortable. I encourage managers to schedule regular check-ins with new employees. New organ rejection can sneak up on you, so you need to ask questions to make sure new employees are in the stream of communication and building relationships with their new colleagues.

Feedback and discussion provide a constant stream of data for the new employee to consider. For example, I try to foster ongoing conversations around expectations, what I am seeing, and a few things I suggest trying. When there is a gap I see between what an employee is doing versus what I expected, I express it rather than wait. As a new employee, there is no way to graft yourself onto a new team without a sense of how you're doing and coming across to others and what you could do differently.

With every new member, your team's DNA changes. When you attract new talent, you must adapt your chemistry and culture ever so slightly to allow the new organ to take hold. Talent doesn't graft on its own; you must help it happen. There is always the chance that new blood will kill you, but without it, you'll die.

Foster apprenticeship.

Once upon a time, we learned only by doing. A quality education meant finding an expert to take you under his or her wing. Whether you wanted to be a blacksmith or a shoemaker, the ultimate break was ultimately a relationship. In exchange, your capacity would be stretched. You would learn in real time, soaking up knowledge through trial and error. You would learn the trade in practice rather than theory. You would build a network and gain respect based on your performance rather than where you received a degree or who you knew.

This era of apprenticeship is now a relic of history. Somewhere along the line we decided to economize and scale education. Given the time-intensive and intimate nature of apprenticeships, and the rise of the knowledge worker, we sought to train more people at once with a streamlined curriculum. Even technical and craft-based educations have become less one-on-one and more institutionalized. As we scaled learning by bringing it into the classroom, we compromised the intense learning that happened in the field. We traded experiential learning for a more standardized but less hands-on approach to education.

Healthy teams find ways to have new engineers work with seasoned engineers, even if it means a short-term compromise in productivity. They seat new designers next to experienced designers to foster the ambient knowledge exchange that only happens in proximity to one another. They create lengthy rotational programs for new hires to gain real-time exposure to different parts of the business. Apprenticeship is an investment in future talent, so actively encourage it.

I was indoctrinated with the values of experiential education during my three years working in Pine Street, an initiative that started in the executive office of Goldman Sachs to help identify and develop senior leaders across the organization. I joined the team to work with Steve Kerr, the leadership development guru who had helped former GE CEO Jack Welch found the company's learning initiatives—including its leadership development center, Crotonville—before he came to Goldman Sachs. While working with Steve, I learned about the 70/20/10 model for leadership development. The model suggests that when it comes to training leaders, only 10 percent happens in a classroom through formal instruction, 20 percent is all about feedback exchange and coaching, and a whopping 70 percent is experiential. Following this premise, some companies create "stretch assignments" for employees—bold projects that purposely expose you to leaders in the field, push comfort zones, and maximize exposure to lessons learned the hard way. Experiential on-the-job learning is the most natural conduit for developing such an expertise.

All too often, the classroom and formal training underserve us. We become dissuaded by theoretical lessons, disenchanted teachers, and a reward system that is all about the grade and not about our love for the trade. To offset this, as a leader on your team, a certain percentage of your energy should be devoted to mentoring others. Apprenticeships are mutually beneficial, as you'll prepare emerging leaders on your team to take more senior roles while developing a culture of constant learning and teaching. Make apprenticeship an expectation.

Shed the bad to keep the good.

Firing people is extremely difficult.

The optimist in me sees the potential in people and always imagines a path to help them be successful. But when the team or the project is suffering, you must act, and swiftly.

As much as you may like to think of your team as friends, you came together around a mission as opposed to circumstance. Your job as the leader of this team is to optimize the capacity of every individual, and the group as a whole, to be more aligned with the mission, productive, and to achieve greater results together. Doing so requires making difficult decisions.

I recall Netflix's Reed Hastings at an event called Founders in Dublin, Ireland, talking about the differences between a family and a sports team. In a family, he explained, you accept people for who they are—and you can't change them. If you have an uncle who shows up every Thanksgiving and gets inappropriately drunk, for better or worse, he's still your uncle. But in a sports team, you have high expectations of one another and have an obligation to change and improve the inner mechanisms of the group. Everyone needs to pass the ball. Your position is never set—and you're always out to win. You can drop a defender who isn't pulling his weight, but you can't sideline your uncle from the clan. You need to manage your staff as a sports team, not family.

If you don't weed out the sources of angst, you risk losing your key players. People join an exciting project or high-performing venture to do the best work of their lives. If they're not working with people they admire—creators who are fully committed to one another and to the work—they leave. If you're hesitant to let underperformers go, you're punishing the best performers by limiting their potential, and you're strangling the team's prospects. The best reason to fire people who are not performing well is to keep your best people. The short-term pain of letting a troublesome employee go outweighs the long-term gain of keeping the rest of your employees engaged.

Teams with strong immune systems also improve themselves naturally, and as much as it hurts, you need to let it happen. While your impulse is often to retain everyone on the team, sometimes it is best to let people move on. I remember a junior project manager in Behance's early years who was well intentioned and ambitious but was still trying to find the right role on the team. On a few occasions, he came to me expressing frustration. I was a young CEO and felt my job was to hold on to every member of our team and not let them leave. If they left, I would have failed—both them and myself. I feared the fallout of someone leaving. Would other team members see it as a sign of weakness and start to consider leaving as well?

Eventually I realized that I was striving to keep him in a job that wasn't a good fit for him. And so we lost him. But after the initial shock of someone leaving us rather than being dismissed, I realized that our team's immune system was working as it should. As you lose people who aren't a good match your team becomes stronger. Be great at retaining your A players, and less so with your B players.

"You have to constantly be reevaluating the people you have," says Anne Wojcicki from 23andMe. "Figuring out talent is hard. You never want to set someone up to fail. Doing so only hurts them and the company. One of the hardest parts of leadership is not getting attached to people. Even the people you enjoy the most may face a point where they become too specialized for their role or not specialized enough. You need to always be evaluating each person in their role—and be willing to make the change."

Despite how uncomfortable and disconcerting it is to let people go or have people submit their resignations, it is the only way to strengthen a team over time. Of course, you should provide ample support and guidance to anyone who needs it. But some people grow out of their roles, or their roles outgrow them. Others become destructive to a team's chemistry or develop into a liability. Your job is to keep your finger on the pulse and make the additions and subtractions to keep your team operating at the peak of their potential.

A steady state is unsustainable; keep people moving.

People get comfortable with where they sit, what projects they work on, and what teams they are responsible for. For leaders, no-drama days where everyone is just happily doing their thing feel great, so they assume a calm, hassle-free existence is the one that produces the best work. They optimize for a *steady state*, when there are no surprises and people do as they're told.

But comfort also breeds complacency. As learning curves plateau, we lose interest in learning for the sake of learning, and our curiosity wanes. We stay engaged as we attempt to master something that interests us, but we start to disengage as soon as we gain control over tasks and our interest dissipates. Periodic disruptions of various kinds provide perspective and make people stay fresh and alert.

The only way to stay strong is therefore to keep shaking things up.

As a young manager, I viewed my job as keeping people engaged with their respective responsibilities. But I eventually realized that careers cannot sit stagnant—people want to see opportunity ahead of them, even if they're comfortable with where they're currently standing. If you don't give them that opportunity—or occasionally challenge them to step up to it—you lose the upward mobility of junior people who are waiting for promotions and new opportunities, and your senior staff can tend to get bored and start looking for new jobs.

Despite knowing all this, I was devastated when we had the first couple of departures from our core Behance team about two years after our acquisition by Adobe. At first I felt abandoned: I couldn't imagine how we would plug certain holes in our team and culture. But as I saw emerging leaders step up and make some positive changes, I realized how much I was underestimating the bench strength of talent in the team. Unexpected movement on the team empowered new people to step into roles both they and I hadn't thought they had the capacity to fill. Had the original team just stayed where they were, as I wanted them to, we would have failed to evolve.

Promotions and moving people to different roles is one way to push people out of their comfort zone and into a new growth period of their career. For example, General Electric is known for their rotational programs, where leaders in the turbine business will be moved to the lighting business. The programs are designed to not only spread best practices across business units and develop leadership capability but also to retain key talent. Other companies assign "stretch assignments," which are special projects that take people out of their expertise and comfort zones, like exploring new business opportunities or regions. These assignments expose team members to other parts of the company or industry and help retain them by presenting new challenges and steepening the learning curve.

Teams benefit from changes to their environment and processes. As you observe your coworkers and glance around your office, look for the things that were once exciting but have now become commonplace. Are there outdated charts on the wall that once monitored progress? Take them down and redo them. Are certain regular meetings or rituals now taken for granted? Switch up the format. Have little cliques formed based on where people sit? Move desks around. Though having a sense of community is important in the workplace, if your staff become too comfortable socializing only in small groups, you lose the opportunity for cross-collaboration and overall team building that comes from chance meetings. In order to promote this, consider redoing seating assignments every nine to twelve months (or, in a larger company, every few years). Sitting next to new people in a different part of the office is an easy way to prompt new relationships and perspectives and keep things fresh.

Change is painful and especially unwelcome when there is nothing dire to fix. But what you must realize—and relay to your team—is that proactive changes that feel premature are far better than reactive changes that feel inflicted upon you. As my friend Tim Ferriss once said, "The more voluntary suffering you build into your life, the less involuntary suffering will affect your life."

Your challenge is to develop a healthy rhythm to keep your team in a constant state of motion. If you don't shake up life every now and then, life will shake it up for you. Too much calm exacerbates any disruption, so building up your and your team's tolerance for change is a positive long-term strategy for increasing tenacity.

CULTURE, TOOLS, AND SPACE

Culture is created through the stories your team tells.

The term "culture" is casually thrown around as if it can be designed in a conscious way: a cocktail hour here, a foosball table there. But culture is not in any manager's control: It's organically formed through the stories your team tells.

The stories a team recalls and shares about itself serve as a continual reminder for everyone of why they're there and what makes the team special; they reinforce the foundations of a business and the aspirational elements that tie people together.

Stories also teach lessons and create texture in time. Without stories, the past is just a blur, never revisited and refined. But with stories, the past becomes something tangible you can stand on. They orient new employees and provide institutional knowledge. Even amid long periods of ambiguity and uncertainty, a healthy culture built on stories provides the context and comfort everyone needs to stick together and keep moving forward.

As a company grows, culture becomes less impacted by everyday stories and is floated on the remnants of the stories that happened early on. Tales from "in the beginning" tend to have an outsized impact on culture as they reflect the core, founding values of why and how this whole thing got started in the first place. For more than a decade at Behance, we would retell stories from the early days, like how my cofounder Matias and I met each other in Union Square one evening, how we all saved up money to buy Dave, our first engineer, a less unsightly pair of jeans, or the year of eating salads for breakfast. These small and seemingly insignificant stories became part of our cultural knitting.

Our core values of loyalty, eccentricity, and determination were imparted through these stories and the traditions that formed alongside them. For example, we have always had running bets among the team for how long it would take to reach milestones. I recall promising the team that, as a lifelong vegetarian, I would eat meat if we ever reached one million members. In 2007 I figured, with barely twenty thousand Behance members, I was pretty safe. And then, maybe three or four holiday dinners later, I had to deliver on my promise in front of the whole team. (I haven't had a bite of chicken since, but I ate it graciously.)

The culture that forms in the wake of these stories is one of a kind. In the aggregate, these quirky exercises are what differentiate one team from the next. Looking back, I now understand how our culture helped us develop a collective gut instinct when it came to making decisions. When a potential partnership or new idea felt either "uniquely Behance" or totally foreign, our culture at work helped us know right from wrong.

Ben Thompson, writer of *Stratechery*, one of my favorite technology analysis publications, wrote about the value of retelling those early moments:

> Culture is not something that begets success, rather, it is a product of it. All companies start with the espoused beliefs and values of their founder(s), but until those beliefs and values are proven correct and successful they are open to debate and change. If, though, they lead to real sustained success, then those values and beliefs slip from the conscious to the unconscious, and it is this transformation that allows companies to maintain the "secret sauce" that drove their initial success even as they scale. The founder no longer needs to espouse his or her beliefs and values to the ten thousandth employee; every single person already in the company will do just that, in every decision they make, big or small.

While I think culture is crafted by all early members of a team, not just the founders—if anyone has an outsized impact on culture, it is because of their character, not their title— Ben makes an important point. Over time, even if the stories themselves are forgotten, the beliefs, values, and nuances of a company's culture are collectively held by everyone.

Don't underestimate the value of a story. Amid the daily grind and the gravitational force of operations, it is easy to ignore, miss out, or altogether obstruct story-making moments. Behance became its own living thing as each person's character was expressed in both the dire moments and celebrations in the seams of our day-to-day operations. If it is any indication of the power of culture, much of our early team continues to work together at the Adobe office in New York, more than ten years later. In the rather frenetic world of tech start-ups, such tenures are rare.

You need to be present for these instances and partake, especially in the early days. You need to recall them on the right occasions. And you need to let go of the reins and allow the characters on your team to begin making their own. Every team has a few "culture carriers" that are especially good at capturing great stories and retelling them. Culture carriers embody the themes that these stories represent, and their unique abilities to reinforce team culture need to be encouraged and celebrated.

As the founder of a project or team, take stories seriously and inject yourself into them—even if it means breaking a twenty-year streak as a vegetarian. Stories are what you make of them, so take some poetic justice and mine every experience for the little gems characteristic of your team, the moments that made an impact. Culture is a naturally occurring phenomenon and simply needs to be nourished, inclusive, and celebrated. The stories in the early days lay the foundation for your culture forever.

Accommodate free radicals.

In chemistry, the term "free radical" is used to describe molecules with unpaired electrons, those that may have a positive, negative, or zero charge. They are highly chemically reactive, and as a result their possibilities are endless when they come in contact with other substances or each other. They can prove wildly destructive or instrumental, depending on context.

I think the term is fitting for a new type of professional that has emerged in the twenty-first century. In the workplace, *free radicals* are the unbound energy sources of the professional world. Instead of operating by the rules many of their colleagues passively abide by, they take their careers into their own hands and put the world to work for them. They gobble up opportunities and operate at a higher risk level for a higher reward. They are not a demographic—they're just as likely to be a baby boomer as they are a millennial—but rather a psychographic. They're resilient, self-reliant, and extremely potent. You'll find them working solo, in small teams, or within large companies, but always untethered. Whether you see them or not, they're everywhere—and they're crafting the future.

Over my years working at and with companies of all sizes, I became fascinated by how misunderstood these free radicals were in the workplace. Some managers dismissed some as selfish millennials while others developed innovation and retention programs that came across as patronizing. At one point, for Behance's 99U initiative to educate creative leaders, I outlined a manifesto of sorts to help leaders build their teams to accommodate the unwieldy but powerful force of these so-called free radicals.

Who are the free radicals?

We do work that is, first and foremost, intrinsically rewarding. But when we make an impact, we expect extrinsic validation. We don't create solely for ourselves—we want to make a real and lasting impact in the world around us.

Whether we work within companies or on our own, we demand the freedom to run experiments, participate in multiple projects at once, and move our ideas forward. We thrive on flexibility and are most productive when we feel fully engaged.

We make stuff often, and we therefore fail often. Ultimately, we strive for little failures that help us course-correct along the way, and we view every failure as a learning opportunity that's simply part of our experiential education.

We have little tolerance for the friction of bureaucracy, old-boy networks, and antiquated business practices. We question standard operating procedures and assert ourselves. And when we can't, we don't surrender to the friction of the status quo: Instead, we find clever ways (and hacks) around it.

We expect to be fully utilized and constantly optimized, regardless of whether we're working in a start-up or a large organization. When our contributions and learning plateau, we leave. But when we're leveraging a large company's resources to make an impact in something we care about, we are thrilled! We want to always be doing our best work and making the greatest impact we can.

We consider open-source technology, APIs, and the vast collective knowledge of the internet to be our personal arsenal. Wikipedia, Quora, and open communities for designers, developers, and thinkers were built by us and for us. Whenever possible, we leverage collective knowledge to help us make better decisions for ourselves and our clients. We also contribute to these open resources with a pay-it-forward mentality.

We believe that networking is sharing. People listen to (and follow) us because of our discernment and curatorial instinct. As we share our creations as well as what fascinates us, we authentically build a community of supporters that gives us feedback, encouragement, and lead us to new opportunities. For this reason and more, we often (though, not always) opt for transparency over privacy.

We believe in meritocracy and the power of communities to advance our ability to do what we love, and do well by doing it. We view competition as a positive motivator rather than a threat, because we want the best idea—and the best execution—to triumph.

We make a great living doing what we love. We consider ourselves both artisans and businesspeople. In many cases, we are our own accounting department, Madison Avenue marketing agency, business development manager, negotiator, and salesperson. We expend the necessary energy to invest in ourselves as businesses, leveraging the best tools and knowledge to run ourselves as a modern-day enterprise.

In the past, those with free radical tendencies were described as difficult or self-entitled mavericks; they were the lone rangers who shunned responsibility. But today, free radicals are emerging as extremely capable leaders across industries.

In large corporations, free radicals question the norms and are regarded as brutally honest and action-oriented individuals. They trade antiquated information-sharing processes for the ease and transparency of tools like Slack and Google Apps; they leverage social media to gain market insights faster (and more cheaply) than the research department; and they always push for more freedom and progressive work practices that value meaningful creation over meaningless face time. They may cause ruckus and force change, but free radicals push you, your processes, and your products forward.

With less friction and fewer obstacles than ever before, free radicals are becoming masterful stewards of twenty-first-century ideas, and, as such, they are one of our greatest assets. As you assemble and manage your team, do whatever you can to accommodate free radicals and keep them engaged.

Be frugal with everything except your bed, your chair, your space, and your team.

In the process of building a business—and in life, generally—you should manage expenses carefully. But sometimes frugality backfires.

For example, given that you spend 30 percent of your life in bed and that sleep has such a great impact on how you feel awake, you should not skimp on your bed. Same goes with your office chair: In this modern age, we often even spend more time sitting at our desks than lying in our beds! So go buy the best damn chair you can find. Beyond your chair, the overall work space matters. While I am certainly not a proponent of expensive offices, the thought you put into the tools and environment you use to build things influences the quality of what you make.

Most companies classify their spaces the same way they do office supplies: negligible. Facilities planners tend to focus on the cost per square foot and logistical efficiencies rather than how space impacts the psychology of its inhabitants. But how you locate and design your space is as important as your team's skills, because your environment impacts how focused, motivated, and creative you are.

The space you use also has a significant impact on the products you create. One of my mentors, James Higa, who spent a big chunk of his career working for Steve Jobs through his time at Next, Apple, and Pixar, shared just how emphatic Steve was about planning the office space for each company. He would take the time to fly around the world to look at sample materials and reference structures, and even once pursued acquiring sculptures by renowned Japanese American artist and landscape architect Isamu Noguchi so Apple employees could have a "daily encounter with beauty" in the lobby. Steve would also spend the energy required to bend the will of headstrong architects until they aligned with his vision. James told me one story about Steve's influence at Pixar. While he didn't get involved in storytelling or Pixar's day-to-day operations, Steve took a very active role when it came to planning the company's physical structure and design. Tom Carlyle, who oversaw facilities for Pixar at the time and would later help with Apple's new Spaceship campus, worked closely with Steve to conceive the vision for Pixar's "town square concept," an area located at the building's center that also housed the bathrooms. The idea was to pull people together every day, whether they liked it or not, to promote "serendipitous idea exchange" when nature called. Collisions between people from different teams, Steve felt, were core to Pixar's creative process. James recalls that Steve also encouraged each Pixar employee to "modify your space and go crazy," recognizing how central freedom of expression was at Pixar. Of all the things Steve could have spent time on at Pixar, not to mention his other responsibilities, including leading Apple, he chose to focus on space because he knew what that meant for the company.

And yet, despite all the good reasons to do otherwise, most teams willfully ignore or just delegate facilities planning and other internal tasks in order to focus on what "ultimately matters": external-facing product and profit. Why the disconnect? Ultimately, it is a mismatch of talent and measures. Information technology professionals are measured by the compatibility of their systems and how well they manage their budgets. Facility planners have backgrounds in planning buildings and are seldom privy to the creative cultures they serve. They are measured by such efficiencies as how many desks can fit rather than whether creative collisions are happening that will enrich the story line of *Toy Story 3*.

Finally, and most important, don't be frugal when it comes to paying your team. When you think about compensation, think about how indispensable someone is—or has the potential to become. Many companies wrongly focus on one's past salaries and assigning people to "salary bands" that allow themselves to be subconsciously biased by age, years of experience, gender, and other characteristics that don't correlate with indispensability. While these companies may get away with underpaying someone in the short term, great talent tends to recognize their own value over time. When they do, their teams pay the price in either attempting to save them or, worse, having to replace them. Your team must feel taken care of and must have no doubt that they are being rewarded as best as possible for their achievements—and then a little bit more.

The products you use to create impact the products you create.

I am always struck and saddened by the old and cumbersome tools I see being used in many large companies and organizations. As a consultant, I was exposed to bulky workflow tools at big companies like General Electric, Proctor & Gamble, and Adidas and government agencies like the CIA (a story I'll get to later in the book) and the U.S. Army. Early in my career, when I worked at Goldman Sachs right out of college, the entire firm was limited to using old web browsers and inferior communications and human resource tools. And when our small and nimble team at Behance joined Adobe, we also had to start using a more constrained set of tools. So many companies and organizations preach the importance of innovation and efficiency, yet they burden their people with tools that constrain flexibility and consume resources.

Practically speaking, there is often a fair rationale for internal tools that are rough around the edges: Budgets are tight, matters like compatibility often limit options, security risks come with switching, and besides, employees will normally put up with and adapt to whatever they're presented with; unlike customers, they don't have a choice.

Start-ups aren't much better, but for a different reason. Rather than suffer from old or bureaucratic tools, they suffer from random, overhyped tools—or no tools at all. Amid the fast pace of a start-up relentlessly building and perfecting a product, who has time to invest in proprietary internal tools?

We vastly underestimate how much the products we use impact the products we create. Just as an artist's painting is directly impacted by the paint's quality and the brushes used, the products we use to brainstorm, plan, design, and execute our work on a day-to-day basis have an enormous impact on the end result of our efforts.

This principle became remarkably clear to me at Adobe when I met countless designers who used our applications, like Photoshop or Illustrator. These designers cared deeply about the user interface of these products because it's where their ideas became realized. As creative professionals, they knew firsthand just how much they were influenced, either consciously or subconsciously, by the tools they used to do their work.

This made me realize how much pressure Adobe was under to optimize their products: The fate of these designers' creations was in our hands. It was remarkable to think about just how much influence our product designers at Adobe had over the broader world of design. Changing an icon, color, or gradient within a tool like Photoshop or XD, the company's tool for web and mobile designers, could have an enormous impact on design in general. Whenever I was persuading a new candidate to join our team, I would make the case of the huge opportunity and responsibility facing those who design the world's design tools.

Internal systems have always been a passion of mine, largely because of how important yet underestimated I think they are. I remember my first few months working with Matias. Behance was still just an idea, but we were already developing a style guide for the brand—and not just because we were building for designers, but we felt such values were critical for a brand professionals would trust. I decided to develop our business plan as a tabloid-size, single-page graphic document rather than the usual document in Microsoft Word: I wanted something visual and alluring, even if it was "internal only." Over the years, whenever I hastily constructed a deck for a team meeting, Matias would insist on redesigning it despite the rush and small internal audience. Every internal cue to our team, he felt, mattered. We had no budget but took great care of what we liked to call "the Behance experience." We knew that the environment we worked in would influence the products we created and the type of people we hired.

Consider the tools you use and your internal documents as crucial to your team's DNA.

These factors will either harm or enrich your team and the products you produce. Internal systems are the first things you neglect when you're busy, which means they are a competitive advantage if you can value and enrich them over time. Employees need to be delighted by their own work experience as much as they hope to delight your customer's experience using your product.

You need to allocate time for optimizing the tools your team uses, your internal communications, and the environment in which you create. If you don't, the products you create will suffer.

Attribute the right amount of credit to the right people.

Your team's performance thrives when the right people are matched with the right opportunities. Perhaps you remember a project that was a perfect match for you? You had the required skills, you had a genuine interest in the problem, you had earned the opportunity based on past performance, there was just the right amount of challenge that stretched your capabilities, but there was also the safety to exercise your creativity. Under such conditions, people are set up to do the greatest work of their lives.

Unfortunately, such alignment is rare. In day-to-day operations, tasks are assigned more arbitrarily, often based on title or availability rather than interest, skill set, and merit. As a result, a lot of projects are led by people who don't want them or deserve them. These conditions breed apathy and will inhibit your efforts to optimize the potential of your team.

The underlying system that helps align work with the best people to own it is attribution. When you and the rest of your team know who did what, a natural intuition develops for pairing projects with people outside of traditional hierarchical structures. Each person's expertise becomes clearer, and the team is naturally supportive of those empowered to lead certain projects, regardless of their seniority. Respect is bred for those at the source of the work rather than those a level up. With such alignment, decisions about who should do what are supported by the larger team rather than being questioned and doubted.

Here are some principles that drive effective attribution in a team:

- Rather than just publicly acknowledging the leader of every project, you should list the broader leadership teams of every project. By explicitly calling out the leader responsible for each function area—whether it be design, engineering, or legal—you can provide a sense of satisfaction for all levels involved and help the group track the output in each area to the person responsible for it. The people who deserve the credit then get it.
- The person who did the work should present the work. For example, if a product manager is presenting his or her team a series of mock-ups and wireframes that were designed by a designer on the team, the designer should present that portion of the deck. This gives your staff ownership over their work and also allows the most knowledgeable person to lead the discussion.
- False attribution can wreak havoc in a team. This applies just as much to congratulating the wrong person as it does putting a success down to circumstance instead of skill. In our effort to optimize whatever seems to work, we're liable to conflate correlation with causation. If things go well, it doesn't necessarily mean someone's tactics worked. Go a level deeper to understand whether a success resulted from good timing, external market forces, great skills and execution, or some combination of the above. Attribute success at the element level: the skills, decisions, tactics, relationships, and hard work that contributed to the outcome. Don't make the mistake of abstracting away the forces driving the success.

Credit is a noisy and misappropriated currency. Without truthful attribution, the forces driving performance in a team become apathetic and ultimately resentful. In a healthy team, people who are accurately recognized for their skills and achievements are given new responsibilities that align with their interests as a result. But we all know that's not how it often happens. To naturally cultivate a team's appreciation of one another, you must optimize how you recognize contributors. The best teams are more *credit sharing* than *credit seeking*; rather than shine a spotlight at the top, they try to trickle the credit as far down as it goes.

Be meritorious by assigning credit truthfully. As you recognize people who work for you, assign credit as you would influence. Ultimately, you want the people who really did the work to get rewarded and have more influence next time around. While you may think assigning credit is about rewards, it's really about assigning influence for future decisions.

STRUCTURE AND COMMUNICATION

When you have the right people, there are no rules for structure.

Some of the most frequent questions I get from start-up founders and new managers in large companies are about how best to structure a team.

"Should I allow remote workers, or should I insist on the whole team working in the office?"

"Should marketing be a separate team or an extension of an existing team?"

"Can my cofounder and I both be CEO?"

"Should designers report to product managers or be the product managers?"

"Should we keep things nonhierarchical or start hiring and appointing managers?"

When structuring our teams, we tend to seek best practices and aspire to put our playbooks on par with those companies around us. We look for so-called rules, like every team should have a single leader, designers and engineers should be on different teams, and there should only be one CEO. While there is merit in each of these norms and I enjoy studying the structures of others, I have always found these questions difficult to answer without the context of the people and circumstances at play. Just as teams must challenge conventional wisdom to build extraordinary products, the same goes for building extraordinary organizations.

The greatest teams I have worked with over the years were all structured with a few remarkable exceptions to the rules. During my years serving on the board of sweetgreen, a chain of locally sourced seasonal-food kitchens, I was struck by how well the company's three cofounders, Jonathan, Nic, and Nate, functioned as tri-CEOs. When I first joined the board, many of my peers told me "Good luck—that is nuts!" But the three of them had transformed the traditional CEO role to uniquely serve the company. They divided and conquered most functions in the business but shared the same core values and intuitively knew which decisions could be made by any of them, only one of them, or required all of them. "I feel like we're pretty lucky because we can share the responsibility of taking action. It's not just one person's job to figure something out. It's not just one person that has all of the weight on their shoulders," Jonathan told me when I asked him about the arrangement. Nic added, "We can have a CEO in three times the number of places and moments... we cover three times the surface area of a normal CEO." For a period of time, this was an advantage.

There are many horror stories about coheads of teams and companies, but there are also so many examples of such arrangements being a strength. Why should there be any rules either way?

In the early years of Behance, we had five leaders of our engineering team rather than a single chief technology officer (CTO) managing them all. There was a comfortable tension I was optimizing for having a leadership team that had to work together to build out our various engineering functions, such as front-end development, back end, systems architecture, and mobile. The personalities of each leader, and their varied level of management experience, also factored into my approach to structuring the leadership team.

Another norm I broke was having our senior designers report directly to me. While designers don't normally report to the CEO, I knew that our business was different. We were serving the design community and were very design driven as a company. Being close to designers helped me ensure that design was, in fact, at the heart of our priorities.

When I first joined Adobe after Behance's acquisition, I continued to step out of bounds when it came to structuring the organization, which ultimately grew to almost five hundred employees. I had some designers report to me rather than work in the company's central design unit, just as I did at Behance; I created very small teams to explore the largest strategy shifts first rather than include every stakeholder at the onset; and I developed a marketing role within some of the product teams to ensure the copy and campaigns were aligned with the product vision. Of course, breaking norms in big companies causes the occasional fire; I had to explain myself quite often. But I tried to mold structure to the kind of work we were doing rather than the other way around. Just as it is remarkably hard to innovate using the same code or materials as your competitors, it is hard to build something new within the confines of a structure built for the past, or later stage products.

When you have the right people, there are no rules for how the team must be structured. When your A players are playing their A game, you can be creative with how they work. In fact, you need to be. The extremely talented people you love and trust know how good they are, and they thrive working on their own terms. As the leader, you need to carefully balance the need for structure with the need to accommodate the autonomy and idiosyncrasies of your team. Optimizing how you work requires unconventional experimentation while letting go of norms.

As I think about the nature of the advice I give to start-ups and the number of times I defy my own advice, I am struck by how frequently rules should be broken. For example, while I feel strongly that you should never outsource your competitive advantage, sometimes the perfect designer—or other domain expert—insists on working on her own as a freelancer. Sometimes the circumstances necessitate defying your own beliefs. The willingness to break your own rules and keep structure permeable to circumstances is as important as the rules themselves. Exceptions shouldn't happen too often, but when they do, they could be differentiating and critical to your success.

So long as you have the right people aligned around the right objectives, be flexible. If superstars insist on working remotely, let them. If two people with complementary skill sets make great candidates for the same leadership role, experiment with coheads. Observe, learn, and then adjust. Despite all the conventional wisdom out there, you're allowed to change the rules. These tweaks could help you or hurt you, but you've got to take some risk to achieve an irregular outcome. Embrace best practices until you need to change them. Then break them.

Process is the excretion of misalignment.

In start-ups, "process" is a bit of a dirty word.

When you bring a small group of the right people together (and they all join the effort for the right reasons), you'll find yourself free of burdensome process. When you're all working toward the same goals and deadlines, fueled by real-time communication, transparency, and a shared sense of urgency, you'll feel efficient. Oftentimes, you're even all sitting next to one another! In these early stages, teams are miraculously productive. Small teams run circles around big teams not because they are so small but because they are so aligned that there is only thought and action without anything in between. It's a beautiful thing.

But as a team grows, misalignment happens. People's engagement slips to varying degrees. Objectives are clear to some and less to others—and can change regularly. Deadlines need to be mandated rather than suggested. Communication is inconsistent by the sheer fact that everyone isn't sitting together. As goals and priorities become crooked, performance suffers.

What's the solution to the misalignment that comes with growth? Process—the very thing you didn't need in the early days. Training programs, daily staff meetings, organizational structure diagrams, approval processes: These are the mechanisms we throw at misalignment to ensure that a group of people think and act in tandem. Process is how we force alignment when it doesn't happen naturally. You schedule meetings, you embed systems for tracking and accountability, and you install more managers.

But if not implemented properly, process slows down progress. It can be painful, especially as teams that grew up eschewing mandates mature. Nobody likes more obstacles to doing the real work.

The conundrum of process is we all need some, but too much is lethal. The more aligned your team is, the less process you need. Here are some principles to consider as you thoughtfully apply process:

Install process for your team, not for you.

A lot of wasteful and painful processes are born from anxiety. When leaders feel insecure about losing touch with parts of their business, they're liable to create more bottlenecks. I've seen some leaders schedule redundant "sign-off" meetings, run daily check-ins, and implement other mechanisms just to achieve peace of mind—for themselves, not for the team. But process tolls imagination and agility and should be applied only to prevent problems. If deadlines are being missed, goals are variable, or legal and financial functions are being sidestepped, installing a process will help. But when you introduce process to your team, do it to solve their problems rather than quell your own anxiety.

Spend more time on achieving alignment than imposing process.

Doing more work to help everyone understand the goals and plan will foster a natural alignment among the team. How often are you merchandising your mission and road map to your team? Likely not enough. Are you ensuring that every new member of your team is adequately caught up? Are you proactively identifying people who seem misaligned and taking the time to get them up to speed? Such alignment will expedite progress and boost quality better than any formal process could.

Audit your processes frequently and always try to cut them down.

Just because a process was necessary at one point in time doesn't mean it always will be. Constantly question the necessity of the policies and procedures you impose on your team. Do you still need to have that morning scrum meeting? Do people still need your sign-off on certain actions? Periodically audit the processes around you and look for ways to either kill or improve them to free up your employees' time where you can.

Your challenge is to lead an efficient team that is fully aligned with as little process as possible. Knowing how to respect process while not letting it inhibit progress is one of the holy grails of management. Introduce process to counter misalignments only as they emerge.

Don't rob people of their process.

As you can tell, I'm wary of adding processes as the perpetual solution for internal challenges. However, I have also learned over the years—often the hard way—how important it is to let people have their own process.

Matias and I often butted heads when it came to aligning the Behance design team's efforts with the broader company early on. While certain business and product decisions could be made in a single meeting, design decisions required a more iterative process of mock-ups and feedback before anything conclusive. However, I always wanted to find the answer fast. Since our team had so little time and resources, I was always pushing for the quickest responses with the largest outcomes. I considered myself the pacemaker, and in my effort to keep the team moving, I would push for a solution without regard for the steps Matias's team needed to take to find the best one.

But my effort to speed through—or steamroll—another team's process would often backfire. Matias's team had developed ways to explore different approaches to problems before choosing a solution. Similarly, our engineering team had developed their own processes for quality control, training, and keeping the right cadence for their own productivity. These processes were working. I had to learn how to temper my bias toward action with a respect for the processes of those around me.

It is healthy to have some degree of *process intolerance*—an innate disdain for undue procedures and waiting; after all, waiting for a green light never gets you there first (though red lights certainly prevent accidents). But interfering with the order of operations of those around you has negative consequences, even if you think your initiative will save time and effort in the long run. People incorporate process into their work as a patch for their own misalignments, and to override such mechanisms without considering why they are there is problematic.

Many issues between leaders and their teams track back to robbing team members of their processes. While you want to avoid layering on too many processes, you must respect the work styles that people adopt to keep themselves aligned and engaged. "Give your staff the context they need for why you're asking them to do what you're asking them to do, and then get out of their way and make sure other distractions are removed from their plate so they can focus on what matters most," says Ben Erez, whom we met earlier in the book.

Therefore, let people self-correct and keep their working quirks—they know themselves best. Process is often there for a reason, even if it's not clear to you. When time is of the essence, find a way to rework and expedite process in a mutually agreeable way instead of eradicating it entirely. Process can and should be augmented over time, but it shouldn't be aggressively ripped away.

Merchandise to capture and keep your team's attention.

Perhaps one of the most important unspoken roles of a leader through the messy middle of a project is that of internal marketer. For all the emphasis around obsessing over your customers and your public brand and message, there is surprisingly little focus on the internal brand and message. What do your employees think of their work, the team's productivity, and their mission? Do they even know the mission?

With all the systems to manage teams and projects these days, we sometimes forget what traditional marketers know: If it's memorable or big and in your field of vision every day, you're more likely to do it. Creating the equivalent of billboards, commercials, and hypertargeted subliminal advertising within your team helps foster alignment and productivity. Seriously!

The best leaders of productive teams are constantly devising new and clever ways to get us to act. This could come in the form of a graphic representation of milestones and deadlines hung on walls, a communications campaign that repeats goals and the progress to date, or in the form of pithy time-bound declarations, like Pinterest's "Year of Going Global," which pushed every team across the company to reprioritize efforts to internationalize the business, or Uber's "Year of the Driver," which they rolled out when they realized they had fallen behind on developing tools and better policies for drivers on their platform.

Other times it is a statement or edgy visual that sticks in peoples' minds and becomes ammunition against old and stodgy thinking. For example, when cloud business services company Salesforce launched their customer-relationship management service at a time when big companies preferred traditional boxed software, they used the classic "no smoking" symbol with "software" in place of the cigarette image. This antitraditional-software sign served as a rallying cry to push both employees and customers beyond the old software mentality.

When I was tasked with rebooting Adobe's mobile products in 2013, I found a few phrases to be especially effective in changing assumptions and mind-sets internally. For example, in advocating for design principles that would keep our products simple yet powerful, we would repeat the phrase "Powerful enough for professionals, accessible enough for everyone" in product-review meetings as well as onstage at product releases. When we embarked on a project called Creative Cloud Libraries, a service designed to help users of products like Photoshop access their fonts, colors, brushes, and other assets across different applications and devices, we used the phrases "Your assets, always at your fingertips" and "Ending the era of the blank page" as sticky statements to keep teams aligned. When features needed to be prioritized, we would always come back to these simple statements to check ourselves against our vision.

Merchandising is also the best tool to get your team's attention on the most important information, especially in an era of information overload. In 2013, just a few years after my first book, *Making Ideas Happen*, was published, I was contacted by the Central Intelligence Agency (CIA) to visit and help an internal team focused on using design and marketing tactics to better disseminate critical information to officers in the field and analysts around the world. Much like any other organization, the CIA realized that its information was effective only if it ultimately reached and engaged its audience. The team was exploring how the use of pithy headlines, infographics, and design principles could grab an agent's attention the same way marketing and advertising does.

Be creative in how you merchandise tasks and progress to capture and keep your team's attention. When you must implement a new process, give it some beauty. Loyalty to a new system comes from believing in it and being attracted to it. The design, nomenclature, virtual confetti that explodes from a completed task—these little touches can go a long way in spurring utilization.

Similarly, when your team makes meaningful progress, you should merchandise their achievements back to them. Give your team the gratification of seeing their progress rather than just moving on. At Behance, we had "Done Walls" that were decorated with a collage of completed project plans, checklists, and sketches that literally surrounded us with the sensation of progress. And whenever I'm presenting a forward vision presentation to my team, I try to start with a few slides recapping what the team has already accomplished. Progress is the best motivator of future progress, but it must be merchandised sufficiently so that people feel it.

While studying at Harvard Business School, I had the opportunity to work with Teresa Amabile, a professor who conducted extensive research on creativity in business. In one study, Teresa had more than two hundred professionals in large companies track their thoughts, motivations, and emotions in a simple diary format for a period of four months. From more than twelve thousand entries, Teresa observed the role of progress begetting future progress. "Of all the things that can boost emotions, motivation, and perceptions during a workday," she concluded, "the single most important is making progress in meaningful work." She went on to explain, "The more frequently people experience that sense of progress, the more likely they are to be creatively productive in the long run. Whether they are trying to solve a major scientific mystery or simply produce a high-quality product or service, everyday progress—even a small win—can make all the difference in how they feel and perform."

You may have a colleague or department that oversees external marketing, but you are the chief internal marketer. The active efforts and campaigns you make to internally promote your plans and progress will help people stay motivated and make better decisions about what to do next. Your team's understanding of priorities and perception of their own progress is in your hands.

A mock-up > Any other method of sharing your vision

If a picture is worth a thousand words, then a mock-up answers a thousand questions.

When it comes to strategy and planning, there is too much talking. I recall meetings at Adobe, board meetings at nonprofits like the Cooper-Hewitt National Design Museum, and brainstorming sessions with countless start-ups where all people do is pose questions in different ways: "Maybe it should do X?" "Maybe the better approach is what Y company does?" "Why don't we try doing Z instead?" Often the different parties aren't even in agreement on what exactly it is they're trying to answer. The discussions therefore stay at a very abstract, conceptual level until someone has something visual or tangible to react to.

Ideas are misunderstood unless they can be visualized. Doubts and confusion can be cleared in one fell swoop by a simple image of visualizing a potential solution. When a visual is put up on a screen or a prototype is passed around, the whole conversation becomes more productive and specific.

During the summer of 2013 at Adobe we were imagining how creative apps on tablets and mobile devices might work with their desktop counterparts, such as Photoshop. We had about a dozen Adobe executives in our New York office along with some of the smartest computer scientists and software architects in the business. We also had two of my best senior designers, Clément Faydi and Eric Snowden, in the room, as well as Matias.

The first four hours of our discussion were mostly dominated by the executives and engineers in the room and seemed to run in a loop. Concepts were pitched, quickly scrutinized, and cast aside, then pitched again with a different lens. There was no anchor for the conversation except for an abstract problem, and I remember feeling deeply frustrated that the team wasn't latching onto anything concrete. And then, with a huff of frustration, Matias started taking the random concepts we had been sketching on a dry-erase wall and mocking them up in an Adobe Illustrator document. (We always used Illustrator at the time for mock-ups; now we use AdobeXD.)

As soon as he did, the group started looking over his shoulder. The conversation suddenly narrowed as a consensus was reached around some elements of the concept he was illustrating in real time. As soon as I saw this, I realized that a few hours of work on some thoughtful mock-ups would probably save us many more days of wayward deliberation. I stopped the meeting and suggested that Clément and Eric, who were leading the project, take some time to construct a concept deck. Going forward, every meeting for this project started with our lead designers "showing" the rest of the group where we were and what we had to discuss rather than just telling people.

It's as if buy-in and alignment come only from being anchored by something in the visual cortex. "When evaluating a product or a service, [one's] brain is working to understand and make conclusions, to come to a decision. Imagery is a superb way to demonstrate something and to provide answers to the questions your brain is asking," explains Peep Laja, founder of ConversionXL, on his conversion optimization blog. Neuromarketers are well aware that our "old brain"—which includes the brain stem, the oldest brain region controlling such automatic functions as breathing and motor responses—powerfully influences decision making. Given the "old brain" evolved to quickly assess visual and sensory threats, it prefers visual stimuli, which are processed faster than words and concepts. Thus, to capture your audience's attention, you should always couple abstract descriptions with concrete images or physical representations of your idea—as these visual aids appeal to and satisfy our most primal neurological instincts.

Sharing a design, a series of samples, or a rough prototype quickly aligns people. Without it, much of a discussion is spent orienting a group around a concept and addressing basic questions and misunderstandings. Without a mock-up, people are trying to interpret something in the dark by feeling one edge at a time. A mock-up or prototype is worth countless meatings and debates. A mock-up turns the lights on.

Present your ideas, don't promote them.

A very simple and common mistake I see among passionate founders and designers is to present a new idea in the best possible light to the point of promoting rather than explaining. Something so polished, without any blemishes, is harder to grasp. The roughness of a new idea provides the texture your team or potential investors need to believe in and latch onto.

At Benchmark we called these CEOs "promoters." They would come in with a seemingly perfect story, broad generalizations about their industry, and would presumptuously disqualify competitors. It was hard to engage with their pitch emotionally, as we couldn't see room for ourselves within it, so we spent our time trying to poke holes in it. We couldn't grasp how they would react during the inevitable tough times that were to come. Would they be able to face reality when it hit? Would they gloss over conflicts and ignore concerning data in favor of sustaining the perfect story?

The founders I get most excited about are the ones who are grounded in reality and equally focused on both problems and solutions. I recall one such founder, Sam Hashemi, from a company called REMIX, who gave one of the more confident yet understated pitches I've seen. Sam has a background as a designer and had spent a couple years volunteering with Code for America, which taps the country's design and engineering talent for the public good. During the program, Sam envisioned a better way for cities to plan their transit systems and ultimately turned the idea into a company. In our first conversation, Sam was matter-of-fact about what his team had accomplished and the parts of his business plan that were clear or still uncertain. He had raised a large seed round prior to our meeting and was so focused on the new problems he wanted to solve that he nearly forgot to mention that his revenue stream was so strong that he hadn't even touched his seed capital yet.

Sam exuded a quiet confidence that reminded me of my first meeting with Ben Silberman, the CEO and cofounder of Pinterest, back when he was raising his seed round in 2010. Ben was visiting New York City to bring on some seed investors with product and design experience. Before our meeting, I spent some time poking around Behance's web analytics to see whether Pinterest was driving any traffic to Behance users' portfolios. The numbers were small, but the growth was strikingly steady. Ben didn't come in with bold growth metrics or a series of slides about how Pinterest would become a massive company. Instead, Ben talked about his love for collecting things and his value for design. A long brainstorm on the design of Pins and Boards led to more calls and my first ever investment in a company other than my own. Over the years since, whenever we catch up, Ben starts with a problem or question. Despite Pinterest's success, Ben's interest is still in studying what works and in fixing what's broken. He wants to engage people, not impress them.

Whether you are sharing an idea with colleagues or pitching an idea to investors, be less polished and more real. A little texture in the form of uncertainty and admission of challenge is helpful for everyone. The right partners will see your challenges as potential rather than weakness, and your honesty will set the right tone for future collaboration and navigating the ups and downs of the journey together.

Delegate, entrust, debrief, and repeat.

As you scale your project, you'll need to rely more on others. While it never feels entirely natural to hand off a responsibility—especially an important one—developing the intuition of what can be delegated and what should stay under your watch is the only way to scale your own capacity and that of your team.

Consider the cost-benefit analysis: New problems will never be solved and your project will never reach new heights unless other people can take on your duties. When you look at it like that, you realize that you have to learn to let go. While I struggle at times to entrust others to make certain decisions, every time I do I feel liberated. I remind myself that the costs of decisions being made a little differently are usually exceeded by the benefits of my newfound capacity to innovate and solve new problems. And it's all thanks to delegation.

The word *delegate* suggests that a leader is single-handedly deciding who should do what, assigning tasks, and then holding everyone responsible as any prototypical boss would. But among high-performing teams, delegation is as much sought as it is received.

In such teams, there is a genuine collective drive to free up those with the rarest or least scalable talents. For example, you want your data science experts or programmers to be analyzing data and programming—not expending their precious energy on administrative work. If everyone is aligned with the mission and the market forces and is determined to do whatever they can to make the greatest impact, then the pressure to delegate should come from below as well as above. In such an environment, everyone is seeking control for what they think they should be responsible for—often the work they can complete the fastest and at the highest quality, or work requiring skills unique to them.

Only when your team members feel in control of their own projects will they feel sufficiently motivated and accountable for completing them.

David Marquet, the former commander of the nuclear-powered submarine USS *Santa Fe* and author of *Turn the Ship Around!*, shared with our team at 99U his insights around delegation from his time in the military:

> The problem is that, in the heat of the moment of conversation, our leadership brains are wired to take control and give direction. It feels good. We get to solve problems, reduce uncertainty by giving instructions, and raise our level of status and authority. Unfortunately what feels good for us feels bad for our people. No one ever did anything awesome or great because they were told to. The degree to which we order people around suppresses any opportunity for greatness. Telling people what to do is the opposite of responsibility.... The danger is people are "doing" their jobs, not "thinking" them. Often these actions inadvertently have the effect of reducing the employee's drive toward empowerment.

Delegation and job titles aren't enough—employees must feel empowered.

In nonhierarchical teams or in big matrixed projects that include leaders from different parts of a company, another problem emerges: Employees struggle because they don't have control over what they are ultimately responsible for. Perhaps your project is dependent on work done by people in other departments, and you have no idea who is responsible for what. Without knowing who is responsible for every dependency, your team will not feel in control of their own responsibilities. Your job is to find and identify a single person to be responsible for every kind of task being completed.

Adam D'Angelo is the founder and CEO of Quora, an online knowledge-sharing community, and is also the former CTO of Facebook. He has long advocated for every function and project in his company having a "DRI"—a Directly Responsible Individual—whom the entire team knows to go to and rely on for that particular area. The key practice, Adam explains, is to not only streamline decision making but also heighten the level of accountability each DRI feels to their peers. As Adam explained to me, there are three things leaders must do to make sure DRIs are effective. "First, make sure responsibilities are clearly defined—well known by the person who is responsible, but also by others. Second, make sure it is also clear who the person is accountable to—the person who is responsible for holding the person responsible. And, third, accountability is about understanding why something didn't work and what needs to happen to make sure it doesn't happen again. Depending on the severity, accountability could be poking fun at someone, a postmortem, or a serious conversation, or an apology to the whole company, or a change in role, or a termination." But, Adam emphasized, "the principle is 'what needs to happen to make sure this doesn't happen again and maintain the expectation that people will meet their responsibilities?'"

There is a point in every project, especially among highly collaborative and passionate teams, when everyone's desire to discuss and influence every decision backfires. Decisions stop getting made out of fear of excluding someone. The quick solution is to assign a DRI to everything—answering emails from customers, handling press, recruiting, functions, every major part of the product. While titles are all-encompassing and matter very little in early-stage teams, yet alone large companies, DRIs are assigned at the task level. The more collaborative your team, the more important it is to know who is responsible for what.

Scott Heiferman, the CEO and founder of Meetup, sees another advantage of DRIs at all levels: making sure that everyone is aligned on how their role within the company matters.

As Scott explained to me over lunch one day in downtown New York City, "I love the idea of every person understanding how their small role aligns with the broader mission.... Elon Musk says that you can stop anyone on the SpaceX factory floor and ask them what they're doing and why it's important. Someone could be making bolts and you could say, 'Why do you do it? What's your job?' And they'll say, 'Oh, I'm making these bolts so that we can have a landable vehicle, because if we do a landable vehicle, then we can get to Mars. And if we can get to Mars, then humanity will da-da-da-da...'" When people know where their small part fits in the whole, they recognize how indispensable their work is. They feel more accountable.

Ironically, when something goes wrong or a member of your team was careless, sometimes they need more authority, not less. By giving them more autonomy and control, they'll either seize it and work hard to keep it, or they will fail faster, which is a good thing for weeding out who is on your team for the right and wrong reasons.

However, you'll never feel comfortable delegating an increasing amount of responsibilities to others unless you can trust that the work is being completed. When you delegate to others and entrust them as authorities, you must foster accountability and apply some degree of quality control. Writing up handoff notes and determining DRIs is just half of management—and it's the easier half. Giving the feedback to refine how others are taking your direction is more important and comes less naturally.

My preferred method of evaluating delegated tasks is holding debriefs after both major milestones and fiascos. Asking questions like "How did it go on a scale of one to ten?" "What should we have done differently?" and "What worked surprisingly well?" will naturally hone a team's instincts, capture what they learned, and foster accountability without challenging the new leaders' autonomy or micromanaging them.

As your project and team scales, get into a rhythm of distributing responsibilities to others, entrusting them enough to feel ownership, and then debriefing to increase the quality and efficiency of the execution. Great management is this *delegate, entrust, and debrief cycle* on repeat.

Know how and when to say it.

In our digital world, communication has never been easier. Remote teams can work together throughout the day without feeling out of touch, issues can be resolved without hearing a dial tone, and conversations can pick up right where they left off across many different mediums.

However, it has also become too easy to reach people. As the time between our thoughts and actions shrinks—and the effort in which to act does, too—our margin for error grows.

There have been many instances in which I've been too haphazard about how I communicate with my colleagues, clients, friends, and family. Oftentimes, a casual text should have been a longer email. Or that email should have been a phone call. Or that phone call should have been a face-to-face meeting.

For sensitive topics, the nonverbal cues you can see only in person are extremely important. However, sometimes the formal nature of a meeting or long email can make a small issue seem like a bigger deal than it actually is.

Knowing what to say and when to say it is incredibly important to maintaining relationships. But it's not enough. How we say it is just as vital. As the trope goes, "The medium is the message."

Before shooting a blasé email to a new client or pinging a colleague about a problem on Slack, consider the following:

Is this a one-way share of information or is it conversational? Email is a great way of blasting off information for people to consider on their own schedule; they can respond whenever they like, and you are likewise not pressured to reply until you've gathered your thoughts. As casual as it can sometimes feel, however, emails are not conversational: They lump all of your thoughts together rather than allowing two people (or more) to spar point to point. This means they also come with a high chance of misunderstanding. Email is an effective way to inform people of something, but if you're aiming to influence others and generate a deep understanding, choose a conversational format instead, like back-and-forth messaging, picking up the phone, or an in-person conversation.

Is the topic collegial or is it sensitive and potentially controversial? Whether it is via Slack, Facebook Messenger, WhatsApp, iMessage, or whatever your preferred texting service, casual conversations best take place over a real-time messaging system. However, the bite-size quality of this form of messaging means it's not well suited to discussing complex matters. Its text-based nature also strips away the tonal nuances of voice and the inaudible visual cues of discomfort. If your topic is sensitive, push yourself toward a more intimate medium—especially if you find yourself preferring text-based communication as a way to avoid the confrontation, as that seldom ends well.

Can the topic be addressed spontaneously, or does it require preparation? When you decide that a direct conversation is the way to go, consider whether or not the other participants will want time to prepare—mentally or otherwise. The more dynamic or controversial (or emotional) the topic, the more you may want to give participants time to gather facts, refine their position, and mentally prepare for the exchange. Without prep time, people are liable to be defensive or overwhelmed.

Planning an in-person discussion ahead of time allows both participants to think about the topic in advance. Privacy ensures comfort. Deep connections cannot be achieved efficiently; they are reached only through advanced planning and investing time.

A scheduled discussion doesn't have to be formal, either. I prefer planning important conversations over coffee, a walk, or a meal. The productivity of a conversation is largely dependent on the permeability of its participants. In most cases, an informal conversation supports a more candid exchange with less defensiveness.

In addition to intimacy, inflection and visual cues allow you to gather nonverbal intelligence to ensure clarity. As Vanessa Van Edwards, a body language expert and author of *Captivate: The Science of Succeeding with People*, wrote, up to 93 percent of our communication is nonverbal, which "means that our body language, facial expressions and other nonverbal behavior is even more important than our verbal content." However, as Edwards, who specializes in emotional intelligence and research, continues, "most people don't even think about what their body language is saying to others. As a result, many businesspeople don't ever realize how much their body language is holding them back at work."

With so many options for how to communicate with your team, it can be easy to choose the path of least resistance rather than focusing on your objective and which type of communication will help you achieve it. We get in trouble when we choose to communicate the easy way versus the right way. As our channels for communication expand, we must endeavor to be more thoughtful about how and when we communicate.

Nothing beats explicitness. Aspire to say it like it is.

Communication often contains too much couching and disclaiming. Everyone has a different style of working within a team dynamic, but the more you can just say it like it is and foster a working environment where people are straightforward and honest about where they stand, the better your team will function, and the faster you'll solve problems.

EXPLICITNESS WHEN YOU'RE SOLVING A PROBLEM

Refrain from using too many niceties that obscure important messages. This doesn't make for a good politician, at least not in difficult moments. But over time, people come to respect candidness and directness. When you feel like a problem is being obfuscated by disclaimers, delicateness, or a lack of intellectual honesty, try to simplify it and compartmentalize the issues. One of my most frequent questions to our dev-ops team at

Behance—the folks responsible for keeping our services up and running for millions of people to use every day—was "What's keeping you up at night right now?" I was always trying to get beneath the surface of the progress we were making to unearth the real vulnerabilities.

When you're proposing a solution to a problem and meet resistance, take a step back to make sure everyone understands the problem first. People tend to dislike solutions until they feel like they understand the problem itself. Proposals must come after personally postulating the problem and the consequences of not solving it. Simple truths resonate; they stick in your mind, whether you like it or not. And that's all the more reason to seek them and state them.

EXPLICITNESS WHEN YOU'RE BUILDING A PRODUCT

Most people's natural tendency is to please and accommodate others. In the process of creating a product, this tendency often manifests itself as a generalized product vision that accommodates too many kinds of customers a little rather than one particular kind of customer a lot. The more wide open a product vision, the less likely it is to revolutionize one particular use case.

For example, while Instagram was certainly not the first way to share photos with your friends, it was one of the most specific, clear ways to do it. Instagram was defined by an explicit purpose—to share a simple photo with a limited set of filters to a specific group of people—and intentionally let go of the many other use cases and kinds of customers it could accommodate. Similarly, Pinterest was designed explicitly to find and pin images in an organized fashion. Delicious, and many other sites and tools, performed bookmarking and offered a visual form for it, but Pinterest was explicitly visual as a default. This made it stand out and helped customers know exactly what they would accomplish at the offset.

Aspiring to accommodate many needs and use cases will make it hard for anyone to identify your specialty and feel compelled to engage with it. I call it the "NYC Deli Problem." If you have signs outside for a salad bar, pizza, Chinese food, and sushi, you're liable to not be taken seriously for any one of those cuisines despite how good your food may actually be. By attempting to engage with too broad a customer base, you fail to engage with any one customer base deeply.

We'll talk a lot more about product optimization in the sections ahead, but there is nothing more important than erring on the side of being exclusive rather than inclusive. In the early stages of articulating a product vision, don't shy away from being explicit about who you serve and who you don't. What are you doing and what aren't you doing? Don't hedge—you must choose.

EXPLICITNESS WHEN YOU'RE COMMUNICATING YOUR INTENTION

When you're asking your team, investors, or community for something, be explicit with what you want rather than optimize for optionality. "Let's close three of our target customers this month" is more effective than "Let's make a lot of progress on closing customers this month." Being specific removes all ambiguity from what success looks like.

Similarly, when you're asking for help, be explicit with your intentions, and what you need to achieve them. Don't ask for general support or feedback. Ask for help in a specific area you know someone is especially qualified to provide. Otherwise you'll get general responses and not specific, actionable support. For example, when I get emails from founders I've invested in asking for help with networking and hiring, I am far more engaged by a specific question like "Do you have any leads for a junior designer with experience developing brand identities?" than "Any talented people I should meet as I build the team?"

Be explicit, and you're more likely to get what you want.

There is power in brevity.

Just a quick reminder:

Shorter emails get faster response times.

Fewer words go further (and are listened to more intently).

Standing meetings (where your knees get weak) prioritize the point.

The less preamble, the more focused your team will be on your message. Most attention spans don't even make it to the end.

Start with your point; don't end with it.

CLEARING THE PATH
TO SOLUTIONS

Tackle "organizational debt."

Leaders who can't make tough decisions cause their teams to accumulate "organizational debt." Like the notion of "technical debt," which is the accumulation of old code and short-term solutions that collectively burden a team over time, organizational debt is the accumulation of changes that leaders should have made but didn't.

Silicon Valley entrepreneur Steve Blank, who first coined the term, described how "all the compromises made to 'just get it done' in the early stages of a startup . . . can turn a growing company into a chaotic nightmare." A lot of these actions (or the lack thereof) are less about the pursuit of productivity and more about avoiding conflict. As a result, the most common decision is to not make a decision yet.

At big companies that pride themselves on having a friendly culture and comfortable work environment, leaders are liable to refrain from causing a ruckus. In any large company, managers often opt to isolate or transfer underperforming staff to other projects and teams rather than deal with the difficulty of firing them. Oftentimes, they're dissuaded by the time it takes to plan, coordinate with HR, and communicate such changes, especially if the communication involves upsetting someone. The Band-Aid is applied, the underlying problem never gets solved, and the burden gets passed on to the next decision maker. Too many companies are plagued with middle managers who take pride in circumventing internal politics and third-rail topics. As a result, productivity can seem at a peak while organizational debt accrues.

Eventually, the mountain of organizational debt compromises the team's operations and product. Progress slows as people become misaligned, and motivation dwindles as bureaucracy sets in.

What to do? When you come across an obstacle in your organization, clear it instead of going around it. Perhaps it is a legal process that required too many calls and could be expedited with a new process? Perhaps you spent a long time finding the right person to solve a problem and could document the solution to save others the hassle? It'll take more energy, but it means that everyone else who faces the same obstacle can move past it faster. When I meet with teams, whether they are my own or part of other companies, I eagerly look for the elephants in the room. The natural tendency to circumvent seemingly irreconcilable topics means that you need to look for clues. When people get quiet or smile uncomfortably about a particular topic, you know it's worth probing. Sometimes you need to ask point-blank: Who is holding up progress?

You should encourage others to follow your lead and take the time to call out inefficiencies and propose ways things could be done better. Small companies with a culture of honesty and a commitment to continual improvement have an advantage at this game. My friend Aaron Dignan, who runs a consulting firm for organizational improvement called The Ready, suggests the idea of a "bounty program." In this system, "any employee who encounters a policy or process that is hindering their ability to deliver value to the customer can submit the policy/process (and a recommendation) to the program website." I like the idea of incentivizing everyone to bash inefficiencies and dumb practices that contribute to organizational debt.

When you're unsure about something, whether it be an email or a comment made in a meeting, act on it or ask about it. Stuff that sits idle, misunderstood by you and likely others as well, plagues progress. Handle something once, not many times.

A lot of big problems don't get solved because we can solve small problems faster.

In the drive to feel productive, we're liable to focus on tasks that can be completed quickly over tasks that need to be completed.

Writer and researcher Charles Duhigg describes productivity in his book *Smarter Faster Better* as "the name we give our attempts to figure out the best uses of our energy, intellect, and time as we try to seize the most meaningful rewards with the least wasted effort." In our efforts to feel rewarded with the least effort possible, we often fail to make progress in solving the hard problems that need our energy the most.

I recall many relatively minor decisions working in a big company, like where to position a logo at the top of an outdated website. This kind of minutia generated long email chains debating the position of the logo, but it never addressed the more difficult—and prominent—issue of what to do with the website. Of course, where to place a logo is a much easier problem to solve than how and when to redo an entire public-facing web experience. As a result, leaders in various marketing and product teams gravitated toward the smaller problems they could solve more quickly. The feeling of being "done!" is seductive. Extinguishing a small brush fire will make you feel accomplished more quickly than making a small dent tackling a forest fire. But one causes much more damage when left unchecked than the other.

Our desire to make progress unfortunately often compromises real progress where it is needed most. Blame those hits of dopamine, firing whenever we feel like we're achieving a small win. Or blame the perverted measures we apply to our own productivity, like how many emails are left in our inbox or how many to-do boxes get checked.

As my former colleague and 99U director Jocelyn Glei explains in her book *Unsubscribe*, email taps into our brain's "urge for completion"—the instinctive drive to finish an activity once we've started it. (This urge is also how technologists keep us engaged in applications like LinkedIn, using progress bars that track our percentage toward a "successful" profile.)

"Chipping away at our inbox gives us a sense of satisfaction precisely because the act includes such clear progress indicators. You started out with 232 email messages and now you have 50—progress! You're advancing toward that holy grail of email productivity, inbox zero, and your brain is compelling you to see the job through," Glei writes.

"The problem is that while winnowing down your inbox gives you a strong feeling of progress, it's just that—a feeling. Because unread message counts do not obey the golden rule of progress bars: Thou shalt not move backward. Instead, your unread message count is always a moving target. While you attend to it, you have the false sensation of advancing toward a goal, but the moment you look away, the target shifts farther into the distance as more messages roll in," she continues. And not all emails are equally important.

Conversely, progress often feels elusive in our most important projects because meaningful work takes a lot of time, and because the applications we use to do our most meaningful work "hide" progress from us: In Word or Google Docs, we delete and write over the same files until we're satisfied, and in Photoshop, we cut and paste our progress away, rarely saving earlier drafts.

"This is the progress paradox," Glei writes, "by dint of technology, it's easy to see our progress when we're doing relatively meaningless short-term tasks, while it's quite difficult to see our progress when we're engaged in the long-term, creative projects that will ultimately have the most impact on our lives."

We need to combat such tendencies with an appetite for the meatier problems before us. Meaningful productivity starts by defining the things that make a big difference and prioritizing them one at a time. Some teams I have worked with call the difference between the big tasks and the little tasks "boulders" and "pebbles."

In every project, there are a few boulders and lots of pebbles. The boulders are hard to move up the hill, but they materially impact your project and differentiate you from others. Boulders could be a major new feature, a new architecture for your service, or writing the initial draft copy for your website. By contrast, pebbles are the innumerable little tweaks and changes you could quickly make that are rarely differentiating.

I try to spend 80 percent of my time on boulders and 20 percent on pebbles. But that's easy to say, hard to do. Even though we know that time is best spent on the big and important challenges, we're still drawn to the quick returns. Resist.

Break bureaucracy by piercing ambiguity with questions.

Too much process leads to bureaucracy, and any team of size is plagued by it. Bureaucracy is like a frigid ocean with an icy surface that is just about to freeze over. Big companies are like big ships. Big ships can go far but are also the slowest. If you sit stagnant for more than a moment, you risk getting stuck. But if you're headed in the right direction and keep moving, you'll get there eventually.

Most new initiatives within large companies get stuck and are forgotten. Instead, you must keep new projects and ideas moving forward, inch by inch.

If you work in or with a big company, it may be tempting to blame the bureaucracy—the company's size, its excessive procedures, the layers of management needed to sign off on decisions—for the lack of innovation and agility you feel. However, the culprit is often our own inability to keep projects moving. Big companies can innovate—it just takes small groups of people willing to sustain motion. The motion that keeps the ship moving is persistent questioning.

"Why does it feel like we are having the same meeting and discussion, over and over again?"

"Why don't we just try it and see what happens?"

"Specifically what (or who) is getting in the way of us making a decision? Let's go meet with them now!"

"When exactly will we have a final answer on this?"

You don't have to be the boss to ask these questions. On the contrary, these questions are best asked by those tasked with operations and execution. Former CEO of American Express, Ken Chenault, once shared what he considers one of the secrets to a fast career progression and reputation as an innovator in a large bureaucracy. "I would make my bosses make decisions," he said. "You can't just sit around and let people think about stuff, you must make them make decisions."

Keeping the ship moving, and breaking ice at the bow, is a painful responsibility, but the person who does it is the person who transforms big organizations. Be the person who asks the persistent, and often annoying, questions. Don't try to get everyone to agree. Instead, put people on the spot to share their objections. When there is ambiguity about the next step, call it out. Ambiguity kills great ideas, and great leaders kill ambiguity.

Conflict avoidance stalls progress.

Fighting is uncomfortable. When you're working alongside people stuck in their ways or overwhelmed by sunk costs, it is tempting to surrender to save the peace. Perhaps you're willing to compromise on your vision and "meet in the middle" to keep people happy? Or perhaps you find a way to circumnavigate the issue and focus on the parts of the project that everyone is more aligned on instead? Neither of these options actually address the problem at hand, though; they avoid it rather than solve it.

I recall some of the more complicated product launches at Adobe during the company's transformation from selling software to providing services. Projects that were once owned and controlled by individual groups, like the Photoshop team, were now highly matrixed with stakeholders across the company. Whenever a launch was in sight, there was always someone saying, "We're not ready yet!" and coming up with more reasons to wait.

"Critics won't like it." "The team is not fully confident in scalability." "We haven't tested enough." Such proclamations yield a series of discussions about what still needs to be done to get us "ready." But these discussions quickly become increasingly heated as launch deadlines fall into jeopardy. As tensions rise, participants start to back out. Meetings fall from calendars. Progress stalls.

These situations always left me in a difficult position. I understood why the desire to avoid conflict was obstructing our progress. Stakeholders were opting for amity with their colleagues rather than dealing with a short period of strife to achieve a more optimal outcome. After all, they had career-long relationships and a friendly work environment to protect. It felt natural to choose peace over progress.

But your job as a leader of change is to challenge peace as a default. Create an environment where people can withstand a fight and engage in friction as it arises. Rather than passively surf the whims of people's hesitations to take action, bring the conflict to the surface with questions like the following:

"Let's talk this out—what is the worst thing that will happen if we launch a bit early? Is scrambling a little bit after launch really worse than punting the project for additional months?"

"Who exactly claims we're not ready to launch this? What, specifically, needs to be done for us to be ready?"

"What is our MVP? Have we not achieved that yet?"

Ultimately, you want a team that values conflict as a means to make bolder decisions and take the required risks for a more exciting end. Disagreement is great, so long as the team shares conviction when a decision is made.

Former Rhode Island School of Design (RISD) president and one of my longtime mentors John Maeda once observed: "A good team does a lot of friendly front stabbing instead of backstabbing. Issues are resolved by knowing what they are."

Straightforward conflict happens when people care enough about their work and bring tensions, ambiguities, and tough realities to the surface. Confrontation tends to be most needed when it is most uncomfortable. It's the truly tough issues, the ones most likely to advance our potential the most, that we avoid. I am still determined to get a sign someday for my office that simply states NO ELEPHANTS. To eliminate all "elephants in the room," your team must commit to as much front stabbing as possible.

Channel competitive energy.

All too often we despise competitors—within our companies and beyond—without appreciating how much we need them.

Competitors boost your productivity by keeping you on your toes. They help establish your market to attract capital and talent. And multiple teams competing to offer a better and more affordable experience is great for customers and healthy for your industry.

Nevertheless, we oscillate between trying to diminish our competitors, trying to copy them, and trying to ignore them. What we should be doing is using them to better understand our market and improve our execution.

OBSERVE AND LEARN, DON'T EMULATE

Behance has had many competitors in the portfolio-display and creative-network space over the years. Some, like Krop, Coroflot, and Carbonmade, fell by the wayside or became quite niche due to bad timing or inferior technology or branding. Others, like

DeviantArt and Myspace, acted more like existential threats, but they never focused on the needs of creative professionals.

However, a few years after Behance launched, Dribbble (spelled like the basketball motion with an extra *b*) emerged as a quick way for interactive designers to show tiny "shots" of their work in progress. The restricted size of the images their customers could upload was a helpful constraint that made it easier for designers to contribute content. More important, such tiny snapshots often made work look better than it was. Rather than be subject to a review of their entire project and how the elements integrated with one another—the ultimate measure of skill—designers could showcase a series of nicely crafted icons or a small corner of something they were designing. As a result, junior designers could post a higher volume of content and look far better with less effort on Dribbble than they did on Behance.

Our team became concerned. We saw more and more junior interactive designers active on Dribbble while their portfolios on Behance went dormant. We philosophically believed that a collection of snapshots was not indicative of a designer's ability to solve a problem or tell a story. But Dribbble's approach made it undeniably easier to add content and look better than you were. Ease of engagement and quick return to one's ego are two tried-and-true tenets of any successful social product, regardless of its purpose.

Strange emotions, reactions, and potentially perilous ideas emerge when you become fixated on a new, shiny competitor on the horizon. At Behance, we debated the philosophical approach versus the practical reality. Should we stick to our convictions and continue building the best platform to showcase and discover creative projects? Or should we provide a feature that mimics Dribbble's snapshot approach?

In the end, our desire to stay competitive and play both strategies prompted us to add a new set of features to display snapshots. This allowed our members to display snippets of their work without the context of the broader project. While it was different from Dribbble, it had the same goal: letting our users engage more easily and, some might say, more carelessly with Behance.

Now, with hindsight, it's clear that our snapshots feature was an emotional reaction rather than a move aligned with our strategy, which was already working so well for us. Sure, it was easier to post more content daily, but the content wasn't serving our mission to help creatives showcase their best work as a story with context. The content our users uploaded felt against our principles. A year or so later, and after much wasted effort, we killed it.

If we wanted Behance to be known—and highly regarded—as the world's best way to showcase your portfolio, why did we spend so much time developing a way to show a lesser type of content that we fundamentally believed was inferior? If we had stuck to our convictions and simply let our competitor own a space we didn't believe in, we could have used those resources to pursue our own, stronger strategy.

Dribbble's growth slowed, but the product remains beloved by a small but active community of designers. Looking back on the whole saga, we should have studied Dribbble to better understand our market without feeling the urge to react to their audience and their use case. Because it wasn't ours. With a little more time, we would have validated our original thesis: that a portfolio's richness and context would serve creative careers across disciplines more than snapshots ever could.

Dribbble should have strengthened our convictions rather than shaken them. Behance's goals were different. Be curious about competitors' moves, but don't emulate them.

Instead, look at what your competitors do, and ask yourself a series of questions:

> **"Are their strategy and goals the same as mine?"** If their strategy and beliefs are different, and you still have conviction in your own, then you shouldn't be distracted. Stay the course. Google launched in 1998 as the twenty-first search engine after other search engines like Alta Vista and Yahoo, but they took very few pages from others' books because their strategy was unique and required entirely different tactics. Rather than simply index the web, Google was organizing the web in a way that improved the quality of search results over time. Google wanted to give you one great result first rather than a list of all the results. This alternative approach made all the difference.

> But if your competitor's strategy and goals are the same as your own, then you need to ask yourself another question: **"Is their tactic better?"** If so, you should consider taking the same tactic yourself. In 2016 and 2017, Instagram infamously copied Snapchat's tactics over and over again. Both apps were playing in the same field, and Instagram used what Snapchat learned to get ahead of it in its own game. Instagram implemented Snapchat's "stories" and augmented-reality features, like facial overlays, because these tactics were directly aligned with its strategy: to host the media friends share with one another. Instagram was getting ideas from Snapchat, but these tactics advanced their strategy rather than diverted it.

Sometimes the thing you admire most in your competitor isn't smart or scalable. They may be doing something that is temporarily advantageous to their interests but, over the long term, unsustainable. I saw this a lot among the first crop of so-called unicorn companies that raised money at billion-dollar valuations and were using their swashes of venture capital to acquire customers at unsustainable prices. The leaders I knew at these companies were vigorously focused on their competitors' market share and tactics to acquire new users rather than the long-term economics of their industry. These short-term tactics proved unsustainable, and entire cohorts of companies diminished their profit margins. When funding dried up, most of them lacked a sustainable business model to attract new investors.

SEEK THE IMPETUS TO ACT

Chances are you already have a surplus of ideas for how to improve your product and a sense of what comes next in your industry. But these thoughts and instincts are worthless unless they are pursued. Amid day-to-day operations and the effort required to execute near-term projects, a lot of good ideas and long-term pursuits fail to gain traction. Oftentimes, pressure from a competitor provides the impetus to act on an idea.

In my book *Making Ideas Happen*, I profiled Noah Kalina, a Brooklyn-based photographer who had photographed himself every single day for many years but had never done anything with the pictures. Then, one evening while surfing online, he came across another photographer talking about a similar project, but with far fewer years in the making. The prospect of another photographer beating him to the punch prompted Noah to construct a montage video of every photo in rapid succession and upload it to YouTube in a matter of a week or so. His video, "Everyday," is now one of the most viewed YouTube videos of all time and became a platform for his now very successful career as a photographer. The sense of looming competition was Noah's motivation to complete a project that he had been silently tinkering with for more than five years.

Competition can turbocharge longer-term efforts that lack short-term rewards and provide a sense of urgency that normally stops you from pursuing your priorities. Pacing yourself against your competitors can be a source of productivity—so long as the tactics being prioritized are aligned with your goals.

KEEP YOUR OPPONENTS IN THE GAME

Aside from being a source of energy for your own productivity, your competitors play a critical role in the health of your industry. Over time, every company in a field builds on one another and helps expand the potential size of the market. For example, in the ride-sharing space, Uber launched on-demand cars before Lyft, Lyft launched a carpooling option before Uber, then Uber launched a tool for drivers to pick up fares at the end of their shift on their way home before Lyft, then Lyft provided "prescheduled rides" before Uber, and the list goes on. Of course, the real winner here is the consumer, who gets a more evolved product offering from the endless competition between two companies.

Be grateful to your competitors for never letting your product—and process—become too comfortable. Isolation and the lack of any credible threat leads to complacency. I'd prefer competitors over complacency any day—and yes, over the long term, it is either one or the other. Great competitors help you win. Competition helps validate the market's need and keeps you ambitious in meeting it. You therefore need to teach your team to respect the role of your opponents rather than ignore them or wish them away.

BE YOUR GREATEST COMPETITOR

Although you should follow them closely, don't become defined by your opponents. If you focus more on your competitors than on your own customers and your own unique approach to serving them, you lose your identity. Stay tuned but not governed by what's going on around you.

If you have conviction in your own ideas and approach, then you should be the most competitive with yourself. Your past personal best—your most productive week, your most efficient sprint, your best-executed event—is what you need to beat. Competing with your past is the purest and surest way to make faster progress without compromising your vision. The greatest successes are the aggregate of persistent optimizations of personal bests.

Creative block is the consequence of avoiding the truth.

I recall hearing from a few different writers that American novelist Joyce Carol Oates once remarked, "Writer's block occurs when the writer believes the idea is fraudulent." Indeed, creative block is the consequence of avoiding facts that provoke uncertainty, fear, and confusion. Avoiding these obstacles to focus on the task at hand is appealing and can work in the short term. But avoidance creeps up on you. Your clarity, vision, and the free reign of your imagination will become crippled as you struggle with your doubts. Your judgment will become flawed, and your insights less potent and clear. You'll start reusing old tactics and material, and then your creativity will stall. Disbelieving your own ideas diminishes your creative energy and sets you up to fail.

To conquer creative block, you must ask bold questions and shine the spotlight on the elephants in the room. Perhaps the product is shitty. Perhaps your business model and all the assumptions leading up to it were fundamentally flawed. The truth will hurt, and it may set you back temporarily, but it will ultimately set you free.

Entrepreneur and investor Paul Graham, founder of the start-up incubator Y Combinator, once remarked in an interview about Facebook founder Mark Zuckerberg: "It's easier to tell Zuck that he's wrong than to tell the average noob [new] founder. He's not threatened by it. If he's wrong, he wants to know." Paul goes on to say, "What distinguishes great founders is not their adherence to some vision, but their humility in the face of the truth."

The greatest thinkers I admire anchor their ideas around a central truth—often one they believe is unique and unrealized by others. Whether it is a thesis for a new product or a future world they can envision and believe in wholeheartedly, it's that vision that drives them. But when something or someone challenges their mental model of the truth, they embrace the new questions rather than look the other way. Rather than confront the tough questions defensively, they get insanely curious about what they might be missing. Rather than ask leading questions, buoyed by hope that their assumptions remain true, they switch into learning mode and open their mind to a possible new truth—a new anchor that could change everything.

Extracting truth is a delicate balance of curiosity, restraint, and compartmentalizing hope. Take great care to ensure past assumptions and old truths never obstruct new discoveries. Be open, humble, and eager to learn that you're wrong—before someone else does.

Moving fast is great, so long as you slow down at every turn.

Ambitious teams often struggle with speed—but being too fast, not too slow. Indeed, speed brings you to inevitable realizations more quickly. If you're able to just try things rather than spend time thinking about them, you rapidly learn if they work or not and can course-correct. But for all the benefits of rapidly testing ideas, iterating quickly, and optimizing for efficiency, sometimes you need to force yourself to slow down. The creative aspects of some projects are best cooked slowly.

Facebook's infamous "move fast and break things" mantra, which graces everything from posters to coasters around Facebook's campus, establishes a mind-set in technology and start-ups that the best path forward is always the fastest one, even when it's reckless. This line of thought has inspired countless practices for how to manage projects, conduct meetings, and develop new products. The "lean start-up" methodology, which became a playbook on how to build a product efficiently, was popularized by Eric Ries's book by the same name and has since spread beyond the start-up world and into the boardrooms of Fortune 500 companies. And for good reason! The bulky, slow processes that have long inhibited launches and learning in big companies were overdue for an overhaul. But, like most rules, there are critical exceptions.

When it comes to speed and efficiency, the greatest risk is taking a shortcut in the one area that distinguishes you the most. While most of a new product's components are commonplace across many companies and should be achieved as quickly and leanly as possible, every product has a few differentiating attributes. It might be your brand, a novel design or user experience you are applying that is remarkably different from others in your industry, or some new technology that provides a vastly better option for potential customers. Those aspects that differentiate your product are your chance to create something valuable and warrant a disproportionate amount of investment. You therefore shouldn't take shortcuts, rush, or strip down the process of creation for these features.

In the relentless effort to get a minimum viable product to market, many teams cut or compromise on the key attributes that are likely to differentiate it from their competitors. For example, I've watched a few mobile social networks over the years launch a very stripped-down "first version" of their product that lacked the features in which they expressed such pride during their initial pitch to me. When asked, they would explain this was "just their MVP." But most of them didn't last long enough to launch the features that truly differentiated them. What most teams underestimate is just how much staying power an MVP has. Whatever you build and launch to the world becomes much harder, both logistically and psychologically, to change after launch. If the uniqueness isn't already baked in, and instead only gets sprinkled on top, it's likely to taste bland.

Speed through the generic stuff, but take the time you need to perfect the few things that you're most proud of. Remember that customers don't engage with functionality. They engage with experiences. They are moved not by features but rather by their experience of using your product. Moving a mile a minute is great, so long as you slow down when you're crafting something that will ultimately become your competitive advantage.

Value the merits of slow cooking.

Chefs will tell you that the secret behind many of the greatest dishes is patience. When you cook something slowly at a lower heat for a longer time, the flavors and textures that marinate yield culinary masterpieces.

Your own creations aren't much different. At the opposite end of the spectrum from "moving fast and breaking things," your creative endeavors need moments of your deep attention and patience. While we intuitively know that great accomplishments take time, we're always anxious when the end is out of sight and the path of progress feels out of our control. Harvard psychologist Dan Gilbert, author of *Stumbling on Happiness*, argues that human brains are adapted to respond more to some threats than to others. "Human beings are very good at getting out of the way of a speeding baseball," Gilbert explained on NPR's *Talk of the Nation*. "Godzilla comes running down the street, we know to run the other way. We're very good at clear and present danger, like every mammal is. That's why we've survived as long as we have. But we've learned a new trick in the last couple of million years—at least we've kind of learned it." Our brains, says Gilbert, unlike the brains of almost every other species, are prepared to treat the future as if it were the present.

"We can look ahead to our retirement or to a dental appointment, and we can take action today to save for retirement or to floss so that we don't get bad news six months down the line. But we're just learning this trick," he says. "It's really a very new adaptation in the animal kingdom and we don't do it all that well. We don't respond to long-term threats with nearly as much vigor and venom as we do to clear and present dangers."

Thus, the evolution of our brains accounts for our tendency to intensely respond to immediate threats, while struggling to focus on long-term dangers or goals. This is why we take such alarm to terrorism but much less to global warming, even though the chances of a plane bomber, Dan Gilbert claims, are far less than the chances of the ocean consuming parts of Florida or Manhattan. It's also why we are such fools for instant gratification, but struggle to manage slow-burning success.

Miraculous things are possible when you allow yourself to pursue an idea slowly. Like fine wine, the longer you can leave the grapes on the vine—and the wine in the bottle—the more complex the flavors become.

Rarely do we get the chance to create something over the arc of life itself, outside of any deadline looming. Our personal projects are often the ones that enjoy the benefits of slow cooking—but by necessity, not by choice. While these projects tend to be neglected, when (and if) they actually come to fruition, they are often extraordinary.

I am reminded of one of the first hit projects on Behance: "Alison," published by photographer Jack Radcliffe. In the project, Radcliffe presented a series of moments in his daughter Alison's life, from early childhood through adolescence and into adulthood as a married woman. While there is nothing extraordinary about each photograph in isolation, the magnitude of time the project represents created a sense of awe and respect from more than 1.3 million viewers around the world. Time adds a value to creative work that cannot be replicated any other way.

For me, writing has always been the one thing I cook slowly. While building Behance, everything was a race. Sure, we iterated each product carefully and paced the critical decisions, but we always did it with an eye on the clock and a declining balance of funds to build the business. Our 99U conferences ran up against a hard deadline that forced quick decisions. Our product updates had a community of impatient customers. Every feature felt overdue. The only thing I could work on slowly was my own writing. Ideas for articles, observations from other entrepreneurs, insights for starting and leading a business . . . I write down thoughts and then come back to them again and again without an end goal in mind. Sometimes I'll jot down a question or an inkling in a quick Evernote and then, two years later, I'll come back to add more or finish a sentence. Over the years, I've refined these little musings, deleted pieces, added layers, and have let them evolve.

This book was a slow-cooked stew sitting on a low burner for a many years.

Unless you're a legendary painter, tenured professor, or a *New Yorker* writer on a yearly retainer, few of us can slow cook for a living. But we can round out our work with a few slow-cooked projects—you just can't forget what you've got on the stove. You must keep coming back to it, checking it every now and then, adding a dash of salt here, skimming off the foam there. Over the course of your life, these projects could become your greatest creations.

"Ask for forgiveness, not permission."

We might never know who said it first, but "Ask for forgiveness, not permission" was our team's key principle immediately after we were acquired by Adobe. We were eager to maintain our start-up ethos, to keep growing our business and developing our products without too many meetings or processes from our new corporate overlords that could slow us down. If we took steps to get every change approved, the product would have stagnated, and our team would have started counting down the days until their stock vested. I wanted everyone to feel empowered to make decisions with their best judgment rather than get lost in the bowels of a large organization.

Sometimes we stumbled and stubbed our toes, skipping a legal process or forgetting to incorporate a sponsor's logo in a flyer. When we screwed up, we apologized and learned from it. But the team remained empowered to pursue their ideas. Sure, we made some wrong choices—but we also made a lot more right ones than we would have if we'd waited for sign-off on everything we did.

This is especially true when you are changing something that already exists rather than creating something from scratch: You're working against the grain of what already works just well enough, as well as the existing structure's comfort and complacency. Asking for permission to do what you know needs to be done will yield hesitation at best or rejection at worst. When I started making changes to the products and teams I inherited at Adobe, I quickly learned that seeking consensus from others around the company prompted too many conversations and meetings. I learned to choose carefully which decisions needed consensus and which could be made on intuition. The former tack was always my first preference, but when I had extreme conviction and believed that the company's immune system might extinguish the spark before it had a chance to take hold, I'd pursue early explorations under the radar... without permission. If such decisions were challenged after the fact, I would engage in debate and revert the change if need be. To give bold ideas a chance, sometimes you need to act first and then adjust them as necessary.

The bolder your idea—and the more foreign the change—the more pushback you should expect. Look no further than the world of architecture, where every great breakthrough seems to be accompanied by acrimony. Two of the most iconic pieces of architecture in the world—the Eiffel Tower and the Louvre Pyramid—were conceived in controversy. In May 1886, three years before Paris planned to celebrate the one hundredth anniversary of the French Revolution by staging a Universal Exposition (the Exposition Universelle), the organizing committee called for proposals for a fitting monument to be built on the exposition site, Champs de Mars.

Having designed the interior of the Statue of Liberty and built iron bridges around the world, Gustave Eiffel was already a famous engineer. His team dreamed up a concept for the world's largest structure: an iron tower climbing more than 984 feet into the sky. The committee awarded them first place.

However, the Eiffel Tower's construction had barely begun when scorn and rejection began to flood in. Most notably, on February 14, 1887, a contingent of famous French artists and writers, including novelist Alexandre Dumas, author of *The Three Musketeers*, delivered a petition to the director of the Exposition Universelle condemning the monument design. Published in the newspaper *Le Temps*, it translates as follows:

> We, writers, painters, sculptors, architects, lovers of the intact beauty of Paris, protest against the mercantile imagination of a mechanical engineer who wishes to make our city ugly. Just imagine this ridiculous tower which, like the black chimney of an industrial plant with barbaric dimensions, will humiliate all our monuments. For twenty years, we will be taunted by the atrocious shadow of this metal pillar, which will soil the city like an inkblot.

One of the petition's authors, the French writer Guy de Maupassant, compared the tower to a high, thin pyramid of metal steps. Others regarded it as a "hole-riddled suppository." Despite such critique, the "eyesore" tower persisted, opening on March 31, 1889. It surpassed the Washington Monument as the tallest structure in the world, a rank it held until the Chrysler Building in New York City was constructed in 1930. During the Exposition, more than two million people visited the tower, many journeying to the top.

The Louvre Pyramid, designed as a grand entrance to the more than two-century-old art museum, also endured significant condemnation upon its opening in 1989, the bicentenary year of the French Revolution. Designed by Chinese American modernist architect Ieoh Ming Pei, the glass pyramid sparked hatred from the general public. François Mitterrand, then president of France, was criticized for announcing the pyramid's construction by Pei without organizing a competition.

"As soon as the project was announced, it was accused of disfiguring the architecture," explains Parisian history tourist bureau Paris City Vision. "Officially consisting of 673 glass panes, it is commonly reported that there are in fact 666. This is the number of the demon and the beast in the Apocalypse. Was the construction of the Pyramid therefore a bad omen announcing the end of the world?"

At one point before opening, up to 90 percent of Parisians are said to have been against the giant glass structure. In 1983, Andre Chaubad, then director of the Louvre, even resigned to protest the "architectural risks" posed by Pei's vision. "I received many angry glances in the streets of Paris," Pei later said. He confessed that "after the Louvre, I thought no project would be too difficult." However, like the Eiffel Tower, Pei's glass pyramid quickly drew adoration from Parisians and visitors alike.

Today it's hard to imagine Paris without the Eiffel Tower and the Louvre Pyramid, two of the city's—and the world's—most iconic structures.

Society tends to eventually celebrate what was, at first, shunned. Companies are no different. If you can withstand some tyranny, you'll be rewarded for it. Oftentimes, the best way to proceed is by charging ahead without too much reliance on the processes developed to maintain the status quo.

Conviction > Consensus

Optimization requires decisiveness. As you improve your product, you will be torn between appeasing your customers and sticking to your own beliefs. You will look to groups for decisions when you should be looking to them only for guidance. The best decisions tend to be the hardest and least popular. When you feel like you're on your own, you'll question yourself.

As humans, we find comfort in groups. And while no great achievement is possible without a group working together, very few critical and difficult decisions can be made by a group. As comedian Milton Berle once quipped, "A committee is a group that keeps minutes and loses hours."

Of course, committees have other purposes that are far less innocuous. By gathering a group with a shared interest, you can generate a sense of inclusiveness, gather perspectives, and tap expertise. Ultimately, the knowledge around you is greater than the knowledge within you, and your job as a leader is to tap your team's knowledge as best you can. But don't avoid difficult problems by designating a group of people with less authority to make the decision for you. While you can gain much from conversations and fact-finding in a group setting, you will not get swift, conviction-driven decision making by kicking a tough problem to a committee.

Decisions based on consensus typically end up with an ordinary outcome because by seeking to please everyone, you boil your options down to their lowest common denominator: whatever option is most familiar to the most people and therefore gets the least protest and the fastest support. As British author Aldous Huxley once observed, "The vast majority of human beings dislike and even actually dread all notions with which they are not familiar. Hence it comes about that at their first appearance innovators have generally been persecuted, and always derided as fools and madmen."

When working in a group, innovators must be willing to be the fool.

The best investors don't grasp too tightly to any given playbook. As a seed investor, I am always trying to use my pattern-recognition abilities without holding on too dearly to whatever worked before. None of my best investments were alike, obvious, or fit a popular rubric. Some, like Warby Parker, struck investors as too crowded a market and too commoditized. Others, like Pinterest, Uber, and Carta, initially appeared too niche with limited markets. And some, like Periscope, defied social norms and made people scratch their heads whenever I'd describe them. You can consult groups, history, and common knowledge, but the tough decisions and crazy notions of future possibilities come from within.

The same is true for ventures of all kinds. I like how Mark Suster, a two-time entrepreneur who sold his last company to Salesforce before becoming a VC himself, made the same case for teams in a blog post:

> No answers are obvious or everybody would be doing these things. I am amazed at how some entrepreneurial teams dither. I watch founders who want to get "air cover" for hard decisions by getting too much input from their teams or boards. I watch management team[s] hedge by building multiple products and spreading resources too thinly versus having strong conviction in their core ideas. Often I think this is because poor leaders are too worried about being loved. Respect > Love.
>
> I watch CEOs who know they need to fire senior staff but avoid doing so instead convincing themselves that they need just six more months because this executive or that one is too valuable to lose. This drives me nuts. When decisions are clear—act. You're a startup, not GE.

I want strong leaders. I want deciders—even if they don't agree with me. I want "benevolent dictators."

Don't get me wrong, I believe that founders should seek lots of input. Then they need to take all the input they received, mix it up, apply a framework for how the information affects your decision and decide. All advice you receive is too generic to help you—you need to decide for yourself in your exact situation.

Only conviction will take you somewhere the group never anticipated. Sometimes you need to forget everything you've learned—all the classes, the "rules of the road," conventions, what investors are telling you—and just go with your gut. It is your intuition, formed from your entire life's experiences, revealing something that nobody else can see. Take it seriously!

Of course, defying consensus carries some risks as well. Conviction leaves your biases unchecked. The patterns of your past and what you see around you can inform your instincts in counterproductive ways. Are you biased against certain kinds of candidates in the hiring process? Are you subconsciously lowering or raising the bar for people you meet based on their accent, background, or how similar they look to you?

We all have biases; they are a natural result of patterns we have experienced ourselves or been trained to believe. But you can recognize your biases only by seeking input from others and inviting them to challenge your convictions. Herein lies the most important nuance of leading with conviction: You must surround yourself with others who also have conviction. Strong gut instincts surrounded by weak people or people afraid to speak up are bound to lead you astray.

For extraordinary outcomes, seek conviction in your work and build teams that value conviction over consensus.

Don't give those resistant to change false hope.

When you make a bold decision that changes your strategy and the day-to-day responsibilities of your team, your job is to foster alignment.

At Adobe, during the 2012–13 transition from selling boxed software like Photoshop to offering an annual subscription delivered online, many employees and customers were resistant to the change. I recall many heated meetings where community evangelists would express the concerns of our less modern customers. As we drafted website copy and customer communications, there was always the temptation to hedge our message: We weren't "changing" anything—we were "evolving our offering." But in our attempt to be delicate with the message, some customers were holding on to the hope that we might abandon the changes and go back to selling software the old way.

Customers are more forgiving than you might think when you share your thought process with them.

I empathized with our customers' concerns. They didn't want to start paying monthly for something that they used to purchase all at once. They were happy with the way our products worked and didn't yet see the need for cloud services and new functionalities that required an internet connection. But we knew that the future of creativity was about collaboration and connecting the creative process across different devices. The future of the industry required our products to change, and the most effective way of communicating this vision was to declare it. In hindsight, my most productive conversations with customers and journalists were declarative rather than blunting the blow with a narrative that made the changes sound less drastic.

Similarly, I noticed that the internal resisters and skeptics within Adobe had a tendency to avoid discussions about the implications of the switch to a subscription model. Some managers who led desktop product teams couldn't imagine adding servicelike features in their products. "The customers don't want these panels to move around," they would say. "The customers don't want to log in." While many of these proclamations may have been true, the decision had already been made, and now we had to execute the vision.

I remember weighing the right response from company leadership in my head. Do you confront the naysayers and force reluctant teams to accept the implications and start changing their products despite their reservations? Or do you acquiesce and just focus on the few modern products that were less controversial? In retrospect, I believe avoiding these confrontations gave the resistant teams a sense of false hope that they wouldn't have to change much after all. This may have set us back years. Sometimes you let your customers and team lead, and other times you must push your customers and team into the future. Hesitation breeds incrementalism—the tendency to make changes too muted, too slowly, and too late. You need to attack the hesitation and galvanize the troops to move forward without looking back.

Great teams implement change when it's still uncomfortable to do so, ahead of the realized need. Don't give those resistant to change false hope for things staying the same; when a decision is made, declare the implications and chop off the rearview mirror.

OPTIMIZING PRODUCT

A quick note before we begin. This next section is all about optimizing your product. The journey of building and endlessly iterating a product or service is a field unto itself, flush with best practices in design, product management, customer research, and psychology. I have approached this section as a book within the book, recognizing that some readers deep in the process of building products may skip to it while others skip it altogether. Regardless of the nature of your work, these principles demonstrate how remarkable products are made in the messy middle. All right, let's talk product.

● ● ● ● ●

The honeymoon phase at the start of a venture is known not only for its boundless energy but also its remarkable clarity. In the beginning of your journey, simple solutions come easily. But as the middle becomes volatile and more problematic, we have the tendency to add complexity. We solve problems by adding more options, more features, and more nuances to our creations.

While a new product's simplicity is a competitive advantage, it evolves and becomes more complex over time. The unfortunate result is what I have come to call "the product life cycle" and it applies to any type of service or experience you're creating, your "product."

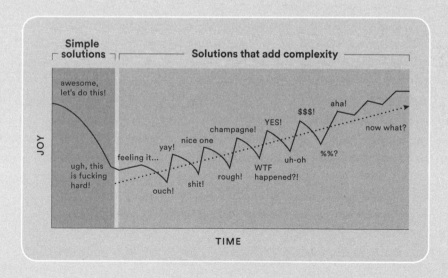

The Product Life Cycle

1. Customers flock to a simple product.
2. The product adds new features to better serve customers and grow the business.
3. Product gets complicated.
4. Customers flock to another simple product.

Simple is sticky. It is very hard to make a product—or any customer experience—simple. It is even harder to keep it simple. The more obvious and intuitive a product is, the harder it is to optimize it without adding complication.

Successfully optimizing your product, whatever it may be, means making it both more powerful and more accessible. The key to striking this balance is grounding the decisions you make with simple convictions, the absolute simplest being *Life is just time and how you use it.*

Every product or service in your life either helps you spend time or save time. The news channels or shows you watch, the social apps like Facebook and Snapchat that you use, the books you read, and the games you play all compete for how you spend your time. Other products, like Uber (getting a car faster), Slack (communicating with your team faster), and Amazon's Alexa (buying things faster) exist to help you save time. And it's not just digital ventures: Businesses like bakeries and restaurants that sell prepared foods fall into this category as well. The only exceptions are rare products like Twitter (a quicker way to consume more information) or Blue Apron (a quicker way to cook at home) that add a time-consuming action to your plate while also making that experience faster than it normally would be.

The fact of the matter is that we are constantly battling time, whether to save or spend it. We're fiercely aware and protective of our time. The only time we're not focused on time is when our natural human tendencies—like wanting to look good, satisfy curiosity, or be recognized by others—make us lose track of it. Natural human tendencies are the twilight zone for time. When you account for these tendencies when developing your product, you win your customer's time.

As I reflect on the new products that have improved my life the most over the years, they ultimately removed a daily friction. Apps on my phone like Google Maps brought the city to my fingertips and helped ensure I'd never get lost again. Products like Uber eliminated the burden of arranging transportation or finding a cab. Decades earlier, companies like FedEx and UPS enabled people to ship something anywhere in the world by filling out a simple form rather than dealing with multiple carriers. Throughout history, many of the best businesses have hunted friction and eliminated it to save people time.

Optimizing the product you're making is ultimately about making it more human friendly and accommodating to natural human tendencies.

The insights ahead are intended to fine-tune your product logic. How do you improve the first mile of your customer's experience of your product? How do you maintain simplicity in the face of new challenges and accommodating new types of customers? How do you make your product increasingly relevant and engaging? How do you keep optimizing your product and marketing to better serve your customers' needs?

Optimizing product experiences is a field of study in itself. While the next two sections on optimizing products have a bias toward digital products, I believe that these insights apply to all kinds of products, services, and experiences.

Take great pride in your product, but not at the expense of failing to see its problems. As soon as your product stops evolving, you lose. As soon as you are satisfied, you become complacent. Never be truly satisfied. When you're creating, the current version of your product should always feel underwhelming. In many ways, the state of your product is a mirror of the state of your team. All that we have talked about when it comes to enduring the middle miles and optimizing how your team performs comes to the surface when your customers experience what you've created. The pursuit of a great product requires discipline, endless iteration, and grounding your objectives with your customers' struggles and psychology.

SIMPLIFYING AND ITERATING

Identify what you're willing to be bad at.

I remember one of my wife's colleagues from her clinical psychology PhD program remarking, "To be a great psychologist, you need to be great with patients and just fair with paperwork." Their thesis was that if you're too organized with your administrative tasks, you're liable to not be as present and focused with your patients.

Productivity and performance are too often conflated. Instead, you need to decide what aspects of your team and product distinguish you most—and what you're willing to be bad at. Your competitive advantage is a conscious admission and acceptance of your weaknesses as well as a recognition of your strengths; it's as much about what you focus on as it is about what you choose to let go.

I recall an exercise I did at Harvard Business School where we examined a group of companies that were known for excellence in certain areas at the expense of others. One example was Southwest Airlines, which was launched at a time when the commercial aviation industry was defined by a common set of values: the quantity of routes offered, the quality of food and service, competitive pricing, and safety. Very early on, Southwest chose to differentiate itself by focusing on just a few of these values at the expense of others.

Of course, safety was never compromised. But when it came to things like food options or number of routes they flew, Southwest shifted their resources to be more competitive on price and quality of service. They simplified their in-flight meal offerings and reduced their routes to cover only the Southwest of the U.S. rather than try to compete with every other airline in all regions. As a result, Southwest became known as the airline with the best service at an incredible price for a specified set of routes. Southwest optimized around its competitive advantage.

Here's a quick exercise. First, make a list of the key characteristics and values of the major players in your industry. (If you're a freelancer, this could be other people your clients consider hiring. If you're a start-up, it could be the industry incumbents or your competition.) Perhaps they can offer a cheaper price to their clients, a focus on customer service, the speed of delivery, or the variety of different services offered. These are the factors that customers and clients weigh when determining who to work with.

Now, make the same list for yourself and your business, but focus on the things you want to be known for. Perhaps you want people talking about the quality of your work, but you don't mind if it takes a little longer or is more expensive. Or perhaps you want to be the go-to provider for last-minute projects and refuse to take on larger projects that would compromise your flexibility. Conscious trade-offs are a competitive advantage when the result is dedicating more focus and energy to what you're best at.

This exercise should reveal some industry-wide values that you don't subscribe to and others you aspire to be known for. The former is a group of things you can be bad at, so long as you outperform on the values you hold dear. Of course, it is important to identify and address your weaknesses. But spectacular achievements are ultimately the result of doing something different exceptionally well.

Make one subtraction for every addition.

Great products don't stay simple by not evolving; they stay simple by continually improving their core value while removing features and paring back aspects that aren't central to the core. The earliest users of a new product tend to be more visionary and tolerant of friction than later users. Over time, you will need to remove the friction, in the form of killing or reducing parts of your offering, to keep growing.

When I compare Behance's network today to the one we had six years ago, I am struck by how much simpler the product is. We eliminated our "Tip Exchange" feature, our "Groups" feature, the ability to customize the colors of your Behance portfolio, and countless other features and experiments that didn't serve the core experience. A small number of customers complained each time we reduced our offering, but a much larger segment of customers became more engaged as a result. The simpler our product became, the more it resonated with people. When we did add a feature that withstood the test of time, it did so by being essential rather than novel.

The creative process is a little dreaming followed by endless editing—but the tendency to edit does not come naturally to creative minds. On the contrary, the discipline to cut and refine your ideas can feel demoralizing—but this is about the customers, not your creative genius.

The paradox of product success is that when you focus on pleasing your most engaged users, you stop engaging new ones. The sad reality—and the opportunity for start-ups—is that most established products take their large user bases for granted and fail to maintain simplicity over time. In the introduction to this section, I outlined the "product life cycle" in which users flock to a different simple product after an existing product takes them for granted and adds unnecessary complexity.

Products that retain their greatness over time tend to hold simplicity as a core design tenet. As a sweetgreen board member, I always admired the way our cofounders Jonathan, Nic, and Nate held on to their original values regarding simplicity, initially forced on them by circumstance, as the company grew along with the temptation to expand the offering. As Nate explains it, "We were lucky with the limitations of our first space, which was only five hundred square feet. We always knew we wanted to be really good at one thing, and the companies we admired were those types of companies. We talked about that, but then what forced the discipline was the space itself. In later years when we had more space, it was like, 'Well, should we do a retail store? Should we add this, that, smoothies?' These are all things that we can convince ourselves fit into the core, but that first restaurant demonstrated that they weren't necessary and the brand was strong without it. We couldn't do anything else, so I think it was a blessing in a way." The original constraints that forced simplicity became a core value rather than a hindrance.

Such constraints also spur innovation without deviating from the core product. Luke McKenna, cofounder of Coco & Co, a New York–based coconut company (that's a lot of co's in one sentence!), makes this case for his product category:

> Our narrow focus (all things coconuts) keeps our supply chain simple. . . . Our challenge as coconut entrepreneurs is to take something that everyone thinks they know inside out, and continually unpack it to find unexpected new ways to create value for our customers. Expanding beyond coconuts would detract from the simple, novel dedication that people find so appealing. . . . We have never felt limited by our narrow scope. In fact, it's this defined focus that has made us so determined to find new and inventive ways to keep things fresh. . . . This is how we have been able to build solar-powered coconut bikes; to partner on a coconut farm in Sri Lanka, where we will be working with war-affected communities to produce the best coconut oils, butters, and coconut products; and bring to life imaginary machines and contraptions to pierce, process or present coconuts in inventive new ways.

Why is it so hard to keep a product simple? A big part of the problem is that you become intimately familiar with your "power users," the small number of customers who use your product the most. This group of customers is also often referred to as the "vocal minority." Power users have so much to say about the product you're responsible for, and as a result, you will start to consider their complaints and requests. If only to feel like you're doing your job, you'll explore solutions to the problems they voice instead of focusing on the opportunities to engage the customers you have yet to reach. In the process, your prioritization and judgment is liable to be taken hostage by the vocal minority, whose desires stem from a deep relationship with your product, and you fail to take your newest customers into consideration.

You can defy this outcome only by devising ways to maintain simplicity. In the world of digital products, one of my favorite tactics is to compare every new feature on your road map to the features that already exist. For example, if you would choose to create this new feature instead of something you've already done, consider killing the live feature.

Forcing yourself to have a "one feature in, one feature out" guideline will help you develop your product with a bias toward simplicity. While simplicity benefits your newest customers and the majority of your current customers, it also benefits your own process to grow your product and solve problems as they arise. The more dynamic your offering is, the harder it is to diagnose what's working and why. But with fewer moving parts, you'll have a better understanding of which levers to pull at which times for which outcomes. Your intuition is sharper when your product is simpler. For the sake of your own focus and ability to make great product decisions, reduce and add to your product in parallel.

Kill your darlings.

Cutting off a tree's newest branch is painful, even if you know that doing so will strengthen the tree's core. As you experiment by pursuing and testing new projects and features liberally, you'll need to prune back most of what emerges—even when it excites you.

It is easy to kill things that straight up don't work, but it's disheartening to nip a blooming bud—something that is showing early promise but isn't good enough to merit your singular focus. Most teams keep nurturing any features or projects that show any capacity for potential, if only to keep their options open. I see this in early-stage companies that tout their "multiple revenue streams" and "suite of features" for different kinds of customers; I also see artists I know recite a laundry list of projects whenever they're asked what they're working on. When you are mid-journey with multiple projects that could potentially be "the one," your instinct is to keep them all afloat. Pursuing a few paths in parallel keeps your options open, and it feels safe.

But it's not. The flaw with pursuing and preserving many options is that doing so stunts your progress in any particular direction. When your energy is split, so is your speed and focus, and the resources around you are harder to tap when your narrative is too broad. Instead of pitching one cohesive vision to your team, you confuse them with two (or more!). Instead of one fifteen-second elevator pitch to a potential investor, you muddle your story with a hybrid. Instead of your friends and professional network all spreading the word about the single thing you hope to achieve, they will be sending different messages.

But the greatest cost of trying to sustain multiple initiatives is having too little thrust behind one goal. When a goal is simple and singular, every realization builds upon the one before it. By having only one problem to crack over an extended period of time, your brain enters a state of deep crunching that is just not possible with too many projects and problems under way. When you're all-in on one project or approach, you have a better chance of reaching escape velocity, when everyone is focused and aligned.

I fell victim to the allure of optionality in the first few years of Behance. While our mission "to organize and empower the creative world" supported all our initiatives, in reality we were splitting our energy across too many things. We built the Behance Network for millions of creatives to showcase their work and get attribution in an organized fashion—but we also developed and marketed Action Method as a project management tool for creative teams; launched a line of notebooks and other organizational products; and created 99U, a conference, website, and magazine about management and organization in the creative world. While all these efforts contributed to our brand and mission, our energy was severely divided. We had no problem killing things that didn't work—and there were many—but we struggled to kill things that worked just well enough. Looking back, I now refer to years two through four as "the lost years" of Behance. We inched forward too slowly and nearly died trying to preserve more potential paths to success.

The struggle to extinguish great ideas and possibilities for the benefit of a central goal is common in the literary world. In fact, there's even a common phrase for it: "Kill your darlings." American writer and Nobel Prize laureate William Faulkner once said, "In writing, you must kill all your darlings," and in his own book on the process of writing and developing plot, thriller genius Stephen King wrote, "Kill your darlings, kill your darlings, even when it breaks your egocentric little scribbler's heart, kill your darlings." But the author Arthur Quiller-Couch was supposedly the first to make the suggestion, which he did in a lecture to a group of aspiring writers in 1914: "If you here require a practical rule of me, I will present you with this: Whenever you feel an impulse to perpetrate a piece of exceptionally fine writing, obey it—whole-heartedly—and delete it before sending your manuscript to press. Murder your darlings."

Creative writing is a war between simplicity and possibility. An effective plot and engaging characters who drive it must be simple enough for readers to follow, but the creative process of developing a fascinating story line is all about following the whims of imagination. As a result, writers find themselves having to cut beautiful passages and extraordinary characters that fail to support the central plot. Junior writers try to weave them in or justify their existence because they love them so much, but the best writers summon the courage and discipline to kill these "darlings." The same goes for passionate entrepreneurs who can't bear the thought of killing something they conceived, especially if it has some value. But you must.

It's hard to kill your own creations on your own; sometimes you need help. One of my most prolific writer friends, Tim Ferriss, has always been especially good at engaging his community to pare back and refine his ideas, whether for his book passages, titles, or podcast topics. As he explains it, "The question that I find most helpful to ask is, 'if you had to keep 10 percent, which 10 percent would you keep, and if you had to, absolutely had to, cut 10 percent, which 10 percent would you cut?' The interpretation of the responses is just as important as the responses. It only requires one vote to cut. If someone says, 'I loved this, I would absolutely keep this 10 percent,' it stays. Even if nine out of ten people vote cut. It takes a consensus to cut, but it takes only one outlier to keep . . . unless, of course, capriciously and subjectively I decide I fucking hate this part, I want it out. In which case, it's gone. First and foremost, you have to keep yourself happy because everyone else is gonna have an infinite number of opportunities to work with different articles and books, but you are gonna have to live with the consequences of the decisions for this book for the rest of your life."

I've certainly faced (and struggled with) this as a writer as well as an entrepreneur.

At Behance, our task management tool, the notebooks we designed, and our annual conference were all darlings. We had authentic and defensible reasons to love and support each one of these initiatives, but the costs became too great. We ended up killing Action Method despite its loyal fan base. We outsourced the paper product line to a third party and stopped spending any resources on the project. As for 99U, which has now grown to include books, events, and an online think tank, we kept at it; the team found a way to compartmentalize the effort and we validated that the brand and marketing benefits exceeded the costs. These projects slowed us down. But fortunately, we found ways to outsource or kill most of our darlings before it was too late.

I have observed similar murderous moments at other companies I have worked with. At one point, the sweetgreen team spent a lot of time developing a juice line that they were all very passionate about, only to eventually call it quits so they could focus more on their core products. I also remember when Dan Teran, founder and CEO of Managed by Q, a provider of office management and services that I invested in, cut a quarter of the services they offered their customers. As Dan recalls, "Even though we were seeing a lot of growth in these categories, like providing offices with catering and health-and-wellness services, we made a decision to focus where we thought we could be best in the world rather than get into competing outside our core competencies—office cleaning, maintenance, tech support, security, and administration. At the time it was a pretty controversial decision and jeopardized our ability to meet our business goals, but it was definitely the right move and allowed us to double down on where we needed to be the best."

Experiments are important, and you need to try different paths to find the best one. But if an experiment fails to become part of your core strategy, it should be killed. Focused creativity is more important than more creativity.

In my first book, *Making Ideas Happen*, I talked about the importance of killing ideas liberally to keep pace making progress on the few ideas that matter most—and how Walt Disney instituted this practice:

It turns out that Walt Disney went to great lengths to ensure that his creative teams properly vetted and ruthlessly killed ideas when necessary. When developing feature-length films, Disney reportedly implemented a staged process utilizing three distinct rooms to foster ideas and then rigorously assess them.

Room #1: In this first stage, rampant idea generation was allowed without any restraints. The true essence of brainstorming—unrestrained thinking and throwing around ideas without limits—was supported without any doubts expressed.

Room #2: The crazy ideas from Room #1 were then aggregated and organized in Room #2, ultimately resulting in a storyboard chronicling events and general sketches of characters. Rumor has it that the original notion of the storyboard was conceived in this room.

Room #3: Known as the "sweat box," Room #3 is where the entire creative team would critically review the project, again with no restraints or politeness. Given the fact that the ideas from individual people had already been combined in Room #2, the criticism in Room #3 was never directed at an individual person—just at the project in general.

Every creative person and team needs a Room #3. As we build teams and develop a creative process, our tendency is to privilege the no-holds-barred creativity of Room #1. But the idea bloodshed that occurs in Room #3 is equally important as the orgy of ideation that happens in Room #1.

Ollie Johnstone and Frank Thomas, two of Walt Disney's chief animators, once said of Walt Disney himself that "there were actually three different Walts: the dreamer, the realist, and the spoiler. You never knew which one was coming into your meeting." It seems that Disney not only pushed his team through all three rooms, but he embodied the characteristics of the three rooms himself.

You may be telling yourself about the benefits of keeping ideas alive as a way of preserving options, but the truth is that you're failing to kill your darlings, just like an amateur writer would. Your best chance of succeeding is to consolidate your energy around a singular focus and work like hell to achieve it.

If you don't think it's awesome, stop making it.

As an investor, one of the most awkward moments I see is when I can tell that a team no longer believes in what they're building, but they haven't admitted it to themselves yet. Gathering a team and raising money to pursue an idea creates a tremendous amount of pressure to "keep at it," and sometimes the momentum itself keeps us going in one direction even when the data or our gut instincts suggest otherwise.

When you build something, there is an inherent love and loyalty you will have for your original vision, even when you stop believing it. When I find myself with a team that seems to have fallen out of love, I look for the most sensitive way to say, "If it's not fucking awesome, switch it up!"

If your motivation is just to finish something you started, you will fail to inspire and capitalize on the resources around you. Sure, you might stumble into success, make a margin, and fill some niche of opportunity for a subpar product. But how will such a mediocre outcome make you feel?

When you fall out of love with what you're making, your gut is telling you something. If you're a founder or working on a solo project, you have the luxury of abandoning the project and pivoting to something you're excited about; the sunk costs may feel too steep at the moment, but over time, it will feel negligible, I promise. Don't let exhaustion or the lack of short-term rewards confuse your gut instincts. Every venture is hard, and every great team loses momentum once in a while. I think the ultimate litmus test is whether you have more or less conviction about the vision than you had at the start. If you still believe that what you're building needs to exist—and the time you've spent on the project only deepens your conviction for the change you will make with your product—then stick with it.

But you need to be willing to cut bait when you've lost conviction for the end state you imagine and know you can do better. Successful pivots require killing off the old to give rise to the new. I often come across founders who admit that their product isn't working and have begun contemplating alternate ideas for their company. But even when they have an idea they feel is better, they instinctually protect the product that is already on the market, even when they know it is not a winning product. When pushed, their excuses range from "I don't want to disappoint the customers already using the product" to "We want to preserve optionality in case it suddenly becomes popular." Well, you will inevitably disappoint customers when they realize you are no longer focused on improving the product, and it is very unlikely to suddenly become more popular without said improvements.

The same principle applies for making other kinds of difficult product decisions, like end-of-life-ing" (killing) a feature or an entire product. Making the decision to kill a product is far easier than the second step, deciding how and when to kill the product. Once a decision is made, the stream of reasons to wait until acting will flow mightily.

"We need to take this slowly. Rather than kill it, let's just stop making updates to the product for a while so customers get the hint."

"We can't afford to upset customers, so let's craft a compelling story as to why we are doing this."

While some concerns are reasonable, most are excuses to delay the inevitable. Killing a product by ignoring it only prolongs its death. Customers will always be upset. As Aaron Levie, founder and CEO of cloud-storage company Box once noted, "To make everyone happy with the decision, you'll make no one happy with the outcome." When the stakes are high, your natural inclination is to wait as long as necessary to be sure of the choice you're making. You trade decisiveness for certainty, even if it means compromising productivity and your team's engagement in the process. Ripping off the Band-Aid quickly compartmentalizes your pain and gives you more energy to focus on creating what's next.

In his 2016 annual letter to shareholders, Amazon CEO Jeff Bezos pointed out the risk that all organizations, especially large ones like Amazon, face by making decisions too carefully and slowly. As he explained it, "Some decisions are consequential and irreversible or nearly irreversible—one-way doors—and these decisions must be made methodically, carefully, slowly, with great deliberation and consultation. If you walk through and don't like what you see on the other side, you can't get back to where you were before. We can call these Type 1 decisions. But most decisions aren't like that—they are changeable, reversible—they're two-way doors. If you've made a suboptimal Type 2 decision, you don't have to live with the consequences for that long. You can reopen the door and go back through. Type 2 decisions can and should be made quickly by high judgment individuals or small groups."

"As organizations get larger," he explained, "there seems to be a tendency to use the heavyweight Type 1 decision-making process on most decisions, including many Type 2 decisions. The end result of this is slowness, unthoughtful risk aversion, failure to experiment sufficiently, and consequently diminished invention. We'll have to figure out how to fight that tendency."

If you don't think your bold, against-all-odds project is awesome, make a change. And if some aspect of your product isn't working, make the tough decisions to kill it. Without such honesty and decisiveness, your work (and career) will fail to progress. Once you admit something isn't working and make the change, you're liberated. You're ready to consider solving an entirely different problem with your full mind and extending your energy long enough to make it happen.

Beware of creativity that compromises familiarity.

In the early days of Behance and our pursuit to build a network for creative professionals, we got a little too creative ourselves.

On the most basic level we created our own terminology for things that should have been kept simple, for example. We used the term "realms" instead of the more literal "creative fields" for the creative fields users who would use that word to classify their work. Our creative terminology made these features distinct from other online communities, but it also made them less familiar. We learned the hard way that new products are hard enough to figure out as it is without needing to decipher new terminology.

It will be tempting to add your own spin. The more assumptions customers have to make, the less effective a solution is, granted the simpler solution works just as well as the complex one. The best products become more effective over time, not more creative.

In order to disrupt an industry, our instinct is to be different. But the best way to capture the share of an existing industry is to be familiar. The most widely adopted products and services accommodate new customers with recognizable patterns instead of "retraining" users with something entirely new. I recall a conversation with fellow entrepreneur Matt Van Horn about this subject. He's the founder of June, a modern "smart oven" that automatically recognizes food placed in it and automates the process of cooking to perfection. At first, his team of industrial designers imagined a wildly different-looking product that totally reimagined what an oven looked like. But eventually they realized that if they wanted the June oven to be considered as a viable alternative to the traditional oven, it had to look like an oven. They were already trying to disrupt a common, familiar action—cooking—so they didn't need to complicate it even further by persuading customers to place mini spaceships in their kitchens. It's easier to disrupt the norm by being familiar.

Patterns in the physical world are powerful, and the best products tap into them. The early designs of Apple's mobile operating system were notoriously "skeuomorphic," which means they employed a design where an interface resembled its real-world counterpart. While many professional designers scoffed at Apple's efforts to make its digital notepad look like its physical counterpart, stitched leather and all. But by doing so, Apple was able to reduce the cognitive friction experienced by its newest users. Suddenly, using a digital notepad instead of the classic one on your desk didn't feel so different. Great technology, as well as other modern solutions to old problems, capitalizes on our analog muscle memory. Use human existence and muscle memory to your advantage by leveraging existing patterns whenever possible.

The only time you should force new behaviors or terminology is when they enable a unique and important value in your product. For example, Snapchat was the first social network that would open on the camera view when you clicked on the app instead of other competitive products like Instagram and Facebook that open on a feed of others' content. This behavior struck new users as foreign, but it retrained users for an entirely different kind of social experience. Snapchat aspired to be more of a camera than an app, and launching the product in camera mode sent a strong and differentiating message to its users that helped distinguish Snapchat from other social apps—as well as the kind of content created with it.

Don't be creative for the sake of it, despite the urge to do so. Popular terms and actions are popular for a reason. Adopt simple patterns, proven to be successful, whenever possible, and train your customers only when it's a new behavior that is absolutely core to what differentiates your product. Familiarity drives utilization.

Too much scrutiny creates flaws.

As you endlessly evaluate your work to make it better, you'll see more and more elements that need to change. If you scrutinize too much, however, you'll eventually reach what I call the "cohesion horizon," where your scrutiny loses perspective, and you start perseverating over details without context and stop evaluating the whole.

Once scrutiny passes the cohesion horizon, decisions become emotional and destructive. Challenge yourself to move on when you sense yourself obsessing out of passion rather than reason. Engage emotionally as you create, but detach from your creations when evaluating them.

If you look at a product, a paragraph, or a piece of art long enough, something will eventually look wrong. Persistent insecurities manifest themselves as unnecessary debates and you suddenly lose perspective of what matters. Gut instinct becomes compromised. The wrinkle that makes your work special is liable to get ironed out if you keep at it. Scrutiny must have a limit, otherwise everything you make will be critiqued and edited back to the unremarkable mean.

Countless studies have shown that overscrutinizing drains our working memory, which we desperately need to complete cognitively demanding tasks. As psychologists Sian Beilock and Thomas Carr describe in the *Journal of Experimental Psychology*, "If the ability of working memory to maintain task focus is disrupted, performance may suffer." Their research shows that anxiety and pressure—which we experience while overscrutinizing a problem—significantly disrupt working memory.

What's more, studies conducted at Swarthmore College examined the psychological effects experienced by "maximizers" as compared to "satisficers." These studies build on the term "satisficer" that economist Herbert Simon coined in 1956 to describe the decision-making style that "prioritizes an adequate solution over an optimal solution." While satisficers make a decision once their criteria is met, "maximizers" want to make the best possible decision, and so they scrutinize every option even if they've found one that's good enough.

In the Swarthmore studies, as journalist Becky Kane summarizes on Todoist, maximizers reported significantly lower life satisfaction, happiness, optimism, and self-esteem, and significantly more regret and depression, than satisficers. Maximizers were also more likely to engage in social comparison and counterfactual thinking, experienced more regret and less happiness after making a consumer decision, and experienced a greater increase in negative mood when they didn't perform as well as their peers.

Those who overscrutinize are likely to be "maximizers." While such perfectionist tendencies can lead to excellent results, as these studies show, they can also result in analysis paralysis.

Beyond the cohesion horizon, any additional scrutiny backfires as your perspective becomes too elemental and less aware of a unified system. Your obsession and extreme attention to detail will cause small and insignificant things to distract you from the overarching goal, and you'll start critiquing and changing parts without consideration for the whole. If you can't help yourself and must search for ways to improve, at least learn to scrutinize a system rather than its parts. When a structure works, look for ways to make it better according to your mission rather than obsess over the rough edges of segments.

Having a tight deadline and an overwhelming list of tasks to achieve can help keep you moving and stop perseverating. Rather than seeking more options, remind yourself that you make progress only once a decision is made, and you can always backtrack or adjust as you learn along the way. Don't fall into the vortex of navel-gazing; keep moving.

Effective design is invisible.

Over the years, countless industry leaders have ascribed to the theory "The best design is the design you don't see," each in their own way—just as a designer would! Or as Dieter Rams, author of the canonical *10 Principles of Good Design*, famously said, "Good design is as little design as possible."

Over the years, and especially through my time growing Behance, I have had the opportunity to follow and work with all kinds of designers from around the world. I've come to believe that the most effective designers are always solving a specific problem and seem to do so more by removing than adding.

The best design often goes unnoticed because something is removed that wasn't meant to be there in the first place. When a product or digital experience becomes materially easier to use, the design elements—the interface, the color scheme, the typefaces—disappear altogether. Such design decisions may not get awards or be memorable, but they do make a product more accessible to more people.

If design is important to your product or process, challenge yourself to look past the graphics and what's new and shiny at the surface. Reduce elements—and any step requiring decisions—whenever you can. Fewer options, shorter copy, and simpler steps will always bring your product to a better place. In the moment, this will feel counterintuitive—you'll assume that progress means new features and a visual evolution of your product. But over time, you'll learn that the incremental reductions and refinements allow customers to flow through the experience with more ease than most new features or additional copy ever could.

Never stop crafting the "first mile" of your product's experience.

Whether you're building a product, creating art, or writing a book, you need to remember that your customers or patrons make sweeping judgments in their first experience interacting with your creation—especially in the first 30 seconds. I call this the "first mile," and it is the most critical yet underserved part of a product.

You get only one chance to make a first impression. In a world of moving fast and pushing out a minimum viable product, the first mile of a user's experience is almost always an afterthought. For physical products, that could be the packaging, the wording of the instructions, and the labels that help orientate a new customer. For digital products, it could be the onboarding process, the explanatory copy, and the default settings of your product. When we spend so much time focusing on making what's behind a locked door so brilliant, we sometimes forget to give the user the key.

A failed first mile cripples a new product right out of the gate. You may get loads of downloads, presales, or sign-ups, but very few customers will get past the onboarding process to start actually using your product. And even if they do, your customers need to feel successful quickly. You need to prime your audience to the point where they know three things:

1. Why they're there
2. What they can accomplish
3. What to do next

Consider, for example, a product like Adobe XD, one of Adobe's newest and fastest-growing platforms for experience designers (people who design interfaces of all kinds, websites, mobile apps, and anything else that graces a screen or helps people navigate an experience). As soon as you open the product for the first time, you should know **why you're there** (to design that cool app you have an idea for), **what you can accomplish** (the vast array of experiences you can design for, as represented by examples and a list of ways to get started), and **what to do next** (it should always be clear what your next step is—and the sequence of steps you must take to be successful).

Once new users know these three things, they have reached a place in your product experience where they are willing to invest time and energy to build a relationship with your product. They don't need to actually know how to use your entire product at the beginning—they just need to trust you and know what their immediate next step is.

Much of what I know about the first mile of product experience I learned the hard way while building Behance's products and working with other start-ups. In the earliest version of Behance, we had so many steps and questions in the sign-up process. For example, we asked new members to select their top three creative fields, like photography, photojournalism, or illustration. There were a lot of options, and new users took an average of 120 seconds to browse the list and select their top fields. It was helpful for both of us to know who our users were and for the users to instantly connect to communities, but we lost more than 10 percent of new members at this particular step in the sign-up process. We decided to remove it and resolved to capture this information later on, sometime after the first mile once new Behance users were actively using the product and willing to give us the benefit of the doubt. We reduced or altogether removed other steps as well. As a result, sign-ups went up by approximately 14 percent. Reducing and iterating the first mile experience had a greater impact on growth than any other new feature that year.

Over the years since, I have worked with dozens of other companies trying to optimize the first mile of their customer experience—whether it was Pinterest's first version of welcoming new users that aimed to maximize the number of "pin boards" each user was following, Uber's way of describing itself to new users when it first launched, sweetgreen's mobile application for ordering salads for pickup, Periscope's live-streaming application, or mobile creative applications at Adobe—and every product suffers the same challenge: helping customers understand why they're there, what they can accomplish, and what to do next *in as few steps, words, and seconds as possible.*

Established products are not immune to this problem. Consider Twitter, a product that engages millions of people but struggled to optimize the first mile. For a subset of users—perhaps the first 150 million or so—an onboarding experience that required new users to select accounts to follow was sufficient. However, at some point Twitter encountered a new cohort of customers who didn't have the patience or desire to curate their own feed. They just wanted the news, and Twitter's first mile experience was much more difficult than switching on the television or going to a website. Even though their core product improved, Twitter struggled to get new users to build a relationship with the product—and growth stalled as a result.

Especially for new companies, these crucial components of initial engagement are typically addressed in haste as a product is launching. The "top of the funnel" for engaging new people with your product is your ultimate source of growth, and yet such early aspects of the product experience like designing a "tour" for your product and determining what the default experience should be are all too often afterthoughts. In some teams, I have even seen these pieces outsourced or delegated to a single person to figure out on her own.

To make matters worse, the first mile of a product experience is increasingly neglected over time despite becoming *more* important over time. As your product reaches beyond early adopters, the first mile will need to be even simpler and account for vastly different groups of "newest users," not just the power users you were originally hoping to attract. New customers are not the same over time; if they were, you would have snared them in the opening round. The first mile requires continual scrutiny after launch. Just because you're accommodating fresh users well now doesn't mean the same approach will work in the future as you attract wider and different audiences. Without constantly reconsidering your assumptions for what new users need, you'll fail to accommodate the cohorts that will bring your product into the mainstream. As products scale across demographics, generations, and nationalities, your first mile will need to change.

The first mile of your customer's experience using your product cannot be the last mile of your experience building the product. For any product with aggressive growth aspirations, I'd argue that more than 30 percent of your energy should be allocated to the first mile of your product—even when you're well into your journey. It's the very top of your funnel for new users, and it therefore needs to be one of the most thought-out parts of your product, not an afterthought.

Optimize the first 30 seconds for laziness, vanity, and selfishness.

Within that first mile, the first 30 seconds of the sprint determine if people will keep running the whole distance. During these first 30 seconds of every new experience, people are lazy, vain, and selfish. This is not intended as a cynical jab at humanity. It's an essential insight for building great products and experiences both online and off-. It is a humbling realization that everyone you meet—and everyone who visits your website or uses your products—has an entirely different mind-set before they're ready to make the effort to care.

We are *lazy* in the sense that we don't want to invest time and energy to unwrap and understand what something is. We have no patience to read directions. No time to deviate. No will to learn. Life has such a steep learning curve as it is with seldom enough time for work, play, learning, and love. So when something entirely new requires too much effort, we just let it pass. Our default is to avoid things that take work until we're convinced of the benefits.

We are *vain* because we care how we come across to others, at least initially. Mirrors, hair products, and social media all provide a quick return of self-assurance for how we appear to others. For this reason, products like Instagram and Twitter are geared to yield you likes and friends as quickly as possible; no one wants to start using a new product if you have no one to share it with. While the majority of your time on a product like Instagram may be spent browsing your friends' content, if you pay attention to your behavior using the product, you'll notice the tendency to open the app more frequently immediately after posting a new image.

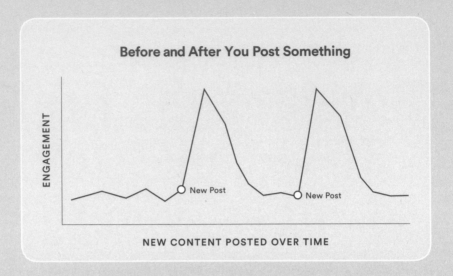

Before and After You Post Something

ENGAGEMENT

New Post

New Post

NEW CONTENT POSTED OVER TIME

You want to see what people are saying about your content, and you'll keep checking. Instagram's activity feed is an example of what I've come to call "ego analytics"; it shows you what people are saying and strokes your ego after taking the risk to publish or share a creation of your own. The same goes for other apps, as well as gallery openings, press coverage, and book launches. We are all hardwired to tune in to what others are saying about us if given the opportunity to do so.

For product designers, ego analytics is a critical mechanism to keep users contributing and engaged. The fact that creative apps are more about seeing who saw your content than seeing others' content is telling. Rather than open our aperture to browse and discover the world's creations, we perseverate over the performance of our own. Our vanity routinely sucks the gravity out of any creative opportunity.

Of course, the more we know our friends and loved ones, the less we judge them and posture ourselves for them—but until they know you, you want to look good. These ego analytics are a very powerful form of engagement because vanity rules the first 30 seconds.

We are **selfish** because we must also care for ourselves. When you engage with a product or service, you want an immediate return that exceeds your initial investment. Instruction manuals, laborious unpacking, extensive sign-up processes, and other friction points that obstruct getting a quick return from engagement are alienating. New customers need something quick, right now, regardless of what they may get later.

This *lazy-vain-selfish principle* is true for all kinds of product experiences, online and offline. In the first 30 seconds, your visitors are lazy in the sense that they have no extra time to invest in something they don't know. They are vain in that they want to look good from the get-go when they engage with your product or service. And they're selfish in that despite the big-picture potential and purpose of what your product stands for, they want to know how it will immediately benefit them.

As a result, every new relationship and resource around us is at a disadvantage. Meaningful engagement with whatever is new to us occurs only when we're pulled past the initial bout of laziness, vanity, and selfishness that accompanies any new experience. Your job is to find a way to reach beyond the surface of every new experience, find its meaning, and express that to the user.

Whatever pulls us past those first 30 seconds is the *hook*. Don't think you're above needing a hook. Nobody is. And most important, don't think your prospective customers are above needing a hook. When you see a prompt to "Sign Up in Seconds to Organize Your Life," it's a hook. Headlines in newspapers are hooks. Book covers, and their lofty promises like achieving a "4-hour workweek," are hooks. Dating sites are full of hooks. An effective hook appeals to short-term interests that are connected to a long-term promise.

Consider your process when purchasing a book. Regardless of how well written and interesting it may be, it is nothing but hundreds of pages—either digital or physical—of black-and-white words. The hook, in this case, is often the cover and title. The cover compensates for the lazy, as it paints a pretty picture that might compel you to reach out your hand and pick it up. Your vanity may be stroked by the prospect of appearing more intelligent or familiar with the zeitgeist by reading what others are talking about. The title and subtitle appeal to your selfishness through the promise of what's in it for you and your self-interests.

Or consider retail. If you run a store, what you display in your windows determines whether or not a potential customer will walk in. The science of window dressing is entirely different from in-store merchandising and the quality of your products—but no one gets to feel the thread count of your sheets or the smoothness of your ceramic kitchenware if you can't get them in the door first.

Your challenge is to create product experiences for two different mind-sets, one for your potential customers and one for your engaged customers. Initially, if you want your prospective customers to engage, think of them as lazy, vain, and selfish. Then for the customers who survive the first 30 seconds and actually come through the door, build a meaningful experience and relationship that lasts a lifetime.

Do > Show > Explain

When bringing a new product to market, you'll be tempted to explain what it is and how it works. Such attempts usually result in extensive amounts of copy, how-to videos, and multisequence digital "tours" explaining the product's purpose and how to make the most of it. For nondigital products and services, explanations take the form of bulky instruction manuals, verbose menus at restaurants, and lengthy onboarding meetings for new clients.

If you feel the need to explain how to use your product rather than empowering new customers to jump in and feel successful on their own, you've either failed to design a sufficient first-mile experience or your product is too complicated.

Having to *explain* your product is the least effective way to engage new users. This realization hit close to home when I joined Adobe and learned how many millions of copies of Photoshop were downloaded every year by prospective customers, opened once, and then never opened again. It happens more often than you think. A new Photoshop document was a blank page, and most people had no idea what to do next. There were no onboarding steps and no templates to choose from first. A quick search for "Photoshop" on YouTube or Google yields tens of thousands of instructional videos attempting to teach people how to use the product, which emphasized how much explanation was required before customers could use the product. There was an entire economy of tutorials, how-to videos, and books devoted to helping prospective Photoshop users navigate the product. Photoshop was a daunting product with no consideration for the first mile.

Over the years since then, the Photoshop team has started designing new onboarding experiences, like a welcome page and tips to jump-start creative projects. But these attempts to *show* how to use the product aren't enough to help new customers achieve some level of success before investing the time and energy to learn how to use the product's vast set of features.

The absolute best hook in the first mile of a user experience is *doing* things proactively for your customers. Once you help them feel successful and proud, your customers will engage more deeply and take the time to learn and unlock the greater potential of what you've created.

For digital applications such as Paperless Post, an online tool to create and send digital party invitations and birthday cards, that means providing customers with templates to choose from and edit rather than explaining how to create a digital card from scratch. For photography-editing applications like Instagram or Google's and Apple's photo products, that means providing smart filters that apply a sequence of effects to an image all at once rather than forcing customers to learn how to use different tools for contrast, brightness, and sharpness. In most of these cases, full personalization is available—but it's not the first option.

The same principle applies to physical products and in-store experiences. When educating customers about which products they should buy, activity-apparel company Outdoor Voices, another company I work with, launched "kits" as a way to help their users save time, and do so stylishly. Kits are essentially a preselected set of matching items that help new customers get the basics without having to navigate across multiple product categories and become familiar with a new nomenclature. The customers feel like they're getting an easy, personalized shopping experience—and the brand is benefiting from fully outfitting them all at once—and they are likely buying a little more than they would have otherwise.

You can't expect new customers to endure explanation. You can't even expect customers to patiently watch as you show them how to use your product. Your best chance at engaging them is to do it for them—at least at first. Only after your customers feel successful will they engage deeply enough to tap the full potential of your offering.

Novelty precedes utility.

As you're building new products and experiences for customers, consider how they will be novel—even gamelike—before they prove useful. Oftentimes, people engage with new products and experiences out of mere fascination and novelty and discover a product's utility only over time.

My first job out of college in 2002 was working on the trading floor at Goldman Sachs, which at the time was located at One New York Plaza. Back then, students pursuing a career in business were encouraged to take a job on Wall Street for a few years despite whatever your longer-term interests were. As a student who studied both design and business, it was a tough compromise to set aside half my interests and immerse myself in a trading-floor culture, but I rolled up my sleeves and tried it.

I found most of my daily responsibilities dreadfully mundane, but I developed an interest in the adoption of new technology on the trading floor. On one hand, the trading floor was powered by incredible technologies that enabled rapid matching of client orders and accounting of positions. On the other hand, the professional traders were remarkably stuck in their old habits and reticent to give new technology a try.

In 2003, Goldman installed a new phone system in our offices. One of its most prominent features was a set of virtual conference rooms that traders, research analysts, and salespeople could hop into at any time using their desktop headset. If some new piece of news broke, people could all join a virtual conference room together to discuss it without leaving their desks. Despite several training sessions and a barrage of onboarding emails, nobody used them—myself included. These virtual conference rooms sat dormant until one day when a senior manager wearing a crazy bright tie covered with various circus acts walked by our team. One of the salespeople, named Rich, yelled out to the entire desk, "Everyone, con 1!" People were puzzled but then realized that Rich was referring to virtual conference room #1. Everyone quickly put on their headsets, clicked "Con 1" on their phone terminals, and hopped in. Rich made a joke about the crazy tie, and the virtual room erupted in laughter from across our desks.

From that day forward, the virtual conference rooms were heavily utilized—and for increasingly professional purposes. Often new technology initially engages users through novelty, and then as they become more familiar with the technology, it results in greater levels of utilization. The same thing happened ten years later, in the fall of 2013, when our team at Behance began playing with Slack, then a new communications tool. The first channels were created for the sole purpose of sharing animated GIFs, jokes, and recommendations for coffee shops in the area—but then after just a few weeks, the whole team was using it to coordinate product releases and road map prioritization.

When it comes to the adoption of new products and ways of working, novelty often precedes utility. As you're building new products and experiences for customers, consider how they will be novel before they prove useful. Don't bury a certain feature or functionality merely because it isn't essential for the intended use of your product. Your most important feature may be whatever gets people through the door. Sometimes the initial reason to use a product, and get through the first mile, is to have fun.

Break incrementalism by questioning core assumptions.

While so much of a great product comes down to your relentless efforts to simplify and refine, you'll also have to make bold changes along the way. The hardest part about bold changes is that they break the systems and measures you use to achieve progress. The practices that keep you on track and improving your product are the same ones that backfire when you need to change. The larger and more successful you are, the harder it is to break day-to-day incrementalism.

Incrementalism is the machine that drives success and scalability, but eventually the growth subsides, and your great product becomes the new status quo. It isn't necessarily bad. In fact, products can become great only through periods of incremental tweaks, updates, and polishes. But the daily drive to optimize your product using metrics, quarterly goals, and other short-term measures will get you trapped in a *local maxima*: You'll feel remarkably successful but only within the confines of the assumptions and market you've optimized around.

This local maxima trap plagues individuals and teams both large and small. Consider Twitter, an extraordinary social product that has toppled regimes and has given both global glory and strife by connecting the world to information in real time. What was once a rapidly growing viable competitor to Facebook has stalled in recent years, as growth in monthly active users has topped out. I believe this is because the company attempted incremental improvements, like optimizing profitability, monthly engagement, and spam controls over bolder moves, such as exploring new markets and redefining the product. Rather than becoming the future of media, reinventing television, or becoming the ultimate source of real-time information on any given topic, the product looks much like it did ten years ago.

Twitter will either stay limited within its local maxima or transform itself. But the organization would need to change before the product ever can. Before underlying assumptions and practices are changed, a team needs to change how they are measured. New goals must be articulated both internally and to external stakeholders, which is no small feat for a public and popular company.

On a smaller scale, I see the same challenges in engineering teams that wish to invest in infrastructure at the expense of near-term and easier-to-measure improvements that advance product and business objectives. If you measure an engineering team by the number of features they release or the speed at which they achieve measurable milestones, then you're disincentivizing any long-term investments that could, over time, truly distinguish your product.

The key to breaking incrementalism and escaping your local maxima is to swap out your underlying assumptions. For example, if your product was founded in the age of social media and mobile apps, what assumptions did you have then that you would now question as voice-activated devices enter our homes and augmented reality transforms our mobile devices?

When it's the right time to make a bold move in product strategy, make a list of the core assumptions your product or service is based on. Many tech companies that spawned early in the internet era have had to reinvent themselves. For example, Scott Heiferman, Meetup's CEO and founder, shared his thoughts with me on the topic of rebooting products and breaking incrementalism one afternoon near his company's headquarters in New York City in early 2017. "Just because you have product-market fit doesn't mean you're going to keep product-market fit," he explained. "That's actually a pretty scary notion. The world changes and people change and society changes and culture changes and moorings change."

A year earlier, Scott became concerned about the company's growth and took a step back to rethink the entire business and how the world had changed since the company's founding. He also acknowledged the fact he was in his forties and more than 60 percent of his company was under the age of thirty-two. He had a feeling, like when you find yourself at a table of PhD-holding professors and feel everyone is smarter than you, that his entire paradigm was off, if only by a little bit. "It's hard to know because you're in the thick of it," he explained. As his new and younger employees posed difficult questions, "I got super defensive saying, 'You don't know what you're talking about.' The point here is to know when to be open to a kind of insurrection. When there was a severe defensiveness, that was the explicit signal to me, it hit me."

In Shakespearian terms, it was a "lady doth protest too much" moment for Scott, where his strong denial of the need to question Meetup's original assumptions was a clue that he needed to. As an investor in the company, I was invigorated by Scott's self-awareness and willingness to reimagine the whole company rather than get stuck making small iterations around Meetup's local maxima.

While Meetup's North Star—to bring people together around shared interests and build off-line communities—has not changed, their product has now changed dramatically. What was once limited to web is now mostly mobile. The brand is new, the discovery experience is easier to navigate, the default experience is different, and the kinds of Meetup's happenings are more diverse than ever. Scott believes that his company's reinvention was powered by the ideas and needs of its newest people.

For instance, when new employees join the company, the entire team of hundreds of people come together as Scott asks them a question in public: "Why is what we're doing important to you?" Scott recalls a time when someone stood up in front of the company and said, "'Hey, I started last week. I'm an iOS engineer. I'm here at Meetup because I've had experiences in my life where, as a transgender[ed person], I went to a Meetup and it was so vital and taught me how important and supportive community is for people to feel empowered.' Whatever the story is, these new employees tell their own version of our vision, and this serves as a regenerative machine to the whole company to understand, in real terms, why what we're doing is important. . . . You can preach or plan until you're blue in the face, but the company won't change unless people really internalize something and make it their own."

Scott's part in the process was accepting the fact that major change was the only way to achieve Meetup's mission better than newer competitors like Facebook ever could. "If you're not embarking on a new major model in pursuit of the same North Star, there's something wrong. But in our case, we didn't go around saying 'Oh, what should we change to? What should we change to?' It was more like art. It was organically making Meetup better for ourselves [as customers]." By proactively integrating fresh talent and empowering its newest people to make the company's mission personal, Meetup escaped incrementalism and made bold changes. In 2018, Meetup was ultimately acquired by the global coworking conglomerate WeWork, in large part due to its renewed growth and relevance in the lives of millions of customers.

Old assumptions don't get questioned enough because we're used to them, and new ideas get dismissed too quickly because they are foreign and challenge conventions. Engaging and empowering new talent is a reliable way to break old patterns. As the leader of a team with new and old talent, your challenge is to balance the need to incrementally optimize alongside the need to change and question everything. Knowing the tendency to be limited by a local maxima, challenge yourself to welcome disruptive forces when you find yourself defensive. Strong denial is a signal for a hard truth.

Foster inbred innovations.

In the everyday minutiae of operating a business, we tend to look outside for innovative ways to improve our products. We attend conferences, hire consultants, and try to reimagine our products to discover entirely new ways of doing things. While these initiatives have great potential in generating new ideas (and acquiring new team members), relying on outside forces to keep your product or service innovative is risky and expensive. Often, the best innovations are sitting right in front of you—literally.

One of my favorite examples of inbred innovation comes from sweetgreen, the seasonal local food chain I introduced earlier. When I walked into a sweetgreen store for the first time, I was immediately struck by the team's attention to design and how they embraced technology in ways that no other fast-casual food chains were. Soon after, I met the team, joined their board, and have since advised the team on technology, design, and marketing matters. Suffice it to say, I was struck by how Jonathan, Nic, and Nate were consistently innovating in a space that most would write off as commoditized and stagnant.

When you sit down with the three cofounders, you can immediately tell how tethered they are to sweetgreen's mission. Whether they're discussing their online ordering system, their selection of lettuces, or how to decrease the length of lines, the conversation comes back to core tenets: providing quality food and experiences for their customers, staying local, and promoting a healthier lifestyle for their customers and employees. When every decision you make is so tightly connected to a mission, the rest of the organization catches on. Employees become not only more loyal and engaged but also active participants in the evolution of the product.

"Some of the best innovations are the ones right in front of your face," Nate, one of the CEOs, said to me. "A lot of the product innovations that you see on our menu today actually happened because a team member or employee was making it in the kitchen for themselves and for [fellow employees]. One example is the 'warm bowl' category where a team member during the winter time was making his own version of stew. We had a chickpea lentil soup that we'd put over quinoa, and the employee was putting chicken and cheese on it. It was this warm version of a salad that really came as an innovation from within. There are lots of examples like that, not just in the kitchen but in other parts of the business, where the innovation is actually already happening— it's just having the clarity to recognize it."

Recognizing an innovation is important. But what makes employees experiment and share their ideas in the first place? How do you ensure that the managers recognize and support a small tweak or inbred innovation that could make a big difference? "I think it starts with our values, and one of our core values is to make an impact through constant evolution," Nate says. "The way we talk about innovation is always through the lens of evolution. Innovation doesn't have to be a shiny new thing. Innovation can be the smallest tweak that feels small but could be transformational." A leader's job is to constantly reiterate the mission and the steps required to achieve it.

Sadly, most companies aren't aligned enough or structured to identify and nourish innovation from within. When people notice something that should change, or stumble upon a new idea, there is no set of values or support system to take those findings to the right people to be enacted. The product and team therefore become stagnant, and innovation must be acquired from the outside.

If you don't align your team with a mission they identify with, they can't help evolve the product. Breakthroughs will germinate from within and, if nourished with enough flexibility, attention, and internal celebration, become actionable. If you don't support inbred innovation, your team's indifference to the future of their own creation will halt its evolution.

ANCHORING TO YOUR CUSTOMERS

Empathy and humility before passion.

Clément Faydi moved to New York City from France to join our Behance team in 2011. He was young and ambitious, and I quickly realized he'd become one of the greatest product designers I'd ever work with. So it was particularly difficult when in February 2015, Clément came into my office to tell me he was setting out to found his own company. I had immense respect for Clément and was excited for him, but I also hated the prospect of losing him.

Of course, my first question for Clément was "What are you making?" He explained his long-time passion for news and helping people connect around their common interests. It turns out that as a student in design school, Clément had outlined a concept quite similar to Pinterest, a company I worked with as one of their investors, years before such sites became popular. Clément had a long-standing passion for designing ways for people to organize and share news and resources, and he was willing to leave a secure job (and a team that loved him!) to pursue it.

My initial reaction was: "Oh no, not another news or collections product." As a technology investor, I had already been burned twice investing in two other news-related start-ups founded by design-driven entrepreneurs whom I respected. And Pinterest, along with many other companies that copied it, had already become popular. I had questions about the news industry in general—about the stability of the business model and the overwhelming power of Facebook—and I didn't believe consumers needed more interfaces for third-party news content. But determination and a dream work wonders. What Clément (and the founders of the other two failed companies I had lost my investment in) had was a passion for the news space and a good thesis for how to improve the way we discover and engage around topics of interest. But their passion was also liable to obscure some of the underlying mechanics for the space and an honest appraisal of their customers' needs.

Unfortunately, passion for an idea doesn't always correlate with the need for it. Clément launched his company, Topick, after a year of some of the greatest design work he had ever done. But ultimately, the product didn't grow as he had hoped and he decided to shut it down. "The thing we were missing all along was the problem we were solving," Clément explained to me one evening over drinks in New York City. "We knew what we wanted to do—organize news by interest and eliminate all the noise in the news space—but didn't confirm whether people were really suffering from this. We focused too much on ourselves, our interests, and our intuition rather than testing the broader market. Even though we found a bunch of other people like us, our interests were not a proxy for everyone else." Had he spent a couple of weeks focused solely on customer needs and problems first, Clément believes that he would have started something different.

Clément's experience reminded me of many other entrepreneurs who were initially motivated by a fascination with a topic rather than a problem. Looking back at my own experience founding Behance, I was no different: I initially wanted to create an online creative community and loved the idea of millions of people showcasing their creativity to one another. But I quickly picked up on a sense of frustration among the customers I was seeking to serve: They didn't want to join new communities; they wanted to get credit for their work and become more productive in their careers. What they really wanted was a utility to manage their online portfolios and get discovered by more people in more places. As I better understood the problem, I adjusted our plan to better address it.

The consequence of starting a project out of sheer passion is making decisions without considering those you're serving. Empathy for those suffering the problem must come before your passion for the solution.

Consider the rise of the popular camera and messaging app Snapchat. There were a lot of start-ups trying to help people share photos and hoping to compete with Facebook. But founder Evan Spiegel recognized the unique insecurities and preferences of its first users: teenagers. At the time of its founding in 2011, teenagers were especially sensitive to leaving a trail of data online that their parents and teachers could see. The idea of ephemeral content that would quickly disappear relieved the anxieties of these teenage users. Snapchat was also empathetic to the fact that many of these teenagers had hand-me-down smartphones with limited storage and cracked screens. The product was designed with a very simple user interface and no dependency on the device's ability to store images.

Having empathy for your customers should come before falling in love with your solution. Likewise, the market dynamics around you should be understood before turning an idea into an active venture. For example, every year, there are a handful of companies that launch iPhone apps and accessories that are ultimately rendered duplicative or altogether useless when Apple launches the next version of the iPhone. There were flashlight apps before Apple launched flashlight capabilities as a part of their operating system. There were styluses of all kinds for the iPad before Apple launched their "Pencil." There were wireless headphones before Apple launched their higher-performing "AirPods." And the list goes on.

While these iPhone app and accessory companies were sensitive to customer needs, they failed to humble themselves in the market and recognize other companies that were better positioned to satisfy the need.

When pursuing a new idea or solution to a problem, run it through three filters:

1. **Empathy with a Need and Frustration:** You have to understand the struggle of your users. Are you empathizing with customers who will benefit from your idea? What is their frustration and where is it coming from? Since you are often a customer of your own product, pay special attention to what frustrates you. As Jerry Seinfeld once explained in an interview with *Harvard Business Review* when he was asked where his best ideas come from, "It's very important to know what you don't like," he explained. "A big part of innovation is saying, 'You know what I'm really sick of?' . . . 'What am I really sick of?' is where innovation begins." What frustrates you likely frustrates many others.

2. **Humility with the Market:** Humble yourself with the market dynamics around you. Is there another company in a much better position to serve your customer than you are? If so, what has prohibited them from doing so? What change in the market could immediately cripple your prospects?

3. **Passion for the Solution:** The final filter for an idea is whether or not you are passionate about the solution. I recall a number of on-demand laundry start-ups that had a market opportunity but whose founders realized, a few years into the journey, that they didn't really care about laundry. Just because you see a market need doesn't mean you're the one to solve it. If you're not willing to spend day and night, year after year, solving the problem, then you're likely to fall short or quit before you figure it out.

When turning an idea into an active venture, you must seek empathy with your customers and humility in your market. Don't let your passion drive you too far ahead of where your customer is. Empathy and humility act as powerful filters. The day you lose empathy is the day you lose.

Engage the right customers at the right time.

Contrary to logic, you don't want to attract all of your customers right away. You want your first cohort of willing customers to be quite small so that you can communicate directly and provide an incredibly high level of touch. At the start of your business, you want to iron out the kinks. As you expand, you want to do so slowly.

One common debate I have with teams at different stages of their journey is about their "ideal customer." There is never just one. The different customers you have at different stages of your business impact how your product evolves and how your team prioritizes. What makes a customer attractive throughout the life cycle of a company varies depending on the stage of your company and product.

Willing > Forgiving > Viral > Valuable > Profitable

As you roll out a new product, you should target different types of customers at different stages. At first you want customers who are more akin to testers, *willing* to try, and likely suffer through, the barely viable version of your product. Then you want customers who may not be testers, but are *forgiving* of the inevitable bugs and gaps in a new product. Once your creation is ready for prime time, your most valuable customers will be those who are *viral*—customers most likely to share their experience with everyone they know. As your business evolves, you'll want to optimize for customers who are **valuable** and ultimately **profitable**. Let's discuss each of these segments of customers in a bit more detail.

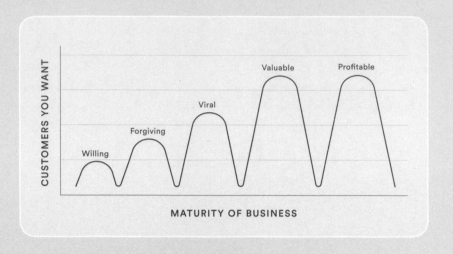

1. Willing Customers: Most willing to try your product, and try again.

In the very beginning, when you're either testing your product or launching it quietly, your challenge is to find customers who love new things and are willing to engage with your newly launched (or prelaunch) product. At this stage of your project, you will benefit most from customers who expect rough edges and are willing to share feedback, and continually give your product more tries as it evolves. In the early days of Behance, I recall certain members of our network who responded to every email and understood what we were trying to build well before it was actually built. I also remember when Periscope was in its early beta test time with a very small but hyper-engaged audience that would jump in whenever a user was live streaming. These willing—and oftentimes visionary—customers are the ones you want to engage first. You don't want too many, because you want to get to know them. These early customers get what you're doing and are willing to participate.

2. Forgiving Customers: Most forgiving of your minimum viable product.

After launch, you will begin marketing your product while it is still rough around the edges. At this point, the ideal customer may not be as visionary and willing to keep trying, but they are forgiving. They are technically capable enough to withstand bugs and mishaps. Most important, they value a better product lacking features more than a worse product with every feature. Rather than look for a perfect fit, they're able to tolerate missing features for some period of time. To engage forgiving customers, be transparent about your road map. Some new companies have an "open road map" or frequently updated blog where they share their lessons learned and progress in real time. One way to make sure your customers are forgiving is to show them that you're aware of what is missing and that you're working hard to improve your product.

3. Viral Customers: Most viral about your product.

Once you have a product-market fit, where your creation has found an audience that is reliably willing to pay or use it, you should do everything possible to spread word of your product far and wide. At this stage, you will benefit most from influential customers who are likely to tell others. These customers tend to not be forgiving because their reputation is at stake when they spread the word. In my experience, sustained, organic "viralness" happens only when a product is polished enough to elicit trust and love from customers who are busy. I encourage teams to engage viral customers only when they feel that their product is ready for it, as these customers may not give you a second chance.

4. Valuable Customers: Most valuable over their lifetime.

As your product matures beyond product-market fit and into a sustainable business, you'll want as many customers as you can handle. As you scale and focus on revenue, you will benefit most from loyal customers who spend increasing amounts of money and time on your products. Ranking customers by LTV (lifetime value) helps sales and customer service allocate resources. New product efforts are geared toward driving LTV, and the best customers are those with the highest LTV. You will need to add new features (while subtracting old ones) and consider offering better services to increase the value of customers over time. Many companies make the mistake of accommodating one type of customer at the expense of new customers. The challenge is to drive value from your loyal customers without alienating those who aren't valuable yet.

5. Profitable Customers: Most profitable over time.

Finally, for mature businesses, the drive is increasing profitability. You will prefer customers who require the least resources to attract and maintain over time. Customers who pay the most and demand the least will drive your profit margin, while earlier customers who may have required more costly hand-holding become less attractive. At this later stage, companies focus on driving value from existing customers more than engaging new customers, which opens up the door for new start-ups to compete and win over the "less profitable" customers whom large companies may ignore. It is wise in the short term, but it can backfire in the long term as new and less profitable customers may flock to a new and shiny competitor.

Reconsider the people you want to engage with your product or service in a granular way at different stages of your journey. My friend and former Adobe colleague Taylor Barada once said it best: "Product-market fit is a journey, not a destination." As your customers change and your product changes, you need to constantly question whom to focus on.

So much of building a business is about patience and pace. You want to build as fast as you can, but not before you interpret the data and gain empathy for the problem you wish to solve. You want to launch as soon as you can, but not before you have a product worth the cost of PR and marketing to spread. And you want all the users or customers you can find, but not before you're able to keep them.

Build your narrative before your product.

Every creation needs a narrative. The narrative is the story of what you're building in the context of why it matters. What inspired the idea? Why does it need to exist? What makes it relevant? How does it make the future better?

The narrative is how early team members and investors make sense of what you're building. The narrative helps you and your team take risks.

The problem is, many founders don't think about the narrative until they're ready to announce or sell their product. It is considered marketing. Crafting the narrative around the product at such an early stage feels, to these entrepreneurs, premature and a waste of time. Big companies are just as bad, often outsourcing the narrative to the marketing department or an external agency. The narrative is not a description of what your product is or does, it is the story of how and why it must exist.

For Behance, our narrative was about the plight of creative professionals around the world whose careers were under siege and too much at the mercy of circumstance. Designers and illustrators and countless other creatives didn't get proper credit for their work. Online "spec contests" had designers doing work for free. In some ways, technology was hurting rather than helping the careers of creative professionals. Our narrative was that technology needed to empower creative people to make ideas happen. By uploading their portfolios, creatives could get more exposure and attribution for their work, resulting in more job opportunities. We called it "creative meritocracy," the idea of creative people getting opportunity based on the quality of their work rather than what agency they worked with, where they went to school, or whom they happened to know.

In many ways, Behance was born out of a sense of frustration with the creative industry and our friends struggling to make a living. Our narrative acted as a compass for us, making it clearer which features we would develop (ones that boosted productivity and attribution) and which features we would not consider (ones that boosted creativity or marginalized attribution). Every product and marketing decision must fit the narrative.

Developing a brand early on, even before the product, helps develop a powerful values-driven narrative akin to the company having its own voice. You will find, when you're making certain decisions that impact the customer's experience of your product, the brand will speak to you. In the early days of Behance, we always felt like the brand was answering certain questions for us. It's probably not a coincidence that Matias, my cofounder, and I spent the first few months of the project building the brand identity for Behance—before we even began product development.

The narrative helps everyone involved—your team, your customers, and potential partners—graft onto your vision. I have seen a lot of other entrepreneurs obsess over things like the brand or logo well before a product vision has been defined. One great example is Garrett Camp, cofounder of Uber, founder of the start-up design studio Expa, and the former cofounder/CEO of StumbleUpon. While most entrepreneurs build their product before even thinking about brand until they're ready to launch, Garrett typically starts with the brand and domain name before anything related to product.

As Garrett explains it, "For all the focus on 'product-market fit' [when a product meets the needs of its users and grows on its own] and 'founder-product fit' [when you have the right founder to lead a particular product], people underestimate the importance of 'brand-product fit'—when you have the right name that can become synonymous with your product and can easily spread without friction." Garrett's first company, StumbleUpon, was four syllables, often misspelled by its users, and Garrett learned from the experience how much easier it is for a product to spread when you spend some time focused on the concept and brand first. Ever since, the companies he has cofounded, like Uber, Spot, and Mix, all started with a simple concept around discoverability and accessibility—and brands that were straightforward, memorable, and easy to associate with a new meaning.

When developing new products, Garrett develops a narrative, which includes the overall concept and brand, even before hiring a team. For the concept, Garrett focuses on something that was small and accessible only to some people—like using a private driver or accessing great restaurants—and then imagines what the world would look like if such experiences were discoverable and accessible to everyone. For Uber, the narrative of allowing anyone to summon (or be) a personal driver was the kernel that preceded even the first inkling of the product. The science fiction writer William Gibson is often credited with having said, "The future is here, it's just not evenly distributed yet," and I think this aptly describes Garrett's approach to weaving early concepts for new businesses—he looks for things that enrich the lives of small groups of people and imagines how to make such things accessible to the masses. With a concept that excites him, Garrett then begins obsessing over the brand and story.

"For a consumer brand that you want a lot of people to know about, you need something recognizable, easy to talk about and share, and feels accessible," Garrett explained. "While it's not essential up front, it's hard to change your name later, and having brand-product fit from the start gives you the confidence that, if you get the product right, you'll succeed rather than wonder why a great product isn't spreading." Garrett also notes the benefits of a great brand when it comes to recruiting a team. "If you're joining a company as head of sales, would you rather be scott@spot.com or scott@discoveraspot.com? The brand matters for the team identity as well, and too many people downplay its importance."

What makes us buy or use a product, beyond its utility? The ethos of a product, the reasoning for why it exists and who made it, and what it is called all give it a premium. When you know your narrative well, it changes not only what you build but also how you market it. Apple's famous "Designed by Apple in California" is an example of a small statement that brings the brand's narrative—a value for design and taking pride in being at the heart of innovation in California—to the product.

As you embark on your next project, consider developing your narrative and building your brand first. If you're already midstream, invest time in it. Doing so will answer questions and help you make better decisions along the way. The narrative should always be framed in the context of life itself. How does your product empower people? Does it help people save time or make them forget time? How does it take natural human tendencies into account, like the desire to look good or make better (and fewer) decisions? And most important, what about your creation will eventually be taken for granted? There's nothing more impressive than inventing what becomes obvious. The only way to create something that withstands the test of time and becomes a critical part of your customers' lives is to understand the broader narrative around your product.

The leaders of thriving communities (online and off-) act as stewards, not owners.

One of the greatest implications of the invention of the internet was the ability for networks to connect online and create a new form of utility—one that was more valuable than the sum of its parts and brought the utility of a large number of participants to your fingertips. Whether it was the new economy founded by eBay, the social network provided by Facebook, or the platform for building your career at LinkedIn, many companies built a business by building a network. Of course, every network is ultimately made possible by its participants. If every LinkedIn member or eBay participant deleted their profile tomorrow, these companies would have no business.

Behance, while smaller in scale than these internet behemoths, was no different. I always reminded our team that the fate of Behance and the businesses we ran out of it was ultimately in our members' hands. The millions of portfolios hosted on Behance didn't belong to us. Our job was to protect and enrich the network, but we didn't own it.

If you're building or hosting a community or network of any kind, you are a steward, not an owner. As businesses become more decentralized, whether through online networks, block-chains, or other methods that connect people, traditional approaches to building and leading communities need to be reimagined.

NETWORKS ARE SERVED, NOT LED.

If so much of the future of business depends on building networks, then we need to rethink the role of leaders in business. For instance, a strategy is less about accomplishing your team's objectives and more about better serving the needs of your network's participants. Whether your network's participants are trying to find their friends, get referrals for a service they need, or build their professional network, the decisions you make must make that easier for your clients, even if it makes it harder on you.

I like to equate serving a network to being in the hospitality business. When customers are in your restaurant or hotel, any iota of discomfort or unnecessary friction can cause them to turn around and walk out—nothing's stopping them, and they have plenty of choices. You can't tell your network what to do, and you can't prioritize your objectives and process over their experience. A community, especially a virtual one, resides where they are respected and their needs are served. You must listen and aim to serve your network's participants knowing that the loyalty and trust you earn will keep the network healthy and valuable for everyone involved, including you.

NETWORKS THRIVE ON TRANSPARENCY AND FAIRNESS.

Transparency in a business is helpful, but transparency in a network is vital. Every comment or like needs to be attributed to a person, and the algorithms at work in determining what we see or who we meet must be somewhat transparent in how it operates.

Many people love Tinder, the original swiping-dating app, precisely because it feels so random. Unlike eHarmony or Match.com, Tinder doesn't suggest potential matches, which means that regardless of your objective attractiveness, education, or wit, you can evaluate the same suitors as everyone else.

Or so we think.

Unbeknownst to most, anyone who's used Tinder is assigned an internal rating: a score calculated by the company that ranks the most (and least) desirable people using the service. These "desirability ratings" are secret, Austin Carr reports in *Fast Company*. Unlike on Uber, Airbnb, or TaskRabbit, no user can know their "Elo Score," as Tinder calls it, or how the algorithm determining this rating functions.

Former Tinder CEO Sean Rad confirmed the rating system to Carr, who was granted exclusive access to his own Elo Score. While Rad wouldn't reveal the algorithm's details, he said it's not solely determined by your profile picture: "It's not just how many people swipe right on you," Rad told Carr. "It's very complicated. It took us two and a half months just to build the algorithm because a lot of factors go into it."

To make matters more convoluted, Jonathan Badeen, Tinder's cofounder and now chief strategy officer, compared the algorithm to the video game *World of Warcraft*: "I used to play a long time ago, and whenever you play somebody with a really high score, you end up gaining more points than if you played someone with a lower score," he tells Carr. "It's a way of essentially matching people and ranking them more quickly and accurately based on who they are being matched up against."

While Carr says he has "regretted learning [his Elo Score] ever since," he couldn't resist the temptation: "The team did a drum roll, and for a brief second I thought by a fluke I'd turn out to be the No. 1 ranked Tinder user," he writes, sardonically. His score was 946, which, as a Tinder data engineer explains, is on the "upper end of average." "It's a vague number to process," writes Carr, "but I knew I didn't like hearing it. Something about 'upper end of average' didn't exactly do wonders for my ego."

As damaging as knowing one's Elo Score may be, it's worth contemplating whether or not you want to know that Tinder—an app millions rely on to find hookups, love, and everything in between—is filtering your potential matches based on measures you'll never understand.

When the inner workings of a network are opaque, participants become more careful. The network's potential becomes limited as they exercise restraint. You shouldn't overwhelm your users with information or make the experience confusing, but building some degree of transparency into the experience engenders trust. The test is whether your participants can figure out why they see something in their feed or how something happened if they wanted to. There must be a path to transparency and understanding to maintain trust. Similarly, when conflicts arise in a network, such as two participants fighting about something, the process of resolving the conflict must be transparent and fair. At Behance, whenever we had two members fighting about an alleged copyright violation or some sort of inappropriate behavior, our community management team tried to engage both participants publicly and chose transparency over serving as an invisible judge and jury.

LEADERS IN NETWORKS EMERGE ORGANICALLY.

You don't appoint leaders in a network. Instead, influence is often determined through community curation. As such, network managers must optimize for forces that drive healthy meritocracy every chance they get to improve network quality and utility. Business management guru Jim Collins once suggested, "You can't really manage a network, but you can help lead within a network." I'd advance this thought further and suggest that you can't even lead within a network, but you can be an effective steward by being increasingly hospitable to your participants. By building features and upholding standards of transparency and fairness, you can help surface quality and opportunity in a network without exerting any degree of influence that would compromise trust.

Natural leaders in a network are those who take the time to report spam, edit entries (like the thousands who do so voluntarily every day on Wikipedia), welcome new users (like active users on certain Reddit channels or the thousands of interest-driven communities powered by online network host Amino), and make an effort to improve the common experience. These leaders gain influence not by being designated leaders, but by gaining the respect and gratitude of their fellow participants.

If you're building a network, be humbled by the fact that you're not in control and that the community doesn't belong to you. Serve your network, promote transparency and meritocracy however you can, and then engage as a proud and committed steward.

Hit the streets, there is no better way.

Toward the end of my second year in business school, just a month or so before graduation, one of my professors summarized all that we had been exposed to in the curriculum—finance, marketing, operations, management, ethics—but noted one essential discipline that was conspicuously missing: sales. The school hadn't figured out how to teach sales, he explained. But it was important nonetheless. Among the business-school crowd, "sales" carried a stigma. The stereotype of "salespeople" was not flattering: always schmoozing clients, focused on a quota, and fending for themselves. Nobody wants to be "sold to," and thus many people avoid being described as a salesperson.

But as a creator of anything new, you're always selling. When you seek feedback or mentorship, you're selling your predicament to those you wish to engage. As you build your team, you're selling your mission. To retain your team, you're selling the notion of progress. If you raise funds, you're selling to investors. And you're always selling to clients and customers, even after they already love you.

It is both ironic and telling that the oft-scorned discipline of sales—the one skill that Harvard Business School doesn't teach—is the most important. We get too cerebral about our business ideas and forget that, when it comes down to it, business is all about relationships between people. Without sharing and persuading, you've got nothing.

An effective creator needs to be a good salesperson—but I don't necessarily mean that in the traditional sense. When it comes down to it, what is sales? If you're not standing in a city square hawking your products to people or cold-calling potential clients from the phone book, what does that mean in the modern business vernacular?

Being a good salesperson means meeting others where they are rather than waiting for them to come to you. It is hitting the streets in every respect, pushing yourself to share your ideas, discussing your progress and inviting questions, meeting people in different fields, and talking to anyone who will listen. You want to understand everyone's problem—the hopes, struggles, and fears of your customers, employees, investors, industry journalists—and you want to connect with everyone you can. At its best, sales is genuine empathy and connection.

It is seductive to sit behind a computer screen and find every way and reason to grow your business without meeting people and being vulnerable, but nothing beats having the hit-the-streets mentality to make it happen. If you're an introvert like me, you'll need to constantly challenge yourself to get outside of your cocoon of productivity and engage with the people around you. What are they working on? What keeps them up at night? How can you help them? Don't write anyone off. A great salesperson or journalist knows that everyone has a story, and every story has a lesson. Every interaction could lead to another if you make it so. When you meet people and determine that they are not worth your time, find something to learn. Whether it is something that reinforces your beliefs or inspires you, something in their story will surprise you.

Push yourself to go door-to-door, in whatever way that applies to you. Spend time sitting next to your customers to better understand their jobs or lives. Push yourself to ask more questions and spend more time building relationships. Connect with people you meet by looking for something to learn. By doing so, you'll feel the granularity of your business, unearth invaluable realizations, and earn new customers, all the while building the relationships that make your creations more viable and sustainable.

Best to market > First to market

Being the first to launch a product and reveal a new solution to an old problem is a thrilling prospect. But over time, being the best in your market exceeds the benefits of being first.

I experienced this firsthand watching several teams developing mobile applications for user-generated live video, and working with Kayvon Beykpour and his company's cofounder, Joe Bernstein, in particular.

Kayvon, Joe, and their team brilliantly designed their product, Periscope, to give users the sensation of "teleporting" somewhere and being able to interact with the broadcaster in real time.

From early on, it was clear that Periscope was onto something special. There were rumblings of a few other live-streaming apps under development, but in the meantime, the private prelaunch testing of the app was performing extremely well: More than half of the one thousand prelaunch users were using the app every day.

The Periscope team and their advisers were not the only people to notice the early traction. We noticed a few familiar names like Jack Dorsey, Twitter's cofounder, and Dick Costello, Twitter's CEO at the time, join the beta test and actively begin using the product. Soon enough, Twitter reached out to learn more about Periscope and ultimately proposed acquiring the company before it launched publicly.

Aside from the difficult decision that Kayvon and Joe had to make regarding their fate with Twitter, there was also the question of whether one of the other similar live-streaming apps under development by competitors would launch before Periscope. There is a reasonable desire among all entrepreneurs to introduce their creation as the first of its kind. Everyone wants to be first—but should they be?

We knew the product was working, and given how carefully and thoughtfully it was designed, we were confident that Periscope, when ready, would be better than its competition. But it was hard to imagine other competitive apps launching first, even if they were inferior. Was it better to be first to market, potentially risking a clean integration with Twitter, or launch a bit later with a far superior product?

Kayvon and Joe ultimately decided to do the Twitter deal and took an additional month or so to make a few enhancements and Twitter integrations before launch. A month or so before Periscope's launch, a similar live-streaming app called "Meerkat" launched publicly. The app received lots of fanfare for being the first of its kind, but it was bare bones and appeared rushed. When Periscope was launched a month or so later, it engaged and retained users on a whole other level. The Twitter integration was a big part of its success, but the carefully conceived features of Periscope became iconic differentiators from its pack of competitors. (Meerkat shut down about a year later, and their team went on to build House Party, a live-video application for groups that has thrived since its launch.)

A cool new product can be an indication of the next big thing—but it isn't always the next big thing itself. You're running a race to be the very first team to get it right, not the first to cross the finish line.

One tactic is to "soft launch" your product prior to announcing it by making it available publicly or by invitation only. Unless you are a large company like Apple under tremendous scrutiny, what you gain in real feedback from customers and the time to improve your product greatly outweighs the cost of forgoing a true "press-worthy" moment of unveiling.

"But what about press?" early-stage teams often worry. "Isn't it important to launch publicly to get the spotlight from day one?" News is relative to when it is announced, not when it happened. Unless you are a celebrity or serial entrepreneur closely followed, nobody cares about your product until you start telling the story. The belief that you should get all the press you can at the moment your product goes live is flawed. What you'll lose in buzz will be gained with a better product and refined pitch.

And you'll want all the extra time you can get. Your product is at its worst when it first launches. Most kinks, software bugs, and overlooked parts of a product tend to reveal themselves quickly in the real world. By launching quietly at first, you can apply the right amount of polish and then solicit press for the "launch" of your product when it's first working smoothly, not when it is first available.

So much money is wasted promoting products before they are ready. In the early days of a business, the best story is about the founders and comes from the founders themselves, not expensive PR firms.

Most journalists I know prefer talking to passionate founders rather than people whose job is to get press. PR is very helpful when a company needs to explain itself. Otherwise, it just gets in the way, especially for early-stage teams. The best press comes when you're ready for customers to judge your product, and tells the story of how your product came about.

As you bring your product to market, don't prioritize launching first and don't obsess over an initial bout of press. The improvements you make after you launch will be more time sensitive than the ones you make beforehand. Don't be "the rabbit," the person who runs as fast as they can at the beginning of a marathon, exerts all of their energy, and then falls behind by mile six. You'll feel eager to be first and get the spotlight for being new, but over time, being the best in your market exceeds the benefits of being first.

Identify and prioritize efforts with disproportionate impact.

While you'll want to make every part of your product better, there is always a specific area of your product that needs your team's energy the most. It may be a feature that has a disproportionate impact on your customer's experience, or a potential single point of failure that could kill the whole product. When prioritizing tasks, focus your team on levers that have a disproportionate impact on your odds of surviving and succeeding.

There are many ways to analyze the opportunity costs of prioritizing certain aspects of product over others. Jeffrey Kalmikoff, who has led product design for teams at Threadless, Digg, and Uber among others in his career, recalled the challenges of leading product development at a geo-location start-up, SimpleGeo, in 2010. With an overburdened development team in a rapidly evolving market, there weren't enough hours in a day for Jeffrey and his team to possibly complete the feature requests and product enhancements they faced. Some ideas were near-term opportunities to generate revenue while others were more strategic. And, of course, some of these ideas were deeply complex and would require multiple developers and weeks of development time, while others were simple cosmetic changes that could be made in a matter of hours.

Jeffrey faced the challenge of prioritizing the team's efforts to make the greatest impact on the business. Easy to say, difficult to do. While everyone in the company shared the same general goal of improving the product, everyone had different preferences: The business managers advocated for some things like new pricing options and marketing pages; the developers, for other things like refactoring code; and the community of early users had an entirely different set of preferences and requests for new features.

To help Jeffrey choose where to focus his energy, he ran an exercise. Jeffrey, who helped lead product and design, asked the CEO and sales folk to review the list of projects and feature requests and assign a level of priority from a revenue and strategy standpoint. The business team looked at each item and assigned a 3 for very important tasks that would make a huge impact on strategy and revenue, a 2 for something with less significance, and a 1 for something inconsequential. Oftentimes, a major feature or design change might get a 1 from this group because, while important for the product, it was not necessarily tied to revenue and overall strategy.

Jeffrey then posed the same list of features and projects to his development and design teams. Once again, he asked them to assign a ranking from 1 to 3 for everything on the list. For this group, he requested that a 1 be assigned to every item that could be done quickly by a small group of people, a 2 for items in the middle that demanded more than a few days but less than a few weeks, and a 3 would be reserved for items that would take significant time and labor to complete, three weeks and up.

With both columns filled out for all features and projects, Jeffrey scanned the list for 3/1s— the items that were both hugely important from a business perspective and easy for the design team to implement. The 3/1s would be immediately prioritized because they were specific items that would require only minimum effort for a huge impact. In most cases, 1/3s would get placed at the bottom of the list, as they would take the most people power for the least revenue output. Others would fall somewhere in the middle.

Other teams I have worked with use the "boulders and pebbles" analogy we discussed earlier to describe equally important items that require vastly different amounts of energy to complete. If you focus only on boulders—the 3/3s—that are both important and costly, you'll never complete the pebbles—the 3/1s—that are just as important but much cheaper to complete. You can't prioritize solely on importance or effort required. You must prioritize across both vectors. Our obsession with avoiding minutiae in favor of large scalable solutions obstructs simple and logical tactics to improve our products.

Measure each feature by its own measure.

While all aspects of your product or service should be evaluated, the measures you use will vary. For example, most features are measured by how often they are used. If a part of your product gets no use, perhaps it needs to be improved, better marketed, or altogether removed. Other features in a product, like a car's "tow mode" that neutralizes the gears, are not intended to be used by the customer on an ongoing basis—they just need to be discoverable and effective when employed. And some features are just intended to initially attract customers to the product but then drop off over time, like a rocket's spent boosters.

If you simply measure all features by the time spent using them, you're liable to miss the more nuanced lessons you can learn from how people interact with your product.

Product development is typically driven by customer needs and nearly all features of a product are what I've come to call *engagement drivers*, intended to drive customer engagement of some kind. Such features can be measured by how often they are used or, when needed, how well they perform (and thus keep customers engaged using your products). The classic approach of marketing a product's engagement drivers—such as a fun new way to customize your photos or better communicate with your team—wrongly assumes that customers get most excited about the features they are most likely to use. On the contrary, the features that excite us most about a new product are often the most novel features that aren't necessarily practical. I call these features *interest drivers* because their intention is not to spur ongoing product engagement or even be actively used, but rather to pique interest.

I've seen this phenomenon when marketing cool new features in creative applications that customers are wowed by online but seldom ever use. I have also experienced them as a consumer. When HBO first launched their critically acclaimed TV series *Game of Thrones*, they launched an enhanced viewing experience for the series in their iPad app, HBO GO. The enhanced version, which included a detailed map of the fictional geography among other features, was a reason for customers to watch the show using the app instead of their TV or laptop screens—and for HBO to develop a more direct relationship with their viewers. It was a great interest driver. But as far as I can tell, very few customers ever used the enhanced-viewing capabilities. It was a smart way to drive users to the app, but few people on social media or in reviews of the app ever reported using them. These interactive features were extremely innovative and compelling but hardly used in practice. Were these features a failure? It depends on whether you're measuring them as an engagement driver or an interest driver. This feature may have failed in engaging users on an ongoing basis but may have been wildly successful in getting customers to download the HBO GO app in the first place. Interestingly enough, after a couple seasons of the show these enhanced-viewing features were removed from the app altogether. They either served their purpose or were being improperly measured.

I've witnessed the importance of interest drivers when Adobe launches new versions of products like Photoshop, Illustrator, and Lightroom. Despite most customers using only a fraction of the products' capabilities on a day-to-day basis, there is always tremendous fanfare around new and novel features such as "perspective warp," where you can alter the perspective of a particular building or scene in an image. While the data suggests that some of these buzz-worthy features are not widely used after launch, they play an important role in advancing the field and getting customers excited about new releases. The true engagement drivers for every new version, whose importance can be measured in traditional ways, are the things that just make the product faster and easier to use on an everyday basis. But incremental improvements aren't sexy and don't make headlines, and prospective customers need reasons to get excited. When you're launching new features, you need both interest and engagement drivers working in tandem.

As you measure your product's success, determine what every feature is intended to achieve and measure it accordingly. As you observe how customers use your product, you may be tempted to remove interest drivers, like HBO GO's *Game of Thrones* integrations or a cool Photoshop feature, when you notice that they aren't being used as much as you'd hope. But be sure to define the purpose of every feature in your product before determining its fate. Is it to strengthen engagement, appease a very small set of important customers, or get new customers in the door? Features with a different purpose require a different measure.

Mystery is the magic of engagement.

When I review marketing materials for new teams, I am struck by their struggle to be clear while also preserving some degree of intrigue. While simplicity and explicitness are crucial, so are the more mysterious forces that attract and engage people.

Curiosity is one of the most effective hooks to pull in prospective customers. It's a paradox because when you launch a new company, you have no demand. Logic would suggest that you tell your story and show as much of your product as possible to engage potential customers; if you don't have much to share yet anyway, you might as well share what you've got! But logic doesn't pierce indifference. Your prospective customers are unlikely to send any attention your way unless something catches their eye.

Any great advertising mind will tell you that a great narrative about your product or service is not a tell-all: It must be short and, more important, it must tap into the natural human tendency to want to learn and understand something that is not fully revealed or infinitely available.

"I have no special talents," Einstein once declared. "I am only passionately curious." This statement probably annoys a lot of evolutionary psychologists. Why? Because scientists still don't really know why we humans are so curious.

Evolutionarily, curiosity seems paradoxical because it runs counter to classical theories of decision making. People chose to do something in order to fulfill a goal. Plus, this inquisitive drive for information makes us utterly unproductive, whether it's scanning Facebook, falling for BuzzFeed clickbait, or in the caveman days, hitting rocks with sticks to see what happens. If evolution is associated with survival of the fittest, it's curious why we evolved to waste so much time.

The leading psychological theory on curiosity, known as the "information-gap" theory, was presented by George Loewenstein of Carnegie Mellon in the mid-1990s. Loewenstein says that curiosity proceeds in two basic steps: First, a situation reveals a painful gap in our knowledge (like a BuzzFeed headline), and then we feel an urge to fill this gap and ease that pain (we click on it), explains journalist Eric Jaffe in *Fast Company*'s Co. Design.

"Such information gaps produce the feeling of deprivation labeled curiosity," writes Loewenstein in the journal *Psychological Bulletin*. "The curious individual is motivated to obtain the missing information to reduce or eliminate the feeling of deprivation." What's more, many psychologists argue that this drive to collect more information enables us to make better, more informed decisions—which, in turn, keeps us safe and thriving.

Per Loewenstein's theory, curiosity isn't much different from other primal desires like hunger or sex drive. "Its onset, like hunger or sex drive, is acutely aversive. Its relief, like eating or copulating, is deeply satisfying (well, sometimes)," Jaffe writes. This theory also posits that we should be most curious when we know what we don't know (those who are too wise are less curious). Loewenstein outlines five curiosity triggers that alert people to information gaps. They consist of questions or riddles, unknown resolutions, violated expectations, access to information known by others, and reminders of something forgotten. The best advertisements, and most-clicked headlines, play on most if not all of these triggers.

More recent neural studies on curiosity support Loewenstein's information-gap theory. In one experiment from professor of behavioral economics Colin Camerer's Caltech lab, "test participants had their brains scanned while they read a trivia question, guessed at the answer, and then saw it revealed," Jaffe reports. "The research team (working with Loewenstein) found that curiosity activated the neural circuitry that's connected with rewards (including the left caudate region)."

This finding is particularly interesting, because the caudate region of our brain sits at the intersection of new knowledge and positive emotions; previous studies have shown it is activated by learning and seeking answers, and it has been closely linked to various parts of the dopamine reward pathway. "The lesson is that our desire for abstract information—this is the cause of curiosity—begins as a dopaminergic craving, rooted in the same primal pathway that also responds to sex, drugs and rock and roll," writes Jonah Lehrer in *Wired* about the same Caltech study.

"The [Caltech] researchers also found evidence for what they call 'inverted-U' behavior," Eric Jaffe writes. "That's the tendency of curiosity to be greatest at some mid-point between ignorance and wisdom—the peak of the inverted U." As the researchers concluded in a 2008 issue of the journal *Psychological Science*, "The fact that curiosity increases with uncertainty (up to a point) suggests that a small amount of knowledge can pique curiosity and prime the hunger for knowledge, much as an olfactory or visual stimulus can prime a hunger for food."

The best advertisers trigger this "inverted-U" behavior, rewarding the viewer by revealing their product just after peak curiosity. Remember the 2017 Super Bowl advertisement about immigration, featuring lumber workers building a door in President Trump's border wall to let an immigrant family from Mexico pass through? "The Journey" was regarded as the best Super Bowl ad because the provocative, emotional story left viewers hanging: Only after the family triumphantly crosses the border do we learn the ad is promoting 84 Lumber.

Evolution made us tickled by learning, and even more obsessed with the reward of knowledge.

When struck by a provocative question or surprising image, we pause our routines and suspend our cynicism and assumptions. We take a moment to unpack what we see and fill the gaps in our mind. We become engaged out of sheer wonder.

Unanswered questions drive intrigue—even if you weren't interested in the answer in the first place. Whenever there's a curtain in front of you, you want to know what's behind it, simply because of the fact that there is a curtain. When you launch a new product or service, presenting unanswered questions may be a more effective means of engaging prospective customers than explicitly explaining your product, which leaves customers with no questions at all.

Movies achieve this level of intrigue with trailers, showing us a glimpse of great characters and scenes without context and leaving us wondering what happened in between. For companies like Elon Musk's electric-car empire Tesla, a sense of mystery has been achieved with features like "ludicrous speed," which has drawn customers in without much explanation as to how it is turned on, never mind what it means.

Perhaps the most famous corporate purveyor of mystery is Apple, whose penchant for secrecy around new products and carefully curated publicity causes millions of people to tune in live to huge product-reveal events to learn about the next iPhone's features. Having worked with Apple's marketing and keynote production teams quite a bit during my tenure leading mobile products at Adobe, I was struck by how carefully Apple decided what to reveal and when. Even after a product's announcement, the reveal of every edge, angle, and aspect was intentional and restrained. As my friend, entrepreneur, and early Apple product designer Dave Morin once told me, "Mystery makes history." When you leave something behind the curtain, people are more desperate to see the full picture.

Ambiguous intrigue has a way of garnering interest better than any product description or list of features ever will. I call this force the "magic" of engagement. It's an illusion, concocted to enchant your prospective audience and break through their rational selves.

Resist the urge to play to the middle.

I've always taken issue with the idea of a company "following their customer," as if a brand and service should constantly adjust to the client or customer's evolving set of preferences: As the needs of a cohort of customers change, it doesn't always mean that you should change with it. Some things should evolve, while others shouldn't.

I've watched this frenetic tendency to follow client needs play out many times in the world of creative agencies, and it seldom ends well. Many great agencies get off to a blazing start by having a strong sense of self. They know the specific type of clients they want to serve and the kinds of services they do—and don't—provide. They build a crack team and deliver an exceptional service to clients. But then something happens. Their best clients ask for different services, and new clients come in seeking services that differ from their core offering. To capture more value from their clients and capitalize on the opportunity to grow, the agency expands their offering. But as their list of services grows, they become generalists and less specialized; their brand stretches to appeal to a broader set of customers, and they lose the edge they are known for. Eventually, they start losing pitches to agencies that are more focused and differentiated and losing clients who feel their coverage is too generic to the new kids on the block. And the cycle begins again.

One creative firm that I have worked closely with and has consistently defied this outcome is Pentagram, the world's largest private design consultancy. Over their many years in business, they have been the creative brains behind the iconic branding for companies like the *New York Times* and Mastercard and Hillary Clinton's 2016 presidential campaign logo, among many others. But despite the opportunity to increase their service list, they've kept it narrow: They seek to design iconic brands and the strategies behind them. They don't offer in-house social media support or influencer management programs. They have not acquired dozens of other smaller agencies to expand their offerings. While the rest of their industry has played to the middle, widening their scope of focus to become one-stop shops, Pentagram has stayed firmly at one edge of the spectrum and is universally known for their specialty as a result.

Benchmark, the venture capital firm I work with as a Venture Partner, embodies a similar discipline. While most firms have expanded their offerings to include conferences, recruiting teams, marketing and public-relations services, and in-house services, Benchmark has opted to stay small and focused. The firm still doesn't hire any associates, and past experiments with a larger fund and a larger group of partners were rolled back. When meeting with entrepreneurs who would like us to invest in them, the partners use the firm's lack of services across the spectrum as evidence for Benchmark's focus on what matters most: the relationship between the investing partner and the entrepreneur. The services an entrepreneur would want from their investor are performed by the actual partner, not other groups of more junior people. As most other venture capital firms have grown and evolved to offer additional services in this highly competitive market, Benchmark's focused offering has become even more differentiating.

Of course, industries change, and leaders must consider when a specialization is no longer an advantage. For example, many of the best hardware companies have needed to become software companies, and some industries have been transformed by new companies that are different from their peers, like Sonos, which competed with other traditional speaker manufacturers by coupling great software with their product. When your competitive landscape changes and your differentiating factor stops being a strength, bold moves are required. Choosing to not evolve either differentiates you or kills you depending on the context. Principles must be consistently evaluated, but don't let the urge to stay competitive compromise the principles that made you competitive.

The greatest brands were developed by playing at the far end of the spectrum and not trying to be everything to everyone. Playing to the middle makes you weak. You'll never be an industry leader if you give up your edge to appeal to a broader audience. As you manage your brand and contemplate your own evolution, hold on to what makes you distinctive. Don't compromise your specialty just to please your market—because if you do, it might not be there much longer.

OPTIMIZING YOURSELF

While we've talked about endlessly optimizing your team and your product, we have yet to discuss the parallel journey and opportunity to optimize your own decisions, planning, and instincts. Just as your team's structure, systems, and product must always be improved, the same goes for your own capacity to lead and make difficult decisions. This section aims to take what you're personally doing that's working and double down to achieve even more.

PLANNING AND MAKING DECISIONS

Make a plan but don't plan on sticking to it.

"In preparing for battle, I have always found that plans are useless, but planning is indispensable."

So said Dwight D. Eisenhower, and his words ring true today in how we approach all kinds of bold ventures. Planning pauses our everyday actions in the trenches and prompts us to take stock of where we are and where we are headed. Even if the plan we make has little resemblance to what ends up happening, the act of planning tunes our judgment.

It's easy to retroactively edit your version of the original plan when reflecting on your journey. I'm certainly guilty of this. I recall one day in late 2012, right after Behance was acquired by Adobe, when Dave Stein, our very first engineer, found a picture of an old 2007 strategy document for Behance. This one-page document from five years earlier outlined all the things we planned to do and (gulp) the time frame in which we would accomplish our goals. He came into my office with it, laughing. Wow, were we off. While our mission to "organize and empower the creative world" had not changed, the initiatives we were planning, the order of operations, and the timing were all, indeed, laughable.

I tried to remember what I was thinking five years ago. I was ambitious and passionate, but completely naive about a few things: how much the feedback we'd get would change our priorities; how much our vision would narrow as our business grew; and the effort required to execute any of these ideas. Nevertheless, the plan served us at the time. If nothing more, it helped us recruit new people and get aligned around a potential future. But every time everything changed, we made a new plan. Priorities change, and the best leaders change with them.

You need to be confident to be willing to change your plan. Being willing to change your mind means you are still permeable and willing to learn. I believe the same to be true in marriage and other relationships: You either change together or grow apart. Trying to maintain what worked in a previous reality will never suffice.

Business plans are a standard part of building a new venture, but they should be approached as a thought process, not a map. Adaptability and instincts make all the difference. You make progress by planning, but you succeed by deviating.

Success fails to scale when we fail to focus.

As your projects succeed and you become known for your work, you'll encounter more opportunities and will face the burden of choice. Successful entrepreneurs and artists attract partnership inquiries, respected leaders are offered new roles and board positions, well-known investors receive a deluge of pitches and invitations to join organizations, and successful authors are asked to speak and write more books. Whether you're choosing when to say yes or no, or selecting from a set of options, your success stops scaling when you can't say no or make a choice.

THE ART OF DECLINING

Over the years that I have known him, Tim Ferriss, a bestselling author, podcaster, and seed investor, has always had a strong compass and discipline when it comes to evaluating opportunities and making the right choices. While I often feel frenetic and pulled from all angles, Tim has no problem saying no. When he's writing a book, he sets an out-of-office email response informing people that he's in "monk mode" and is unlikely to reply. He turns down many paid speaking gigs swiftly, passes on most introductions and inquiries, and seems at peace with it all. So I asked him about how he navigates opportunities.

In his earlier days as a lesser-known author, when there weren't as many opportunities to decline, Tim had a simple litmus test for the commitments he made: Was it something that could be "a first" or a "category killer"? He wanted to hold out for projects that could really redefine a category rather than keep him in a competitive space.

Five or so years later, after publishing his next bestseller *The Four Hour Body*, Tim decided that he needed to become a better manager of his time and, as he explains it, "shifted to what Scott Adams, the creator of Dilbert, calls Systems Thinking: choosing your projects based on the skills and relationships you will develop."

Tim goes on to explain, "This is important because the skills and relationships you develop persist beyond the failure of any single isolated project, so they are cumulative. The snowball of assets in the form of relationships and skills accumulates and presents you with multiple opportunities to take advantage of these skill sets and people with whom you have developed relationships. That is how my podcast started, that is how I choose my investments now in the start-up world after seventy-plus investments . . . I now look at nearly everything through the lens of a question: 'Will I develop relationships and skills that will persist beyond this project and help me even if this project fails?' That is really the hurdle for me saying yes to new options and opportunities."

While I tend to focus on the opportunity cost of saying no to something, Tim simply declines everything that doesn't lead to new skills and relationships that he deems valuable. But what about people you already have a relationship with? It's easy to decline a stranger but much harder when your network grows and you're inundated with asks.

"For friends, if I become close to them, they are almost by definition at this point not people who take things incredibly personally, so I don't owe them much of an explanation," Tim explained. "If they make an offer or an ask that I cannot comply with without sacrificing a lot on my side, then I will simply say, 'Sorry, so-and-so, I'd love to do this but I'm just out of bandwidth. I'll cheer from the sidelines, but I'll have to be a polite pass for now. I hope we can do something when the dust settles on my side.' Something like that. It doesn't have to be a lot. It can just be, 'Hey, man. Wish I could do it. I just can't right now. Too much on my plate. Let's talk soon. Hope you're awesome. Tim.' If that doesn't suffice, if they require a lot of coddling, and a lot of reassurance and they get upset and it causes strife in our relationship then that disqualifies them as a true friend to start with.

"In the case of friends, I will often ask, if someone asks me to do something, 'Zero to ten, how much are you asking me to do this? Because if it's a ten and you need me to do this, I will do it, but I have very little bandwidth right now so let me know. If it's really, really important to you, I will do my best to help and move things around, but if not, I'll pass.' True friends, nine times out of ten, will give you a pass. Then when they need your help, they need your help, and that's totally fine. What goes around comes around for sure."

Like Tim, we should all make a few bold bets early in our career to do something first and redefine a category. But throughout our careers, we should challenge ourselves to say yes only to things that bring our skills and network to a new level. Our natural drive to say yes to as much as possible, if only for optionality, may help us in the beginning of our careers but hurts us later on.

THE ART OF CHOOSING

So much of productivity and decision making comes down to how we manage options. One of the world's greatest experts in decision making is American psychologist Barry Schwartz. In his revered 2004 book *The Paradox of Choice: Why More Is Less*, Schwartz details how considering more options often makes us less satisfied with the eventual decision we make, not more certain in it. For example, throughout the book he uses the example of shopping for a new pair of jeans. Instead of simply walking into a store and picking up something with a 32-inch waistband, we are now given a multitude of options: dark or light denim, frayed or clean, high waisted or low slung, tight or loose, boot legged or skinny? As a result, we're often less satisfied with the choice we eventually make; we're always wondering if there's a pair that would have fit us better or a color that we didn't spot at the back of the racks.

Schwartz divides people into the two groups of decision makers we learned about earlier: maximizers and satisficers (terms we discussed earlier that were originally coined by economist Herbert Simon in 1956). "Maximizers need to be assured that every purchase or decision was the best that could be made," Schwartz says. "As a decision strategy, maximizing creates a daunting task, which becomes all the more daunting as the number of options increases." A maximizer is the type of person who will spend an entire day schlepping around from shop to shop, searching for the best option for the best price, whereas satisficers "settle for something that is good enough and do not worry about the possibility that there might be something better," he says. "She searches until she finds an item that meets those standards, and at that point, she stops." Maximizers may feel like they have reached the right decision—but the satisficers often do so much quicker and end up being happier with the choices they've made.

In order not to be paralyzed by the decisions we have to make, we should often make up our minds quickly instead of surveying every option and weighing them one by one. In the introduction to his book on trusting your instincts, *Gut Feelings*, psychologist Gerd Gigerenzer refutes the latter commonsense model of decision making: "For decades, books on rational decision-making, as well as consulting firms, have preached 'look before you leap' and 'analyze before you act.' Pay attention. Be reflective, deliberate, and analytic. Survey all alternatives, list all pros and cons, and carefully weigh their utilities by their probabilities, preferably with the aid of a fancy statistical software package. Yet this scheme does not describe how actual people—including the authors of these books—reason."

Instead of weighing all options and seeking more before making a decision, sometimes it's best to go with the option that feels most right at first. Otherwise you'll waste time and energy searching for more options that may be only mildly more beneficial (or worse) than the one you started with, and you'll be left second-guessing yourself rather than building conviction.

At some point in every career, lack of opportunity and options stops being the problem. Instead, you're faced with a new challenge: when and how to say "no" and how many options and choices you really need to make a great decision. Most people fail to understand that their past success was likely the result of a more singular focus with fewer options. If you hope to scale your success further, you must choose more wisely and decline more opportunities.

Don't optimize for the best deal now at the expense of long-term outcome.

Negotiation plays a role in every project and is a critical skill for a leader to master. Whether you are hiring a team, agreeing to terms with a client, or ironing out a deal with a vendor, how you negotiate sets the tone for the relationship. Of course you want a good deal—everyone does. But you must also optimize for a relationship that sets you up to succeed in the long term. And sometimes that means taking a hit, right at the start.

Some people take the aggressive approach, asking for more or offering less than they think is fair. Their strategy is to purposefully exceed the boundaries of fairness with the understanding that the opposite party will push you a few steps back. However, by doing so, you're setting a precedent for a tug-of-war; there will always be an expectation that initial offers and claims are not to be trusted. Aggressive negotiations might get you more money in the initial paycheck, but they run the risk of setting a hostile and mistrusting tone for the relationship going forward.

For one-off negotiations, like buying a piece of real estate, the aggressive "ask for more than you deserve" strategy may be the right one. But when it comes to negotiations that spawn long-term relationships, you need to create the best possible foundation and seek out a mutually beneficial outcome. The degree of trust, respect, and loyalty that comes from such negotiations matters more than whatever extra value you can extract from being manipulative. You can evaluate the effectiveness of your negotiation by asking yourself questions like "Did the process increase trust and respect between parties or reduce it?" "Did the negotiation serve to further align interests, or did it create a chasm between them?" and "Did both parties leave something on the table in confidence that doing so will enhance the longer-term outcome?" How you measure the success of your negotiations will impact the decisions you make throughout the process.

When negotiating a deal, I've always aspired to be fair. It's simple: I have a discussion up front with my counterpart in which I make the case that, philosophically, I am interested in an outcome that sets us up to succeed, and I therefore want to reach the fairest deal for both parties. I explain that I want to avoid any possibility of regret on either side, and to build a relationship we both need to believe the deal was fair and that nobody was taken advantage of. Then, in preparing to make my offer, I put myself in my counterparty's shoes to determine what they should fairly expect (and deserve). I do the same thing for myself. And then I lay it out and explain my process in coming to what I believe is a fair figure alongside it. Using this method, you will ultimately arrive at a number that should be backed up with a transparent analysis that you're willing to share.

So next time you enter a negotiation, think beyond the number. Remember that the end of a negotiation is the start of a relationship—one with the potential to create a tremendous value beyond whatever is invoiced.

Don't underestimate the criticality of timing.

With so much focus on trends, new technologies, data, and human tendencies, we often forget to factor in timing. Perhaps, because timing is out of our control, we talk about it less. But the outcome of our work is determined just as much by timing as it is by other variables, so it's worthy to consider more thoughtfully.

THE RIGHT LEADER FOR THE RIGHT TIME

Hiring managers tend to focus on the fit of a particular leader in a company without factoring in timing. Companies have a unique set of needs and opportunities for different phases: Sometimes you need leaders who will drive product innovation, other times you need leaders who will masterfully sustain incremental growth. Sometimes you need a finance-oriented CEO who brings margins and expenses in line and transforms the business model, other times you need a vision- and product-minded CEO who will create a new narrative and reposition the product for entirely new purposes. Sometimes a product needs a "flag planter," and sometimes it needs a "road builder," as Shantanu Narayan, Adobe's CEO, once put it. In my experience, these leaders are rarely the same people. Like dating, a great match is as much about timing as it is about capabilities and shared values.

To lead an industry, companies require different leaders (or different leadership styles) at different times. Which is hard to do because the default of most companies is to cling to a playbook that has already proved successful. Every playbook gets old, and the more successful it is, the harder it is to deviate—especially for the leader (often the company's founder) who wrote it. When I help companies recruit an executive, or hear about a CEO transition, I try to reconsider the company's position with a blank slate. Where is the company coming from and where must they go? What are the new oppertunities and threats? Who is the right leader... now? Can the current leader become that leader, or must we find someone new? The ideal leader for a company changes as the company changes.

THE RIGHT DECISION AT THE RIGHT TIME

One of the most important lessons I have learned over the years, as a generally impatient person with idealistic tendencies, is to wait for a process to unfold. Achieving a vision without breaking the system requires periods of generating buy-in, exhaustive testing, and allowing time to pass for ideas to sink in and the right people to get on board. It is frustrating but true that, in most cases, companies and products should change only in careful increments. Pacing is very important. But sometimes your team and product are at an inflection, and a trigger must be pulled quickly and all the way. The leaders I admire most maintain healthy incrementalism while imposing the occasional transformational jolt when it is needed.

The inevitable outcome of any business governed by too much incrementalism is a limited market size because the local maximum—the one thing that has worked in the past that keeps getting iterated—becomes the ceiling. While I am a big proponent of taking small steps in cautious terrain, and carefully testing and validating new improvements before going all in, new ideas are inflections and must be executed in full before they function. Sometimes you need to take a leap, not a step. The best teams know when the time has come to make the bold move and can reorganize to pull it off. Great leaders are generally even-keeled but able to make an unpopular decision at the right time, even when such decisions break routine and cause discomfort.

THE RIGHT INVESTMENT AT THE RIGHT TIME

Investing is a discipline focused on the future that can be determined only by the present. While you're forecasting and attempting to bet on the future, it's impossible to predict how the variables (the ones you know of) will interact over time. Therefore, forecasts for the future, while good mental exercises, should be grounded with a deep and accurate understanding of present-day problems and humanity. Otherwise, you may be betting on a future that is off by an order of magnitude.

The other key to timing is tracking the tailwinds. My criterion for investing at the right time is whether the team is attempting to defy a likely outcome or make it happen in a better way. I invest in the latter. The best teams I come across are parlaying forces already under way in their favor.

In almost all cases, best to ignore sunk costs.

I get it. You've spent days, weeks, sometimes years working on artwork you love, coding something in your mind's eye, or building specialized hardware for a project, but it's somehow not adding up. Even though it's work that has value, it might be time to let it go rather than continue to hang on. And it's only natural to overvalue what we already have when we're at risk of losing it.

This tendency is referred to as the "endowment effect." This describes how we have an inclination to disproportionately value things because we own them. Numerous experiments have demonstrated our bias to hold on to something we own merely because it is ours—even if we are offered the fair value amount in cash. I like how Tom Stafford, a writer for the BBC, suggests we hack ourselves to sidestep the endowment effect and rationally determine how valuable something really is. He asks himself, "If I didn't have this, how much effort would I put in to obtain it?" As he explains, "more often than not I throw it away, concluding that if I didn't have it, I wouldn't want this." Vetting the true value of what you are afraid to lose is the first step to letting it go. Value is best measured by the resources you'd be willing to spend to do it again, knowing all that you know now.

At a deeper level, ignoring sunk costs is about allowing yourself to change your mind, despite whatever plans are in motion or how strongly you have already advocated for your previous opinion. Jeff Bezos once remarked in an interview that he didn't think consistency of thought was a particularly positive trait. He went on to suggest that the people who are most often right are the people who most often change their minds. Among his executives, Bezos is known to encourage self-contradictions. Given how fast information flows and changes, why should viewpoints have such staying power? In a team working at the cusp of a particular field, all beliefs should be subject to rapid change. If your default is to cling to your original convictions, you're more likely to be wrong in a fast-changing environment.

The real reason we cling to our original convictions is the energy, time, reputation, and money we invested in them. These resources are sunk costs the moment they are spent. Only by allowing yourself and your team to cut such investments loose can you empower people to change their mind when they should.

You must also resist the impulse to make "halfway changes" that attempt to recover some sunk costs. Don't hold on to the progress you've made developing a marketing campaign or a new product feature when you've had a revelation that points you in an entirely new direction. Let go. Instead, revert your efforts to the problem you're trying to solve and iterate from there—fresh. Great work is seldom the result of repurposing stuff that didn't work.

CRAFTING BUSINESS INSTINCTS

Mine contradictory advice and doubt to develop your own intuition.

Having now been an investor in more than eighty different early-stage companies and served on boards or advised a handful of companies through some major inflections, I am struck by how great advice in one context is horrible advice in another. Not only must you discern criticism from cynicism, you must also determine when "best practices" become antiquated.

For better or worse, there is no shortage of advice and people willing to give it to you, often without your wanting or asking for it. I recall Andrew Wilkinson and Jeremy Giffon, partners at Canadian tech and design studio Tiny, summarizing the idea of successful entrepreneurs giving advice to others as the equivalent of someone saying, "Here's the numbers I used to win the lottery."

Investors are also not shy about sharing their wisdom, garnered from years in the boardroom and the patterns they've noticed over the course of their careers. But as my friend and fellow investor Hunter Walk, general partner of venture capital firm Homebrew, once suggested to a group of entrepreneurs, "Never follow your investor's advice and you might fail.

Always follow your investor's advice and you'll definitely fail." That's because the problem with "best practices" is that they are entirely context dependent. As a result, advice should be sought, reconciled, but not necessarily followed. As one of my favorite founders, Joe Fernandez, CEO and founder of Joymode and Klout, once encouraged fellow entrepreneurs, "Look for investors that respect the fact you're not always going to follow their advice."

The best advice doesn't instruct—it provokes. The benefits of soliciting wisdom from others is indisputable, but the real value of advice comes from reconciling its contradictions. The theme of my experience writing this book, which is chock-full of opposing perspectives, has been exploring contradictions and realizing how every insight is situation dependent. Most best practices are, in fact, just potential practices to consider employing. The more potential paths you have to consider, the better you can triangulate your own approach.

To complicate matters, sometimes the doubt you receive from others—early customers, investors, and family included—is actually a positive sign. One of my favorite examples is the early reviews for the iPod when it was first released in 2001. One letter to the editor of *Macworld* deemed it "another one of Apple's failures just like the Newton . . . Apple could have done more-innovative things with an MP3 player than just make it look cool and give it some fast features." More succinctly, one Slashdot iPod review read: "No wireless. Less space than a Nomad. Lame." People love taking down something that is new and unfamiliar.

Society is remarkably hypocritical. We shun things before we celebrate them. We chastise students who drop out of college to pursue a fascination that cannot be taught in school, and then we celebrate them when they become dropout-cum-wunderkinds like Jobs, Zuckerberg, or Gates. Likewise, many new ideas are distinctly unpopular before they become popular. So when you're bearing the brunt of naysayers, it's normally a good sign. When everyone thinks you're crazy, you're either crazy . . . or really onto something.

If you plan to move an industry forward in any material way, you must learn to gain confidence from doubt. The majority of people are pragmatists. They don't like change, and they'll cite history as their argument; they'll remind you that you're liable to fail because "history repeats itself." What they're missing is that history repeats itself until history is made by those who are informed but not bound by the past.

I've seen the life cycle of a few companies now. The first round of doubts boil down to, "I don't get it," "I wouldn't buy it," and the general belief that "most start-ups fail." Then people will doubt your product decisions and marketing as "strange." And if you ever go through an acquisition or initial public offering, you'll hear that "most acquisitions fail" and "public companies aren't innovative." The only constant throughout the journey is doubt. If you're governed by it, you'll be paralyzed and your industry will stop progressing.

As Joe Fernandez once suggested to me, "Believing you can accomplish what others can't is basically the ultimate strength and biggest weakness of entrepreneurs." Indeed, you must learn to hear the constructive criticism but consider doubt from pragmatists as a positive signal. When you feel an onslaught of doubt that runs counter to your own intuition, amp up the volume of your own gut instincts. When something inside feels right, learn to gain confidence from the doubt. Don't complain about the pragmatists—surprise them.

Whether the advice you receive is actionable or just outright negative, reconcile it to conceive your own approach. Always pair what you hear with a different viewpoint. Play contrarian and consider why a tactic worked for someone else but may fail for you. The more you toil over different perspectives, the more you remember what you learn.

Finally, don't value what others do or advise you to do more than the most unique convictions you have for your vision. Don't start to question your gut solely because it is different. Nothing should resonate more loudly than your own intuition. The truly differentiating factors of your project are the ones most likely to be different, misunderstood, or underestimated by everyone else.

Don't blindly optimize, keep auditing your measures.

Because of our love of and dependence on metrics, we can easily forget which goal they're actually measuring. You may be measuring foot traffic to your store, visitors to your website, or clicks on your ads, but perhaps your real goal this year is to make a sales number or establish your brand? The danger with measures is their gravity and how quickly they dictate our daily efforts. It's easier to track the growth of smaller things rather than dynamic systems, so we therefore often default to focusing our efforts on spiking the wrong goals.

Author and marketing wunderkind Seth Godin calls measures "stand-ins." In his personal blog, he writes: "Sometimes, the thing that matters doesn't make it easy for you to measure it. The easiest path is to find a stand-in for what you care about and measure that instead. For example, websites don't actually care about how many minutes someone spends on the site, they care about transactions or ad sales or making content that moves people to take action. But those things might be harder to measure at first, so they focus on minutes. The problem with stand-ins is that they're almost always not quite right. The stand-in looks good at first, but then employees figure out how to game the system to make the stand-in number go up instead of the thing you're actually trying to change."

Stand-ins are seductive because they are easy to measure, and they are dangerous because we get obsessed with them instead of being obsessed with what they represent. Seth suggests a good litmus test for your measures is to ask the question, "If you had to choose between increasing the stand-in stat or increasing the thing you actually care about, which would you invest in?"

Don't let artificial measures abstract your goals. When you're optimizing for a particular measure, reiterate for yourself and your team the real impact you desire to make, not just the metric you're measuring. Always ask "What is the real goal here?" The answer is nearly never as measurable you may think.

Avoid too many measures, because the more numbers you're tracking, the less attention you pay to any of them. Some teams I've worked with, especially in large companies, have built large digital dashboards of dozens of metrics that become the focus of every executive meeting. The problem with reviewing so many measures at once is that the conversation and suggestions are split across all of them rather than focused on the few that matter most. Measures that are easier to move than others will naturally get more focus. But I would argue that there are only a couple of metrics in your business, or perhaps only one, that matters most.

The teams I admire most boil their business down to one or two of these core metrics that they believe represent progress in everything they need to achieve in a given year. For example, Julio Vasconcellos, CEO and cofounder of Prefer, a company I helped cofound that provides a referral network for independent professionals, used a single measure as the key metric for the first two years of the business: the "number of working pairs." A "working pair" represented an independent professional and a client working together using the company's platform and tools. Specifically, the Prefer team measured the total number of working pairs every month, which represented the product's ability to retain its users, as well as "new working pairs," which represented the product's network effect and ability to attract and convert new users. Sure, Julio could have also focused on more traditional measures like number of downloads, monthly revenue processed, total users, total transactions, and countless others. However, by focusing only on measuring "working pairs," he empowered the team to try other tactics that could strengthen the retention and growth of the company's most important metric, and not get caught up trying to increase surface measures like revenue or downloads.

The same principles apply for the measures you use for your own team's progress. Your most precious resource is time, and the most important measure is how effectively it is used. Rafael Dahis, a former product manager at Twitter who joined Prefer as our first product manager, would often remind us that return on time invested is the metric that matters most: "There's a question we should ask every day: Are we investing our time in the most important things?... Simple back-of-the-envelope calculations will help you prioritize features according to their return on investment, making sure the outcomes are the highest possible over a given period of time."

Measures become your anchors and will, for better or for worse, restrain your product and your thinking and determine your blind spots. Set them in the area you wish to explore and in which they can make the most impact with the least time, and keep evaluating their efficacy and alignment with your long-term goals.

Data is only as good as its source, and doesn't replace intuition.

On the topic of measures, the decisions you make based on those metrics are, of course, only as good as their underlying data.

After ten years of working with product teams and reviewing investor updates, I am struck by how many ways the same statistic or piece of data can be used and interpreted to suit different managers' agendas. Data without context is misleading and can be used to illustrate nearly whatever you want; if you know the answer you're looking for, you'll be able to find data somewhere to support it.

Irresponsible data gathering and data presentation aren't just misleading, they're dangerous. Think about the Great American Eclipse of 2017. After the frenzy of educative articles and the race to buy solar-eclipse glasses, the internet lost its mind over a chart created by a Reddit user that suggested that after the eclipse, people searched for "my eyes hurt" online just as much as they had previously been searching for "solar eclipse." After briefly staring at the sun, this chart baited our deepest fear: We are all, in fact, going blind.

Here's the chart, from Reddit user superpaow:

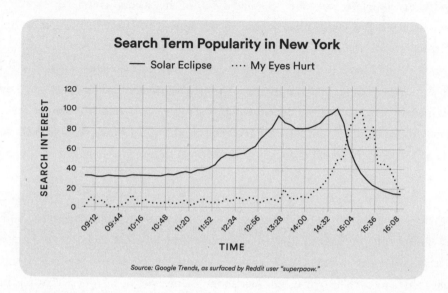

Search Term Popularity in New York

—— Solar Eclipse ···· My Eyes Hurt

Source: Google Trends, as surfaced by Reddit user "superpaow."

As *Quartz* reported, this chart, not the sun, should make your eyes hurt: The data were a bastardization of somewhat confusing Google Trends information, without a defined Y-axis. *Quartz* reporter Nikhil Sonnad got the original data from Google Trends, which, as he reports, showed the popularity of a given search term over time. When he searched for both "solar eclipse" and "my eyes hurt" on Google Trends, he got this chart:

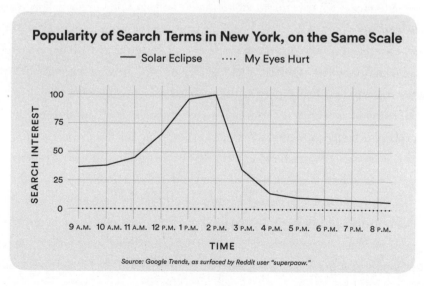

Popularity of Search Terms in New York, on the Same Scale

—— Solar Eclipse ···· My Eyes Hurt

Source: Google Trends, as surfaced by Reddit user "superpaow."

"What once looked like a fascinating trend ('my eyes hurt' overtook 'solar eclipse') now seems to be a complete nonresult," Sonnad says. "In this second chart, 'my eyes hurt' remains completely flat while 'solar eclipse' peaks around the time of the eclipse (in New York)." As Sonnad explains, the confusion is rooted in how Google measures what it calls "search interest." "This is the term used by Google Trends, and it means essentially this: For the given period of time, take the highest volume of searches, and call that 'one hundred search interest'; every other amount of searches in that time period will then be relative to this peak of one hundred," he says. "So in my chart above, for example, 'solar eclipse' was about half as popular around 11 A.M. as it was at 2 P.M. (The eclipse peaked in New York at 2:44 P.M.)"

The original Reddit chart didn't point out this relative indexing. "It did not label the Y axis, giving us no indication of what those numbers represent. That made it seem like the actual number of searches was the same, as opposed to searches relative to the peak for each term," Sonnad continues. Which reveals another problem with the "search interest" Google Trends metric: "It tells us nothing about the number of searches. That means that showing one search term's interest over time is virtually meaningless."

As it turns out, in absolute numbers, even at the peak of 'am I blind,' more New Yorkers were searching for information about the F subway line. Yet, thanks to bad data, we all wasted our time freaking out about going blind because some random Reddit user said so.

Statistics and reports based on data can also be destructive when it comes to creativity. They're liable to create a hard stop in an argument and shut down our will to reason. Instead of having healthy debates to reconcile different opinions and instincts, data-driven facts tend to cut the conversation and subsequent exploration of the full terrain of possibility. One frequent example I observe is the "people don't use this" proclamation. While the raw number of customers using a particular feature can be easily measured, it is a meaningless stat without the context of how many total customers have the need for the feature, what percentage of them know about the feature, and what the usage patterns look like for other features. Despite the drama of a particular piece of data, you can't make decisions until you understand how the data was collected and its full context.

Data-driven arguments can make us jump to potentially catastrophic conclusions. I recall a widely distributed statistic during the 2016 U.S. presidential election that claimed 25 percent of Muslims living in the U.S. supported jihad. Supporters of then Republican candidate Donald Trump cited this stat as a reason to support travel restrictions associated with what would come to be called the "Muslim Ban." Very few people and organizations, such as PolitiFact, took the time to question the source of the data itself.

It turns out that this statistic was extrapolated from an opt-in online survey of a few hundred people who claimed to be Muslim, and one of the early questions in the survey asked respondents to describe how they defined jihad. The majority of respondents defined it as a peaceful pursuit, and only 16 percent of respondents defined it as a violent pursuit. It is not even clear whether any of the people who said they support jihad are the ones who defined it as an act of violence. It is not even clear whether any of the survey's respondents were even Muslim. With only a casual look at the underlying data and methods used to collect and analyze it, the journalists realized that this headline-capturing statistic was meaningless.

We love data. It answers questions. But the definitive nature of data means you must use it with caution. When presented with a statistic that has broad implications, your first question should be about its integrity. Where did it come from? What was the sample size, time range, and breakdown of people from whom the stat was captured? What is the context around the collection of the data? Only when you have interrogated your data sufficiently should you consider how to use it.

But even if the data quality is high, some problems require having a bias toward your own intuition. If there are numbers backing up your direction, it can be easier to feel justified in moving forward. But I have also seen and heard too many stories of product decisions, made from instincts, that initially defied logic but led to success.

One example is Square's ability to sign for a purchase using your finger, which allows hundreds of thousands of small businesses to accept credit cards and manage payments. This may seem totally unexciting now, but Square was a pioneer in bringing a better user experience to real-world commerce when they developed the feature over the course of 2011 and 2012. At the time, nearly every piece of research and data in the world of transactions and user experience suggested that faster was better. But the team at Square weighed this common logic and the data supporting it against an instinct they had for how to make the customer experience more enjoyable, even if it took a little longer and required a finger's flick more of effort. They decided to trust their guts—and the company has been reaping the rewards ever since.

At the time, Megan Quinn, now a general partner at venture capital firm Spark in Silicon Valley, was Square's head of product. "Visa and Mastercard had just decided that they would no longer require merchants to have their customers sign for purchases below twenty-five dollars," she says. "The move was intended to speed up the flow of transactions for merchants (and customers) and their data indicated that overall fraud implications were minimal." The majority of purchases made on Square were for less than twenty-five dollars—coffees, books, trinkets—so to remove the signature requirement to speed up the process just that little bit more seemed like a cause to celebrate. However, the team found that one of their most iconic branding experiences was the ability to sign for their credit card with their finger. And losing it could cost them their competitive advantage.

"Customers would draw pictures and get creative with their signatures," Megan says. "And besides actually having fun with it—imagine, having fun with something as simple and mundane as signing for your credit-card purchase of coffee—it was the only way we had to introduce Square to both sides of the transaction: the customers and the merchants." If you were a merchant, you'd need to ask people to sign, but if you were a customer, that simple step was your introduction to the company and gave you a first impression of interacting with Square's product and brand.

The team debated internally about whether to adopt Visa and Mastercard's new rules, which would eradicate the need to sign with your finger. They knew it would make transactions faster, but they also knew it would make the experience less memorable and interesting for their customers—that it would be just another transaction. "So, we decided not to adopt the new rules," Megan says. "Eventually we made it an option in settings for our merchants, but even then, we kept the default at requiring signatures for all transactions."

Today, Square is a public company powering millions of transactions per day, and has competed successfully against the mammoth credit-card companies by offering a better user experience for merchants and their customers—one that goes against some common logic.

Common sense and near-term metrics help you optimize your product incrementally and reliably—but iconic and breakthrough product insights are not the result of trying to improve a metric. In contrast, great inflections are the result of instincts for what will serve your long-term goals; they're about feeling, not thinking. In some ways, instincts precede awareness and help you make a decision months or years before that data prove it obvious.

Stress-test your opinions with radical truthfulness.

Sound judgment, achieved through aggressive truth seeking, is your most differentiating and deterministic trait. Despite all the hard work you do and the good luck you garner, you can lose it all with a tainted decision—and compound your outcome with an enlightened one. It's all about being honest.

This was the founding core principle behind Bridgewater, one the best and most consistently top-performing hedge funds of all time. From the very beginning, founder Ray Dalio sought to design a culture and set of (rather controversial) practices to foster truth and self-awareness in his organization. As he described in a talk at the 2017 TED Conference in Vancouver, "I wanted to make an idea meritocracy... and I realized that we would need radical truthfulness and radical transparency [to achieve it]."

As someone who believes wholeheartedly that self-awareness is the greatest competitive advantage for a leader, I love the idea of developing tools and norms that promote it. What if every opinion you and your team had was openly scrutinized and had its biases identified? We would reach a point where great ideas and insights transcended politics and prejudices. What if arguments motivated by insecurity or fear were called out as such? What if the best idea had the best chance of happening? While such a high degree of truthfulness comes with its hesitations, it could unlock a utopia of productivity and performance.

Journalists Rob Copeland and Bradley Hope interviewed over a dozen past and present Bridgewater employees and profiled a number of the firm's beliefs and practices in the *Wall Street Journal* in 2016.

> Rules for Bridgewater's staff are laid out in a 123-page public manifesto known as the "Principles," which every employee is expected to know and diligently apply. Along with maxims such as "By and large, you will get what you deserve over time," the Principles are filled with advice from Mr. Dalio such as "Don't 'pick your battles.' Fight them all."
>
> Mr. Dalio also believes humans work like machines, a word that appears 84 times in the Principles. The problem, he has often said, is that people are prevented from achieving their best performance by emotional interference. It is something he thinks can be overcome through systematic practice.
>
> The underpinning to his success, Mr. Dalio often says, is his belief that markets reflect the workings of a misunderstood economic machine, and interpreting its mechanics requires a relentless and often painful dedication to getting to the truth through "thoughtful disagreement." That's why employees are encouraged to challenge each other repeatedly and without reservation.

Bridgewater has developed impressive and astonishing in-house tools for fostering such truth and self-awareness. Employees undergo psychological tests, snap polls after meetings to comment on their peers' contributions, daily quizzes related to management challenges they face, and routinely rate one another's performance in areas such as "listening." Dalio has also made large investments in building a team and internal technology to facilitate these practices. There is an isolated team called the "Systematized Intelligence Lab," led by a former IBM executive who was in charge of Watson, IBM's artificial intelligence system. The Systematized Intelligence Lab analyzes employee behavior and the reams of data generated by all those polls, quizzes, and assessments. The lab has also developed custom iPad applications and programs that employees use to rate one another's strengths and weaknesses. The goal of all this is to achieve a level of piercing insight into individual performance and team dynamics that cuts through the cruft of politics and posturing.

However, it should come as no surprise that some past employees I spoke with say working at Bridgewater can feel like being studied in a lab as much as working at a hedge fund. Practices that strain human norms of wanting to keep up appearances instead of letting guards down do not come without a cost. As Copeland and Hope noted in their profile, "Bridgewater says about one-fifth of new hires leave within the first year. The pressure is such that those who stay sometimes are seen crying in the bathrooms, said five current and former staff members."

One of the most fundamental principles driving behavior at Bridgewater is the notion of "Know what you don't know, and what to do about it." Former employees I know say that this message is a constant theme throughout Dalio's *Principles* and in weekly firm-wide correspondences and tutorial videos. A few examples from the few hundred *Principles* Dalio believes in, that he extrapolated from his years of experience:

> Understand that the ability to deal with not knowing is far more powerful than knowing.
>
> Recognize that your goal is to come up with the best answer, that the probability of your having it is small, and that even if you have it, you can't be confident that you do have it unless you have other believable people test you.
>
> Constantly worry about what you are missing.
>
> Successful people ask for the criticism of others and consider its merit.

The persistent push for employees to question their subjective knowledge and to supplement their ideas with their colleagues' insights demonstrates Dalio's underlying value for self-awareness above all else. It's the closest thing I have ever seen to a mechanism that boosts objectivity and boils politics and emotion-laden opinions down to raw insight. If nothing more, it prompts a feedback loop that is rarely, if ever, thriving in a team.

As you evaluate your ideas as well as the opinions and insights of those around you, challenge yourself to give feedback and absorb as much of what is given back to you. You don't need to agree with what you hear, but you need to know what others think and candidly dissect why you agree or disagree. Build a culture that values alternative viewpoints rather than seeks and rewards those that support your own.

With naivety comes openness.

"Knowing when to ignore your experience is a true sign of experience," observed my mentor John Maeda. Or consider the take of the notable computer scientist who pioneered much of the programming behind graphic user interfaces, Alan Kay: "If you're immersed in a context, you can't even see it." The cost of expertise is familiarity and becoming biased against new ways of doing it.

Ignorance is bliss, and it's the ideal operating state at the very start of a bold project that would otherwise be too daunting with all the facts. Your lack of experience actually gives you the confidence to question assumptions that industry experts wouldn't dare defy. That inexperience can make you more open and confident with subjects you're naive about—but that naivety will become a disadvantage over time as your success is determined less by openness and more by execution.

One of the best ways to maintain (and reclaim) the benefits of naivety is to surround yourself with different people. A team of people from different backgrounds and industries will keep you questioning assumptions. You need to empower new and inexperienced people to follow their logic over industry norms. The "ignorance" that new people bring with them to your team breeds a special kind of insight. Not only will fresh blood offer new ideas, it will help you see what everyone else overlooks. When new members of your team feel like there might be a better way, you should encourage them to explore it rather than advocating for "the right way." Naivety yields an openness not yet tainted by—or bound to—the past.

The science of business is scaling; the art of business is the things that don't.

Art is special because it doesn't scale; it inspires us because it is uniquely personal, emotional, and seemingly scarce. These same forces make a business special, but they don't teach them in business school and they defy conventional wisdom.

Why would Warby Parker, an eyewear manufacturer, create limited-edition stationery or make-a-snowman kits? Why would sweetgreen, a healthy fast-food chain, engage local artisans for each store they open? Why does Gary Vaynerchuk, an entrepreneur and author with millions of followers, take time to personally respond to people who contact him? On their own, each of these actions is unnecessary and quantitatively immaterial; any short-term measures might even deem such actions as an unwise waste of resources. But collectively, these actions distinguish these brands from their peers. The nonscalable artistic elements of a product keep it from becoming a bland commodity.

The best entrepreneurs I know craft and value these seemingly unnecessary and hard-to-measure elements far before they became obvious differentiators. Most industry pundits, investors, and incumbents overlook art until it impacts the bottom line and becomes a true source of differentiation. But true innovators value art up front and compete against incumbents through the *art of business*—the stuff that doesn't intuitively scale.

BE "REMARKABLY UNSCALABLE" AT THE START

The beginning stages of a business are more art than science. You must try to solve problems with new ideas that will feel strange and are in no way economical. You must run manual experiments, spend endless amounts of your own time with customers, and tinker until you find something special.

My Benchmark colleague Bill Gurley advises teams to "do remarkably unscalable things at the beginning of a business." In the early days of Behance, I used to write personal emails to a handful of customers every day introducing myself, giving some suggestions for the portfolio they posted on Behance, and offering to answer any questions directly. Many of these exchanges became relationships that lasted years and yielded customer insights that we would have never garnered from a dashboard. Many other leaders of early-stage teams I know send personal notes to early customers, field customer service inquiries themselves, and encourage their teams to do whatever hand-holding they can.

One of the greatest examples of a nonscalable decision that made a huge impact from the get-go came from Joe Gebbia and his team at Airbnb. After seeing poor-quality photographs dominate the site's marketplace for short-term rentals, they decided to hire professional photographers to capture high-quality images of each home. At the time, Airbnb was competing with Craigslist and was struggling to get the volume of transactions required to be a viable business. Rather than cut costs and further automate the listing of properties, the team decided to offer free professional photography for properties posted. As a result, properties on Airbnb looked far superior to those posted on Craigslist. This level of handholding, while certainly not economically scalable over time, set a level of quality and aesthetic for Airbnb that vastly differentiated their marketplace from Craigslist and other generic listing websites.

Give your customers something precious, something that cannot be easily scaled, automated, or commoditized. The greatest innovations in an industry are strange and artlike before they become the new standard. Do things that your competitors and incumbents wouldn't even think of doing for lack of financial reward. Only through these explorations will you discover the key differentiator—the art—that surprises customers and builds a remarkable product and brand.

DON'T FORGET THE LITTLE THINGS AS YOU GROW

Once your product is in demand and you look for ways to be more efficient, you'll be tempted to develop the "science" side of your business. How can you serve more customers with less effort? What costs can you cut without compromising quality? New projects that encounter early success often struggle with the balance of scaling operations while optimizing the art of their business that got them there in the first place. Viewed objectively as a money-based measure, the art is usually the first thing that gets cut.

The best companies are profitable from their science yet known for their art. As you grow your business, seek to preserve the things that distinguish your brand and service, even if they don't scale as easily. The only way to do this is to proclaim to your team that these projects are a core part of your strategy and create measures that sustain them. In some ways, art is an investment in your enterprise value that cannot be summarized on the balance sheet.

Years into Behance, we made hosting portfolio-review events around the world a core part of our strategy. Looking at the numbers, you'd wonder why spending the resources to host a few hundred events around the world with an average of twenty participants each made any sense for an online service with millions of members. Why commit a team and resources to help no more than five thousand members physically meet up every year when we had more than three times that amount sign up every day? Underneath these metrics was a realization that we learned at the beginning, and it became more important only as the business grew: genuine relationships with and between our members was our competitive advantage against other technology companies like Squarespace and Wix that sought to commoditize websites and online portfolios. We felt like we had a personal element, even if so few people were actually involved. Our in-person events for five thousand people around the world would generate tens of thousands of social media posts, and the images would ultimately reach hundreds of thousands of people. But more important, these events prompted conversations and relationships that went far beyond our brand as a service and instead made it a lifestyle. These people influenced our brand, product decisions, the story we shared while recruiting new team members, and the way we defined our own work.

So don't optimize the art out of your business. Sustain and nourish the little things that make a big difference.

THE LITTLE DETAILS, ALL ADDED UP, MAKE A BIG DIFFERENCE

Obsession over small details is something I look for in entrepreneurs and product leaders. Such obsession means that the founder also sees her business as art. When I first met media entrepreneur Jon Steinberg, the former president of BuzzFeed and founder and CEO of the modern financial news network Cheddar, I was awestruck by his obsessions. Steinberg was infatuated with every edge of his business, including the kinds of cameras they were using, the nuances of the deals he was signing, the quirky characteristics of other people in his industry, and, of course, the content. He was passionate about all the obvious things in his industry, but also maniacal about the little things that, he believed, were important. On their own, his obsessions seemed inconsequential. But in the aggregate, the fine details made Cheddar look and feel different to the younger demographic of viewers he was pulling away from old, stodgy competitors like CNBC. The value of individual details is impossible to quantify, which is why so few people tend to them. But the value of the sum is striking.

In your work, try to find the things you love that nobody else cares about. Your gut fascinations are lead indicators of what may prove important over time. So many things in work and life can be scaled. But when you come across something that cannot, like art, relationships, or details, pay special attention. By preserving the art in your business, you give it a soul that people will connect with.

SHARPENING YOUR EDGE

Your true blind spot is how you appear to others.

It is impossible to know how you come across to others. People see you through a very personal lens made up of their own experiences, insecurities, fears, and aspirations, just as you see others. Despite your best efforts to adjust to those around you, you'll never be seen as you hope you are. You cannot possibly understand how others perceive you, because so much of their perspective depends on what you conjure up for them.

Same goes for your relationships with employees and customers. However well aligned you may be, and despite your efforts to communicate clearly and act ethically, there are other forces that determine how you appear to others—the two biggest being context and psychology.

We take for granted how much context varies for everyone. For example, someone's degree of risk aversion is closely correlated with how their upbringing, financial security, and past experiences impact their confidence. If they've had a string of good luck, they might react to a shaky situation with aplomb; if they've had a couple of unlucky run-ins, they'll see the same opportunity through a very different lens. And then there are those nervously approaching a totally new problem they've never encountered before who could be perceived as having a lack of ambition when, in fact, it is simply the result of a context they lack that everyone else has. As you unearth someone's past experiences and empathize with their fears, you begin to attain a clearer picture of who they really are. But without such insight, you may fail to recognize their value and build a relationship. Without context, you cannot fully engage with those around you.

The other powerful force beyond your control is psychology. The complicated mesh of reactions and biases that are constantly percolating in everyone's subconscious mind determine how you are perceived by others.

Everyone perceives you differently, so acknowledge the blind spot. In order to become aware of what you can't see, attempt to determine how you're coming across. For example, ask people, "If you were me right now, what would you be doing differently?" This question not only yields advice but also gives you a sense of how others view your position and actions. Of course, nothing diminishes this blind spot better than building a personal relationship and getting familiar with one another's fears and insecurities.

You'll never be perceived as you intend to be, so no matter how much control you think you have, stop being presumptuous. Don't assume that the opinions you express are what people hear, or the way you project yourself is what people interpret. Instead, try to see yourself and your message through the lens of those around you. You'll never achieve full resolution, but every bit of contrast helps.

What you agree to do, do right.

There are two kinds of commitments we make: active and passive. If you're like me, you probably make too many of both.

Active commitments are investments of time, energy, and resources in areas you willingly choose to love and pursue. If you're founding a new company or building a dream team, you'll commit yourself to countless emails and meetings to recruit talent. You'll take midnight calls if it means closing the right candidate for a role on your team, and you'll send sneaky emails under the table at family gatherings. Similarly, if you're raising a family, you'll commit to attending school events for your children and planning birthday parties for them and their friends. When you've made an active commitment out of your genuine interests and values, you'll take any opportunity that presents itself. Doing so comes naturally.

But when you commit to doing something that doesn't align with your interests, you've taken on a *passive commitment*. Perhaps you're maintaining an old product or keeping a difficult customer because you cannot summon the courage to say no. Or maybe you agreed to attend a schmoozey event when you'd rather be sleeping, or have to meet with a problematic former employee who you know is looking for a reference. When you operate out of guilt rather than intention, you are making a passive commitment, which is a promise you make for something you wouldn't choose to do but feel compelled to support.

The idealistic advice is to "learn to say no." We're advised by countless books and blogs to make as few active commitments as possible while killing the passive ones, since focusing on the few things that matter most to you is the greatest way to make an impact. But realistically, it's never clear how valuable an opportunity will ultimately be. After all, blind dates are a waste of time until you meet "the one." And introductions in business are no different.

I met Matias Corea through a random introduction from a friend in the nonprofit world. I met Ben Silberman, the cofounder and CEO of Pinterest, as a favor to our first intern at Behance, who knew Ben was visiting New York and looking for a product adviser and seed investors. Both of these chance meetings impacted my professional life in ways I never would have imagined. So much of my life has been the result of taking on more and more commitments—often passive ones—without a clear return. Had I subscribed to the "just say no" mantra everyone else was focused on, I would have missed out on some of my most important opportunities.

Consider whether or not an opportunity is aligned with your genuine interests. A great litmus test for whether you should do something is if it distracts you. Something that doesn't distract you from everything else in your life is unlikely to ever get sufficient attention from others, never mind the attention it deserves from you. Distraction is a form of natural selection. When something or someone persists in your mind, give it more energy. But when you're engaging in a new project or getting to know someone and sense that you're falling short, admit to yourself that what started as an active commitment may have become passive.

For what you agree to do, do right. When you stop nourishing something, let it go. Passive commitments, at best, dissipate into nothing and, at worst, lead to painful extractions and reputational damage. Everything you do should be an active commitment or nothing at all.

An enormous amount of productivity and happiness in business and in life depends on whether you're able to cut out your passive commitments. To do this, acknowledge passive commitments for what they are, and try to understand what's driving your need to entertain them. Fear of disappointing others? Desire to make near-term money even if the work is uninteresting? Unwillingness to bear a small amount of short-term pain for a much greater and long-term benefit? When you feel stuck sustaining certain projects, relationships, or parts of your business, conduct an objective cost-benefit analysis that factors in the value of your attention and the opportunity cost of other active commitments you could make instead.

Build a network that amplifies signal.

The more accomplished you become, the more noise you are exposed to. "Noise" has become a commonly used reference for the incessant banter, marketing messages, and regurgitation of stuff you already know. Noise tends to flow into your in-box and life but does nothing for you. "Signal" is the stuff you hear and learn from others that impacts you: the right question, feedback, or introduction that changes your plans.

As you achieve some level of success in your field, you'll swap from the years of wishing people returned your calls to wishing you could just take the phone off the hook. You must learn to amplify the few reliable sources of signal you have. Your best path to continued progress is to become more discriminate of your sources of information, have a better filter for noise, and be a better seeker and conductor for signal. The best decisions and investments you make will ultimately be the result of instincts informed and opportunities sourced from people and sources of signal that you respect.

There are two ways to build a network and source signal: growing surface area or going deep. In the beginning of your career, optimize for surface area. You'll want to meet many people from all levels and angles of your industry and those ancillary to it. As you're building a team and professional network, and triangulating your own interests, you're often at the mercy of circumstance. By expanding the surface area of what you learn and who you meet, you increase your chances of finding more signal. In the early days of building Behance, I went to industry conferences for advertising and for design and pushed myself to have as many lunches as possible with anyone I could reach (a tall order for an introvert!). While most conversations didn't amount to anything material, every chat gave me a deeper perspective of the industry. I learned how advertising agencies worked, I learned how freelancers found work and the tools they used, and I developed better judgment about the people I wanted to work with and others to avoid. It's hard to differentiate signal from noise in the early days of a project or company, but the more you expose yourself to it, the better you can distinguish between the two.

As you become more focused and a source of signal in your own right, you'll want to shift from seeking surface area to going deep with a smaller group of people whom you respect. Rather than meeting as many people as possible, you'll want to focus on the people you deem the most competent. Competent people understand their field, they have strong opinions, and they have a history of following through with their commitments. They are *high signal*; the information and feedback they share tends to be measured and material. What they say consistently matters more than most of what I read or hear from others.

Of course, a big part of receiving better signal and less noise from others is making sure that you're ready to absorb the sound waves in the first place. The mistake I see emerging leaders make as they build their own network is trying to connect with their peers by commenting instead of listening and sharing original and counterintuitive insights. High-signal people don't want to discuss what's popular; they want to discuss what's not, or why what's popular is wrong. When you meet people you consider to be highly competent and with whom you wish to build a reciprocal relationship, challenge yourself to ask questions and listen. Tune in to their interests and determine what they're knowledgeable about rather than feel the need to showcase yourself.

As your network grows, so will the noise. The sixth-sense-like intuition that leaders get at the peak of their career is the result of developing a network and filter that fosters a high signal-to-noise ratio. By going deeper with those you consider most competent, you are amplifying the power of signal in your life.

There is no better measure of your values than how you spend your time.

When it comes to values, so much of what we tell ourselves is different from what we actually do. For example, if you believe that "nothing is more important than people" in your business but spend most of your day looking at spreadsheets, then you're valuing analysis and paperwork over relationships. If it's that important to you, the amount of time you spend developing people on your team and in one-on-ones should reflect this value.

All too often, our time is spent on tasks with quicker rewards. The decisions we make on how to spend our time are normally more heavily influenced by our desire to feel productive rather than to adhere to our values. The quick hit of dopamine from checking our emails or resolving a small problem quickly overrides what we know matters more.

You can tell yourself all kinds of stories to rationalize how you spend your day, but the calendar doesn't lie. The accounting of how you spend your minutes is the hard truth of your values.

A few years ago, I started the practice of looking back at my calendar at the end of every week and asking myself what meetings and experiences served my priorities and which did not. Something feels right about seeing calendar blocks for when I spent time at my children's school or was home for dinner. Similarly, I feel good about meetings that helped a team get aligned or helped recruit a great leader to join a team. But I often find that too much of my calendar is disconnected from what I am most focused on: my relationships with family and close friends and building teams and products. I instead appease others and keep commitments that I made passively and don't have the gumption to cancel.

One reason we hesitate to audit how we spend our time is because we can't bear the truth. Day to day, amid the gravitational force of operations and the desire to please others and immediately gratify ourselves, we spend time in ways we are likely to regret by the end of the week. Reconsidering your schedule can be a rude awakening, but it's the only way to plan better the next week.

Of course, how you allocate every day will not be a true reflection of your priorities in life. Some days are consumed by a short-term crisis or some other indulgence. Much like the pursuit of balance, priorities are not achieved at every moment in time, but rather over time. Whatever values are core to your work and life should command the lion's share of your attention. The closer you get, the less you'll regret.

Are you keeping track and facing the facts?

The other thing you must do to spend time more wisely is audit your routines before they become mindless habits. Perhaps you have a meeting every Monday morning with your staff or capture notes in a particular format. Maybe you look at a few social media sites every day or check in with a certain dashboard every hour. Eventually, you may find yourself going through these motions and forgetting the reasons you started doing them in the first place. Actions you once took with intention and were determined to iterate become mindless routines that may or may not be effective.

Make an effort to identify the things you do "just because," and audit them. Are your Monday morning meetings actionable enough? Are those dossiers you prepare before meetings worth the time it takes? Are you gaining actionable information from the websites and dashboards you visit every day? Don't feel loyal to routines—question their continued relevance and effectiveness. Some routines become outdated, and nearly all routines can be optimized if you take a moment to question them. Every now and then, break a routine and decide whether doing so was in any way liberating.

Routines backfire when you start doing them without thinking. Throw a wrench in the machine every now and then.

Leave some margin to mine the circumstantial.

Everyone likes a productive day. The idea of squeezing in a few more meetings and getting through a few more emails evokes a sense of pride. I have a drive to maximize what I can get done with the limited amount of capacity I have. But the problem with this relentless drive for productivity is surrendering your flexibility. Without a certain amount of capacity left idle, you are less able to accommodate circumstantial opportunities as they arise. Without fluidity, you're not able to adapt. You need to create and preserve some margin of downtime in your days to reach your full potential.

The invigorating sensation you get from a jam-packed schedule is nothing more than a gamble against the odds. A full schedule, without any margin for error, puts your entire day at risk. When you get away with it, you feel lucky. But when one thing goes wrong, the whole day piles up.

You also need a margin to mine circumstantial opportunities and explore the unexpected. Fashion designer Isaac Mizrahi once explained that his greatest ideas come from "mistakes or tricks of the eye." Many famous innovations started with a mistake that the inventors allowed themselves to explore more deeply: the weak adhesive that became the Post-it note or the melted Mr. Goodbar that signaled the potential of microwaves for heating food. When confronted with the unexpected—and with enough wiggle room to not panic—you have the option to either quickly backtrack and make up for lost time, or run with it a bit. Do you have the time to continue a chance conversation over lunch that could yield a new project or breakthrough? Do you have the capacity to tease out that unexpected result that could shed new insight?

Don't itemize every minute. For example, when you plan your day, double transit time and leave a few blank blocks to accommodate change. To increase your chance of new discoveries, you must preserve the faculty to follow up on mistakes and circumstantial opportunities. As you seek to utilize your productivity to its fullest, always keep a reserve.

Part of managing and auditing your time with great care is making the most of wherever you find yourself. When you're seated next to a random person from an entirely different trade at dinner, try to learn about their specialty. The busier and more ambitious we get, the more protective and intentional we become of our time—but sometimes it's too much. Ambition shouldn't override opportunity.

When you fail to disconnect, your imagination pays the price.

I've long been fascinated by the diminishing returns when you pass a certain point of obsession. At some point, relentless focus blinds your peripheral vision, and your determination becomes a liability. Being a product adviser for a number of later-stage companies over the years has helped me understand how all-star teams can struggle to deviate from their well-tread paths and original convictions. One of the greatest roles an outside adviser can play is sharing observations and asking questions that may be obvious to the speaker but overlooked simply because they are outside of the team's field of vision.

Every leader needs to come up for air every now and then. By temporarily disconnecting from your journey, you're able to take perspective of all the moving parts. Like a view from the balcony as opposed to the dance floor, you come to appreciate your place in the larger system. It is humbling to realize how myopic your perspective is, and it is inspiring to contemplate the expansive terrain of possibility that surrounds you. Distancing yourself from your daily battles and pursuits restores your energy and refreshes your imagination. The peripheral blinders come off and ancillary ideas come into focus. Disconnecting sharpens your imagination.

Unfortunately, it has become increasingly difficult to disconnect. In an age where our devices are always with us, we spend idle time tuning in to what is happening to others and are unaware of what is happening around us. We have started to live a life where we are pecking at the collective in-boxes around us, trying to stay afloat. The magnitude of this problem is larger than we realize as we lose presence and time to partake in deep thinking.

We are living the to-do list of others, always responding and reacting to the latest thing that demands our attention. I call this the era of "reactionary workflow." Through our constant connectivity to one another and endless streams of information flowing around us, we have become increasingly reactive and less proactive. We respond to what others most recently sent us rather than what we believe is most important. We feel most productive when we complete a to-do list rather than make a material impact on long-term creative pursuits. Beth Comstock, former vice chairman of GE and the company's CMO before that, once explained to me that when she needed to take a step back and think about her business—to remove herself from the constant flow of incoming stuff—she would book a trip to China. The ten-plus-hour flight (and the forced disconnection that comes with it) was her oasis of proactive thinking.

But without the time or means to take a quick trip to Asia, what else can we do?

Some people create windows of nonstimulation in their day: periods of time when they force themselves to close their emails, tune out from social networks, and consider a few questions and long-term projects that require deep thinking. Perhaps it is a couple of hours every day—or perhaps one day every week—where you stop living at the mercy of the modern day and be a bit more intentional.

For me, my problem of constant connection has renewed the significance of a secular Sabbath: a day of rest. Many religions have their own version of the "off day," but they all share the fact that it is mandated by being free of work. In 2008, a movement called the "Sabbath Manifesto" was launched by a nonprofit organization called Reboot, and its first project was called the "Unplug Challenge." It was an open dare for participants to go one day without technology. As part of this project, journalists, writers, and bloggers were contacted and challenged to unplug for one day, and then report on it. Almost everyone found it enlightening, or at least refreshing.

The following year, the movement called for a "National Day of Unplugging." It gained coverage all over the world. In an ultimate irony, #nationaldayofunplugging became a trending topic on Twitter. Go figure.

As part of the National Day of Unplugging, the group refined the "Sabbath Manifesto for the 21st Century." The manifesto included ten principles for an effective break from the modern world. They are as follows:

1. Avoid technology

2. Connect with loved ones

3. Nurture your health

4. Get outside

5. Avoid commerce

6. Light candles

7. Drink wine

8. Eat bread

9. Find silence

10. Give back

Whatever your method, we all must force ourselves to disconnect. Ritual, however you define it, is a very effective way of creating a consistent space for downtime and deep thinking. Technology is not a bad thing; it just needs to be used in a way that helps us in our intentions, and works for us rather than controlling us.

One of the greatest challenges of the twenty-first century is to keep your focus and preserve the sanctity of mind that is required to create and ultimately make an impact in what matters most to you. Imagination happens only when your mind has the freedom to run rampant. When you're always connected and able to find an answer, you stop wondering and wandering. Unfortunately, in the modern day of reactionary workflow, our minds seldom run free.

Be aware of the cost of constant connection. To keep perspective and nourish your imagination, create windows of nonstimulation in your day, rituals for disconnection, and periods of time in your life where you get out of your element and allow for new questions and curiosities to take hold.

STAYING PERMEABLE
AND RELATABLE

The more credit you need, the less influence you'll have.

The sun warms us, grows our crops, and makes Earth inhabitable. Our fate depends on its energy-giving rays. But ultimately, in around five billion years, the sun will explode like every other star and turn its surrounding planets into dust. It was nice while it lasted, eh?

What feeds us eventually kills us. It's a theme of dependency-driven reliance that dominates nature as well as our social lives. This same universal truth of science applies to ventures. The forces that feed your progress—rewards, ego, and pride—are often the same that kill it.

Ego is rust. So much value and potential are destroyed in its slow decay. Achievement rarely ages well, unless you keep sanding it down.

The people I admire most in my industry have talents that are less publicly apparent and instead reveal themselves in quiet ways. They have hired and empowered great makers and celebrate the people on their teams. They have created meaningful content and made high-quality introductions. They don't aggressively market themselves. Instead, word spreads naturally. As respect for them compounds without any loss in approachability, these leaders achieve an even greater level of influence.

It's only natural to want short-term affirmation, and you're liable to overattribute successes to yourself and failures to others. But by doing the opposite, you'll feed your team's potential rather than assuage your own insecurities; you'll have a better chance to make an impact behind the scenes without the headwinds of envy, ego, and the natural drive for credit. When credit is attributed to a person instead of a team, it dilutes the shared sense of ownership and openness that drives alignment and execution. Credit for one person depletes ownership by many.

The start of a venture is full of many humbling moments. Humility keeps you grounded, and it helps founders develop real companionship with colleagues and empathy with their potential customers. Most first-time founders I work with have an ear to the ground and are tremendously sensitive. They agonize over any ounce of constructive feedback they're able to extract from new customers and are sensitive to the feelings and emotional status of their team. These sensitivities cultivate the chemistry of a productive and engaged cohort.

A team's success makes a founder feel more confident. While success may be attributed to many factors—including their humility, hard work, good timing, and a lot of luck—most founders tend to attribute success to themselves while attributing failures to others and forces out of their control. As a result, leaders become overconfident and stop listening. Feedback is discounted. Their team's concerns are less tolerated. The product suffers.

Don't insist on reinforcing your independence by downplaying the role of your team. I'm always surprised by how destructive leaders can be just to feed their ego. I've seen family businesses split, incurring tremendous legal fees for both sides, for issues solely related to control and one part of the family not willing to involve the other. All ego. I've seen co-founders pushed out and forced to sell their stake at a discount rather than take an inferior title. In all of these situations, ego quite literally depleted the leader's bank account as well as their future potential.

Success is sustained only by reminding yourself—repeatedly—that it wasn't you. Hardwire this into your brain. Such humility helps you acknowledge your faults, release your disillusionments, and accept an important truth: Your team did more than you think, and you did less than you realize. Your environment is influenced by multitudes of forces more powerful than any singular skill you may possess. The best among us harness these forces.

Nothing corrodes the potential of a team faster than a sense of superiority. Opportunity is lost as soon as you devalue those around you and embellish your own capabilities. When you feel superior, you become numb to your surroundings and miss potential intros to customers and talent, lessons learned from others' experiences, empathy with customer needs, and sensitivity to market forces. You forget that timing was on your side and that you succeeded not because of what you know but despite what you don't.

Keep fighting the construction of your own stoic monolithic story of grandeur. Such narratives make you inaccessible, even to your own friends and family. While you may instinctually wish to appear better than you actually are, doing so distances you from the people and forces you need to sustain your trajectory, both from a business sense and in terms of moral support. The more you can remind yourself how lucky you are and how much self-doubt you have, the more relatable you will be to others: You're just a man or woman in this wild and largely random world with problems to solve. Success backfires as soon as you think you could have done it alone.

Keep reminding yourself that success doesn't mean you know what you're doing. Success means that many forces aligned in your favor, that your team outperformed itself, and that you kept yourself from screwing it up. When you feel yourself becoming headstrong and invincible, shift your focus away from yourself and onto your team.

When you find yourself hungry for credit in the moment, make a long-term investment instead. For your own potential if nothing more, take every chance to shine the spotlight on others.

Remove yourself to allow others' ideas to take hold.

Successful creative teams often have a strong founder who is, on her own, a creative power-house. While it's exciting to work for and invest in such remarkable leaders, the ideas of others on the team can struggle to take hold in such a luminary environment.

On an interview for the Song Exploder podcast series, where artists unpack the creation of one of their songs, Weezer front man Rivers Cuomo described the creative process behind the song "Summer Elaine and Drunk Dori," for which he wrote the original draft of the lyrics and score. I was struck by the handoff he described, in which he let his bandmates play with the first version of his song without him in the room.

"I really appreciate the power of democracy," he said. "The songwriter—in this case me—with the best of intentions can limit the creativity of the other members of the band because you're attached to your original demo. You had this vision for where you thought it was gonna go, and in any case, you're just one brain and you have this one limited perspective. Politically in the room, you have more power than everyone else, even with the best of intentions. Other people are gonna think, 'I guess he wrote the song, so if he doesn't like what I'm doing, maybe I shouldn't do it.' So, it's very helpful for those guys to get time in the studio with our producer Jake Sinclair without me—to come up with their own parts. I don't hear it until they're done with their parts. Then I get to listen back, and in most cases, I am just blown away by how cool and fresh and layered and complex everything has become."

To tap the full potential of your team, sometimes you have to let go of the reins and let people have their own creative process. Even if you think your first draft is perfect (unlikely), allow your colleagues to play with an idea without your presence. This fosters a sense of ownership and alignment that expedites execution. More often than not, great ideas grow out of good ideas—and it keeps the band together.

The danger of getting attention is that you stop paying attention.

Getting attention is distracting. In the early stages of a venture, one of the greatest benefits of isolation and anonymity is uninterrupted focus. The time a well-known and in-demand person spends fielding inquiries or reading about themselves online is time that you're not spending on building your team and product, planning, and learning.

Earlier, when we explored tactics for optimizing products, I explained the importance of "ego analytics," the stuff that feeds an early user's vanity enough to engage them and keep them coming back, whether it be "likes" from their friends or a leaderboard in a game they are playing. We know that Instagram and Twitter users are more likely to use the product after they contribute content because of one major reason: They want to see how other people are interacting with their content. But the cost of basking in a burst of attention from others is becoming less interested in the content that others are posting. The time users spend seeing who liked or commented on their own content is time they no longer spending exploring.

The same can be applied to your life. As you launch your project and receive press and other public accolades, the time you normally have for others will be consumed by your attention to the attention *you're* getting.

I can recall a few moments in my life where I have received press. My email and various social media feeds light up, and I would spend time browsing and responding to everyone's kind (and sometimes not-so-kind) words. At the end of the day I would initially feel elated, followed by the realization that I got nothing done that day. With all the attention, I had tuned out everything else happening around me. For all the excitement, a success can feel strangely defeating, as if publicity stalls progress.

Such attention also tolls your creative process. Imagination thrives when you're fully absorbing everything around you. When you're fully receptive, encounters of chance and mistakes of the eye become ideas. But when you create something new you become, if only for a short period of time, numb to your surroundings. You zero in on the aftermath of your work. Your primal need for validation takes hold and shifts your focus to who is seeing your work and what they're saying about it.

People and companies who work in the limelight every day must find ways to compartmentalize the attention they receive. Some CEOs and public figures appear to overcome the gravity of fame with curiosity. For example, I was once part of a small group dinner with Jeff Bezos, who was an early investor in Behance. I remember being struck by just how many questions he was asking the group about our work and opinions on new design and tech trends among other topics. I recall leaving the dinner and realizing that the conversation had not even touched upon Blue Origin, his private spaceflight company, or the *Washington Post*, the newspaper that he owns. The man is building rockets to explore the final frontier and controls one of the country's largest media organizations, but was more interested in asking us about start-ups.

It dawned on me that perhaps Amazon's persistent growth and Jeff's seemingly infallible grasp of so many different industries was the result of his curiosity overpowering others' attention for him. While most people would allow themselves to be heralded as the expert in their field and share countless stories, Jeff's insatiable thirst for knowledge of others' ventures keeps him learning and exploring—and also keeps the pressure off him.

"Keep making a ruckus."

Years ago, one of my mentors, Seth Godin, sent me a note that simply said this:

Scott, keep making a ruckus. Seth

This note has meant different things to me over the years. But more than anything else, it reminds me to not shy away from conflict. It reminds me to keep fighting. It encourages me to embrace struggle and be wary of complacency induced by comfort.

Sometimes a mentor's advice reveals its value only over time. In this case, "keep making a ruckus" proved some of the best advice I ever got for optimizing teams and products. While at Adobe, I faced the challenge of asking difficult questions and stirring the pot at a time when the company was doing extraordinarily well and the problems I was trying to solve were important, but not urgent. In such circumstances, there is a natural drive to keep the peace and avoid conversations about seemingly unnecessary risks. In certain meetings, when the metrics looked great but underlying questions felt buried, I could hear

Seth's advice in the back of my head: "If it doesn't feel right, just ask!" Sometimes the question did nothing, but other times it acted as a poke to the elephant in the room.

I've faced similar challenges on nonprofit boards for entirely different reasons. In the nonprofit world, where many people are volunteering their time or taking reduced salaries to solve important problems, it is especially difficult to question strategy and criticize leadership. In such environments, it is even more important to muster the courage to speak up. The implications for looking the other way can alienate staff and hurt your constituents in the long run. People, strategy, tactics, and assumptions all need change over time. Responsible leaders can stomach the pain of being the catalyst.

But how much ruckus is too much? Every system has a threshold of stress it can withstand before collapsing. The trick is to pick your fights wisely and know how to push people without depriving them of their own process. Sometimes the best way to instigate change is one-on-one, planting questions as seeds and letting them take root in your colleagues' heads for a while. Reactions tend to overpower rationale, so you can circumvent gut responses to controversial questions by dropping hints and concerns before big meetings. Chances are you're not the only one suppressing a doubt or difficult question. Be the one who shakes things up to keep things moving in the right direction.

Questioning and prodding to uncover the truth is bound to irritate others. As a default, people want to avoid conflict, and it is always easier to confront long-term concerns later on. But being truthful requires a tolerance for disappointing others. It's the only way to optimize. Seek the ruckus.

THE FINAL
MILE

THE STATE OF FINISHING

I t was mid-December 2012, just days before Christmas in New York City.

I was running on less sleep than ever before, unshaven, on the brink of being sick, and off the radar from friends and family. After about thirty days of intense negotiations, diligence, detail defining, and painstaking deliberation, we had signed the final paperwork the night before to be acquired by Adobe: $150 million for a small team that had boot-strapped a business for five years and then raised about $6 million in venture capital. In addition, the team all received generous employment packages. We'd be able to continue working together. Twelve of us would become millionaires.

There are moments in life when motion comes to a full stop. My brain was cycling all the way back to the start: meeting Matias, the first person I hired to help see out a crazy idea, at a Starbucks in Union Square after I had finished my normal work day at Goldman Sachs. For six months we worked late nights after our day jobs, mocking up and debating the plans for Behance over bottles of wine and Chinese takeout. And now, seven years later, it was all coming to an inflection point that would change our lives.

At about 8:30 A.M., riding the elevator in Behance's Soho office up to the seventh floor, it all hit me. The world felt still. Emotion swelled in my throat and eyes from a mixture of elation and disbelief, somewhere on the verge of laughter and a deep, guttural sob. (The fact I had a horrible cold and spiking fever from weeks of overwork pushing the deal through also didn't help.) Seven years of volatility, doubts, and fears welled up inside me, finally having a definitive point through which to exit: We had done it. We had made it.

I walked into the office and assembled the team. People were quiet yet assembled quickly. They already knew it, but it was my news to share. Standing alongside my COO, Will Allen, I looked out at all twenty or so of my teammates and remembered back to the days when it was just Matias and me foraging for free wi-fi in coffee shops. I was choking up before I even began.

I don't remember my exact words. I was out of my body that day. But I remember saying thank you: thank you to the team that had gotten us to this point, and everything they had done to make it happen. I remember telling them that they deserved this, and how proud I was of our team and what we had built. And, as my eyes swelled up, I remember saying that leading our team had been the greatest honor of my life.

It wasn't all euphoria, though. I worried I would regret it. Would Adobe protect the product and community we had built? Would our culture change? Would newfound wealth corrupt our ambitions or values? I was excited, but I was also scared by how our lives would change.

These ups and downs added texture to what the press and public would soon summarize with a pithy headline and a number with a dollar sign. The press ran headlines about NINE-FIGURE TECH ACQUISITION IN NYC! and the phone rang with requests for comment and well-wishes from people who had chipped in along the way. While not a billion-dollar exit, our acquisition was also celebrated by our investors, who had invested only a year prior at a fraction of the valuation of our acquisition. When we all first signed on, we never expected any of this. Most of the team had college loans and dreamed of owning an apartment. I knew life would change, at least a little, for all of us.

It's funny which memories stick with you. There are endless mundane periods that I can barely remember, and there are certain moments and patterns of action that I will never forget. Like printing our mock-ups: We printed out every step of the customer journey for our first website in 2006, hung them up on the wall, marked them up, made changes, and then printed a new set to hang up long before we hired any engineers who could actually help us build what we were drawing. I remember the sensation of pulling out "the latest" from the printer. It felt like progress, even if it was all still on paper. Then my mind jumps to hand delivering orders of our physical paper products ourselves ("Action Books," which we used to bootstrap the company) so that we could pocket the shipping fees. I would stand in line with professional couriers at the service entrances of these Manhattan skyscrapers, waiting to deliver our notebooks into the hands of random advertising agency and hedge fund employees. During these bootstrapping years where every dollar counted, I recall sitting with our office manager, Brit Ancell, discussing how we could stagger our bill payments so that we could make payroll.

I remember the persistent sense of "if I just do one more thing, we might make it." I remember the feeling of my eyes shutting in front of my screen in the early hours of the morning, thinking of one more email to send: one more customer I could follow up with or one more designer I could find online and invite to check out our products. There were many, many years of "just do one more thing."

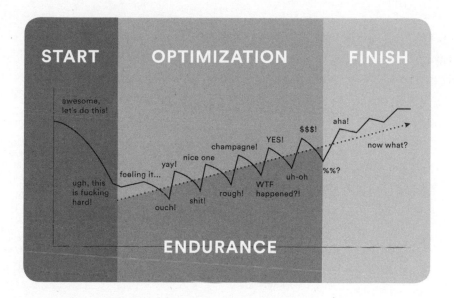

The most humbling part of creation is that you're never truly done. A finish, it turns out, is an abstract mile marker that makes your long journey through life more digestible. Being aware of where you are in that cycle of creation and which way the wheel is turning is imperative to keeping the cogs turning. From every finish comes new possibility, so long as you lead it well and pass the baton on.

APPROACHING THE FINISH LINE

The "final mile" is a different sport.

When an investor gets a text from a CEO wanting "to catch up quickly today," it typically means one of three things: The founder has been approached with an acquisition offer, the company is shutting down or running out of money, or some other important decision impacting the future of the business needs to be made. I received one such call in late 2016 from an entrepreneur working in the security technology space. With a mix of anxiety and giddiness, he informed me that he was in late stage talks to be acquired by Facebook. "That's exciting," I said, and followed up with a few questions. "What are the terms of the deal? Will Facebook be keeping your team together? Have you spoken with other potential acquirers?"

He paused. "Well, we're just getting into that, but I've gotten to know a few leaders over there really well through this process, and their corporate development team came in to meet us last week."

"Us?" I asked. "They came in to meet your team? Do you have a deal yet?"

"No," he replied. "We haven't gotten that far yet. That's some of the advice I wanted to get from you."

I sighed and my head turned down as I realized what was going on. I needed clarification. "So, you've discussed your product with Facebook, shared your road map, let some of their senior leaders meet with your team—and yet you haven't even discussed price or deal terms yet?"

This entrepreneur had failed to realize that Facebook viewed his company as a small talent acquisition, meaning he had accidentally created a major distraction and ultimate disappointment for his team. He had given his potential acquirers tremendous leverage, skipped the process, and ultimately the deal fell apart. The whole thing was a complete waste of time and set his company back months. You can run a race so well and still screw up the final mile and lose.

A great founder isn't necessarily a great finisher. The final mile is a different sport, which means you need to bring on new kinds of coaches and employ different training tactics. With the finish line in sight, your instinct may be to keep doing what you're doing and race toward the light. But at the end of a venture, everything changes. No matter how accomplished you've become over the course of your journey, you'll need a new set of tactics and a ton of guidance. Instead of enduring and optimizing, you're closing.

Behance's final mile began when our third round of discussions with Adobe about a potential partnership fell apart. There were so many reasons for Behance and Adobe to work together, but every time we got close to forming a partnership, Adobe felt they would be best building or running their own portfolio network rather than partnering with one. They were right to feel this way because, as a subscription business, Adobe needed to build relationships with the creative community. Online services like community and portfolio management were becoming a more central part of Creative Cloud, Adobe's main business. They needed to build it themselves or acquire the best option out there.

Several months later, I had the opportunity to meet David Wadhwani, who was Adobe's senior vice president in charge of the company's digital media business at the time. He shared his vision with me for Creative Cloud and the integral role Behance could play as part of Adobe: connecting tens of millions of creative professionals in real time, from the moment they created and published work with creative tools like Photoshop. A few more conversations with David and the rest of Adobe's corporate development team made it clear that this was a major opportunity. I quickly enlisted a group of advisers who could, in confidence, coach me through the process.

For example, I outlined various options with Albert Wenger, our investor from Union

Square Ventures, who sat on our board. I had phone calls with other entrepreneurs who had both completed big-business acquisitions or had decided to stay private and raise subsequent rounds of funding. I recall multiple midnight conversations with Chris Dixon, one of my angel investors, when I was trying to navigate the terms of the deal and find ways to shift more value to certain employees who deserved it.

All the while, I felt outside of my comfort zone, as if the expertise I had accumulated over the last seven years was suddenly worthless. I was a complete novice at one of the most important moments of my career. I wasn't afraid to ask for help (which wasn't always the case earlier on in my career), and I'm glad that I did.

In the final mile, you can't rely on your market experience and confidence in the day-to-day management of your business. Even when you feel like you're ramping up, you need to slow down, enlist help, and boil your options down to simple yes or no questions. Is your project ready to finish or not? Is this move good or bad for your customers? Have you achieved your goals? Will this finish adequately reward your team? As you articulate the right questions and consider your answers, lean heavily on advisers you trust.

In the final mile of any journey, the terrain changes. Psychologically, you'll ponder the implications of finishing and likely have mixed feelings. You'll start to question yourself and your motivations. You may feel inclined to turn inward and bare the new terrain on your own, but you can't. The final mile is not meant to be traveled alone.

Stay in the early innings.

When you walk around the headquarters of Facebook, a company known for its "stay scrappy" ethos, you'll notice the persistent presence of stickers on laptops and sayings on posters that read THIS JOURNEY IS 1 PERCENT FINISHED.

The paradox of making progress is that it moves us past the early period when we're the most willing to make the bold moves that actually accelerate progress. Most companies are more like the Myspaces of the world: They iterate their way to a "successful" product and then focus relentlessly on sustaining it. In contrast, Facebook has consistently acted like they were in the early innings.

Sustaining the "we're still just getting started" mentality keeps people questioning assumptions and always thinking bigger. I believe that Facebook, which was founded in 2004, wouldn't have thrived for so many years had it not completely changed many times over the years. What started as a college directory became a platform that allowed you to log in to other websites and services, then an event discovery tool and a medium for groups to work together. It also grew to include Instagram, messaging platform WeChat, and virtual reality company Oculus. Facebook keeps evolving, and it will only become limited if the team begins to feel and act like they are nearing the finish.

When the public heard about Facebook's acquisition of the global messaging platform WhatsApp, people questioned the accuracy of the headline: $19 *billion* seemed like an obscene price for a company with no revenue. But if Facebook intended to own messaging and how people connect with one another beyond its platform, they needed to own the industry's leading messaging app, WhatsApp. It was ultimately an incredible acquisition and, in February 2018, WhatsApp reported having more than 1.5 billion monthly active users. Only a company that believes they are 1 percent finished would make such a bold bet.

The early innings are your company's most fertile and flexible. You are not feeling entitled by your success, and instead are taking risks and making mistakes. The product is just finding itself and is open to big shifts. You're falling asleep and waking up with ideas and insights for small tweaks that could make a big difference. And in the early innings, you're always selling: Everyone you meet is a potential supporter, investor, employee, teacher, or customer. It's not temporal, it is a mentality.

As you approach the later stages of your project, your challenge is to hold on to some of the openness, humility, and brashness you had in the beginning. Keep repositioning the ultimate goal to be as far away as you can see, and never forget that blind spots only grow as you succeed. In mind and in spirit, stay in the early innings.

Overcome your resistance to a great outcome.

When you pour so much of your life into a project, the final mile can be emotional. For better or worse, a labor of love becomes a part of who you are. As you approach the finish line, it is only natural to wonder how your venture has changed you. You'll face the challenge of reconciling the implications to your own identity.

The impact that Behance's acquisition had was wildly different for each of us on the team. While we were all generally hardened by the experience, some of us felt more confident while others felt humbled. Some of my colleagues upgraded their lifestyle and made large purchases quickly; others tried desperately not to change a thing. While everyone was pleased with the financial outcome and public victory, I observed some very peculiar behaviors during the final mile.

As Behance's acquisition came closer to fruition, one senior colleague displayed erratic behavior in the form of inappropriate conduct and poor judgment. Sarcastic comments that made people feel uncomfortable, occasional outbursts, that sort of thing. People on the team kept complaining to me and I kept addressing it with them, but the behavior persisted. I was perplexed: My colleague intuitively understood the great ramifications for screwing something up during such a crucial period of negotiations and scrutiny; nevertheless, incidents kept occurring.

I recall going home one evening and sharing my disbelief and frustration with my wife, Erica, who is a clinical psychologist.

"He's fighting it," she said.

I was confused. "What do you mean? He's about to have an incredible success that he has worked so hard for over so many years. Why would he be fighting something that he's always wanted?"

When you don't feel ready for an outcome or wonder whether or not you deserve it, you may unknowingly fight it. Our subconscious mind acts upon the insecurities and doubts that we are not willing to admit to our more conscious and rational selves. And if we subconsciously don't believe we deserve it, we are liable to act accordingly.

It became clear to me that my troubled colleague was subconsciously sabotaging himself. His behavior was out of character, and I decided that we needed to address the cause rather than the problem.

The next evening, we sat down together in the corner of our conference room, out of sight from the rest of the office. At first defiant, he tried to rationalize his behavior and insisted it would stop and that I had nothing to worry about. I paused, moved my chair closer, looked him in the eyes, and simply said, "You have worked so hard. You deserve this."

At first, he looked perplexed. He was still in defensive mode, and I was on some other plane entirely. I repeated myself: "You deserve this success. You don't need to fight it: You worked for it." His disposition changed. Tears welled up in his eyes, and I'll never forget feeling that, if only for a moment, we had cracked something far deeper. We stood up and hugged. He apologized, and we walked out together. Whatever actually happened in that conference room, it was enough for him to accept his own progress.

Most lapses in judgment have a deeper psychology to them. I have seen enough leaders do wildly uncharacteristic things at a time when their businesses and lives were on the cusp of major change. There is a part of all of us that fights our own progress. Overcoming this resistance is the first step in setting up your finish.

You deserve it. Sit with that.

Don't underestimate the value of adding a brick.

In 2009, I was thrilled to join the board at the Cooper-Hewitt National Design Museum. Part of the Smithsonian, the Cooper-Hewitt is a heritage institution with a complicated set of relationships with the government, New York City, and its many donors from different locations and generations. I had joined the board out of my interests in design and the rapidly emerging field of interactive and digital design. Despite my excitement about the prospect of these new areas of design being represented in a museum, I walked out of my first meeting deflated.

When you've worked in a fast-paced, action-oriented start-up environment, sitting through a process-driven board meeting for a century-old nonprofit can be frustrating. Some people sit on nonprofit boards because of their financial contributions, while others are invited for their expertise. As a result, the room is often full of players with impressive backgrounds but disparate qualifications and agendas, with varying levels of opinions and communication styles. To keep everyone happy and engaged, the discussion tends to be highly coordinated by the organization's executive director. It's not uncommon to leave such a meeting wondering, "Did anything get accomplished? Was that a massive waste of time?"

While walking through the museum's halls toward the exit, one of my longtime mentors, John Maeda, whom we met earlier in the book, approached me and asked what I thought. I expressed my dismay with how slow and inefficient the meeting felt, and I asked him if his years as a university president at the Rhode Island School of Design had taught him how to withstand the laborious process of managing your expectations in such a huge and slow institution.

He smiled and noted, in his usual calm and wise tone, that I was too accustomed to creating things that are momentary, like digital products and start-ups. "However great and successful such creations might be, Scott, they will likely be gone and irrelevant in a hundred years," he said. "But a true institution sticks around, and every change you make permanently alters something that will exist forever. Even if all you add is a brick to the foundation of such an institution, your contribution will stand the course of time."

John's point changed my perspective entirely. Perhaps an institution's resistance to change is healthy. Perhaps it's a benefit, not a weakness. After all, the stakes are so high when you're changing something that was built to sustain the whims of nebulous leadership and trends.

More important, John helped me appreciate the rare opportunity in life to add a brick—to be a contributor and steward rather than a maker. He also made me realize how absorbed I had become with the start-up world. Amid our dreams to create new things and solve the latest problems, there is a wholly different level of impact we can make in our community and society that lasts forever. Of course, adding a brick doesn't feel like much and may not even register on the normal scale we use to measure day-to-day progress. But such contributions to the world transcend ordinary measures.

Preserve some patience to improve something that will last forever. By adding a brick instead of continually searching to create something new, your contributions may outlast your stay.

Finally, as you seek to make your own creations more institutional to withstand the test of time, turn yourself from the maker into a contributor. Sometimes this means leaving a bit unfinished. Set your predecessors up to succeed by empowering them to build upon what you've done. Don't sign your name on it. If your predecessors feel ownership over what you started, they will nurture it as their own and keep building.

PASSING
THE BATON

If you can't end wonderfully, end gracefully.

No venture turns out as you imagined, and very few turn out as you hoped. If the time comes to wind down, fight the urge to quickly shut it down and move on—especially if it didn't go according to plan. The final mile is rich with lessons to absorb and steps you must take to preserve your reputation and take care of those who helped you.

Some entrepreneurs opt to shut down projects silently; they want to avoid the spotlight on their failure or the need to answer uncomfortable questions. When this happens, silence is the only official word you get as a past customer or investor, and you're left confused and resentful. Others try to make excuses for why things didn't turn out or spin their company's dissolution as an "acquisition" despite their just taking a job at another company. But the entrepreneurs I respect the most own their outcome, no matter what it is. They end gracefully.

I've received my share of emails and phone calls from entrepreneurs with bad news. One such email came from Tim Hyer, founder and CEO of a company called Getable, which envisioned a world where customers would rent things like lawn mowers, barbecues, power tools, and other expensive, space-consuming products that tend to sit in garages, mostly unused. I believed in Tim's thesis and invested in 2012, anticipating the trend of millennials wanting to own less and rent more. But after a couple of years, they struggled to identify the right market to start with and keeping customers engaged. As a result, Tim shifted his business to contractors and construction companies as customers, not your neighborhood woodcutting hobbyist. But not even this pivot was enough: Ultimately, various industry dynamics made it difficult to grow and become profitable, and Tim's team made the difficult decision to shut down the business. In his note to investors, he was reflective, candid, and grateful:

> After eight years of riding this roller coaster, I have just filed the Certificate of Dissolution for Getable, Inc. Anyone who has been part of a startup understands the highs and lows that come with creating a business from scratch. The forces are almost always against you, yet you fight with everything you have. I'm proud to say that I, along with many teammates and co-founders along the way, did just that for nearly a decade with this company . . . bootstrapping, forming an early team, building a prototype, raising capital, establishing a board, signing early customers, growing the team, raising more capital, reinventing the business model, rebranding the company, resetting the team, hiring, firing, achieving milestones, raising more capital, reinventing the business again, exploring acquisition opportunities, etc. Periods of soaring highs followed by abysmal lows. And more effort than you can quantify. In the end, it just wasn't enough. It's difficult to admit this truth, not only to myself, but more so to the people who have supported me and others in this journey. You gave me everything we needed to succeed and I'm sorry to say that we didn't.

A common and noble end to a messy middle. As an investor, I look for entrepreneurs who are empathetic, have a set of customers suffering from a problem, are deeply passionate about solving it, are self-aware, and have been weathered from some real-world experiences that will help them endure and optimize the journey ahead. Tim embodied all of these characteristics. He just didn't become one of the lucky ones. But instead of being sour or making excuses, he owned his misfortune and apologized for those caught up in it. Tim's approach to ending his first venture will, no doubt, serve whatever he does next.

Much like the end of a book or movie, how you end your project determines your chances for a sequel. Don't let your anger, shame, or anxiety prevent you from ending gracefully. If you handle it well, failure is merely a step in the right direction.

You are not your work.

One common struggle among successful entrepreneurs and artists is that their identity is wrapped up in their work. Whether it is a musician feeling forever defined by his band's success a decade ago or a business leader known for a particular venture earlier in her life, great work tends to hijack one's sense of self.

I saw this with my grandfather Stanley Kaplan while I was growing up. Stanley began tutoring kids for standardized tests like the SATs in the basement of his parents' home in the late 1930s. The son of immigrants, he took it upon himself to help provide for his family and ultimately purchase their first car.

For the fifty years he was running his tutoring business, my grandfather was "that Kaplan." I recall getting into cabs with him when I would visit New York City as a child. He would always ask the driver if they or their children had taken the SATs. "How did they do and how did they prepare?" he would ask with a grin, waiting for their response. He taped every interview he gave and relished the identity he shared with his company. Upon his death, I remember rummaging through hundreds of old cassette tapes chronicling every interview he had done. My grandfather Stanley was his business.

More a tutor than a businessman, he sold his business in the early 1980s to the Washington Post Company and put most of the proceeds into a nonprofit foundation. The Washington Post Company went on to transform Kaplan into the global enterprise it is today, with more than one hundred physical schools and a vast online business that has generated billions in revenue. It was an extraordinary achievement for the son of an immigrant plumber, who only became a tutor when he wasn't accepted into medical school because of the limited quotas for Jewish students at the time.

But when he sold Kaplan just as it began to really grow, no amount of money would make up for the part of himself that he lost with the sale. In his old age, he suffered from a depression that I later learned he likely struggled with to some degree throughout his life. I remember his extreme melancholy, and how his eyes would only light up when I asked about the early days of his business. It was as if the sale of his business—the end of something that had so powerfully defined him—was his end as well.

These memories weighed on me as I considered the prospects of selling Behance. I had spent only seven years building Behance, not my whole life, but like my grandfather, my identity was wrapped up in it. Many of my friends were in my industry, and any fanfare I received was because of Behance more than any other part of my life. I was afraid of becoming like my grandfather and being defined by it.

I've seen many friends leave their high-profile jobs or the companies they founded and face similar struggles. Homebrew's Hunter Walk, one of my favorite early-stage investors, wrote a candid blog post after leaving a senior role he held at YouTube for a number of years, which he was widely known for in his industry. He wrote about trying to acknowledge his own struggles with "separating 'where I work' from 'why I matter' and self-worth." As he explained it, "Careers are sets of decisions where you have the chance to emerge from the chrysalis every so often and show the world, show yourself, how you've evolved. You are not your org chart, your department budget, or your title. Don't let success at a company prevent you from pursuing scary and wonderful new opportunities to build. It took me a little longer than it should have, but from the other side, it's pretty awesome."

Having the confidence to leave your previous identity behind is easy to say, hard to do. Having endured a journey that nearly sucked the life out of you, that journey becomes a part of you.

Detaching your self-worth from what you create is complicated, especially for creative people for whom work is very much self-expression. I remember one talk at the 2015 99U Conference from Rohan Gunatillake, a deep thinker in the world of mindfulness and meditation, and a serial maker of products related to mindfulness, including Buddhify, Kara, and Sleepfulness. His talk was about fear in creative careers, and his last point was the fear of decoupling self and work (which is an essential step in developing generativity). How do you build something that is a creative expression of yourself but not fail if it fails? Rohan gave the audience a suggestion for an important first step: Recite a few affirmations while paying attention to how they make us feel.

He put up the first affirmation on a slide: **"I am not my Twitter bio."**

The audience laughed. "This is an easy one," Rohan explained—of course you're not your Twitter bio.

Then he showed the next affirmation: **"I am not my résumé."** People laughed again, but a little less.

Then he switched to the third affirmation: **"I am not my company."**

Backstage, this one made me gulp. So much of my life was my career, and Behance felt a part of me. Other entrepreneurs probably rolled this one around in their brains a bit, too. As founders, when you dedicate yourself to something for so long, the company ends up looking a lot like yourself. It's an extension of your own interests, strengths, and faults. It is therefore hard to detach from something that is, by its very definition, your creation.

Rohan had one final affirmation: **"I am not my work."**

The audience fell dead silent.

"Hold that statement in your mind," he said. "Notice yourself thinking, 'But I am my work, I put everything into it.' The practice of decoupling yourself from your work is noticing that movement, noticing the struggle and the pain of that movement."

When you're finished, your fate and your work's fate diverge, but your identity belongs to you. And you are not your work. Your work, or your art, is something you've made. It can fail, be sold, or be left behind, but it can't be you. A successful final mile requires letting go of what you made and returning to who you are, your values, and your curiosities that are kindling for whatever comes next.

Aspire to finish on your own terms.

While traveling through Japan with a group of other product designers in 2017, I learned about the story of Isuzu Sakurada and his Michelin-starred restaurant in Kyoto from his son-in-law. Sakurada was inspired to become a chef during his teenage years studying at a Zen temple. In his twenties, as a young chef, he opened up a small restaurant called Sakurada in a back alley of Kyoto with four tables and ten seats total. Particularly known for its dashi (soup stock) among other traditional Japanese cuisines, young chefs from around Japan would travel to Kyoto to learn from Sakurada. Word spread of his amazing creations, and a few decades later, Sakurada became a two-starred Michelin restaurant, putting it among the most celebrated restaurants in the world.

Soon after receiving his Michelin stars, to the shock of his staff, community, and the culinary world, Sakurada announced he would close his restaurant in one hundred days.

Going out on top is one thing, but shutting down your restaurant so soon after achieving such global recognition is quite another. Foodies from around the world made a pilgrimage to dine at Sakurada before time ran out. His loyal patrons would come in for their last meal and leave in tears. His announcement attracted so much fascination that a documentary was filmed chronicling the process of shutting down his restaurant. The documentary ends with a scene of him taking down the traditional flag that Japanese restaurants hang above their door.

It's hard to watch a man so talented setting his craft aside. But when I had the opportunity to meet his son-in-law, he talked only about how satisfied his father-in-law felt. Isuzu Sakurada had garnered tremendous respect from his local community and global acclaim from Michelin, all of which had "made him feel so full," as his son-in-law described it. His decision to close his restaurant appeared to be the epitome of going out on top, but it was more so a result of being so delighted and satisfied with all he had done that he didn't need any more of it. He now wanted to spend more time with his family, and in nature. Perhaps these were the only appetites in his life that had not yet been satisfied, I wondered.

In a miraculous twist of fate later in the day, my group happened to run into Chef Sakurada playing in a small square with his granddaughter. I was struck by the man's sense of peace and happiness. His smile and mannerisms carried no weight to them—the man seemed so incredibly content with his world.

So, that's what it looks like to end on your own terms, I thought to myself. It's not just about moving on when you're performing at the level you always wanted to be remembered for—the desire to "end on a high." It's about moving on when you feel fully satiated and can therefore allow yourself to pursue something different.

My own father's retirement from a successful career as an orthopedic surgeon was similar (minus the Michelin stars). He had attained all the titles he had hoped for, including being a team doctor for the Red Sox and Patriots. At one point in his sixties, when he was busier than ever, my father decided that a day in the operating room was less enticing than a day with his grandchildren or engaging in other hobbies. He approached his two younger partners and proposed a time line to eventually stop operating altogether and became more of a mentor than a practitioner. It wasn't an easy decision, but he felt fulfilled by his work and noticed his energy and interests beginning to shift elsewhere. Rather than wait until his work started to suffer, he made the decision.

I remember how much I admired his process. It was difficult for him, but it was deeply thoughtful and on his own terms. He owned the process of finishing rather than let it own him. A great finish is on your own terms, and it starts with that fully satisfied feeling that you want to hold on to. If you can bifurcate your identity and emerging interests from your past accomplishments, you're ready for a new chapter. Your legacy will never retire, but it is set on the note you leave it with.

One of my favorite sayings from ancient times is "Wealth is ultimately feeling like you got your full portion." When I finish a project, I aspire to feel full. And when I lay dying, I hope to look back on what I would consider a full life.

NEVER BEING
FINISHED

Continuing to learn is an elixir to life.

As I write, Warren Buffett is eighty-seven years old and still regarded as one of the greatest investors alive: His company, Berkshire Hathaway, holds more than $600 billion in assets and wholly owns companies like GEICO, NetJets, and Dairy Queen, and is among the largest owners of American Express, Apple, Coca-Cola, and Wells Fargo, among many other companies. His annual letters to investors in Berkshire Hathaway help us understand what keeps him at the forefront of his industry. After reading just a few of these letters, a couple of things stand out.

For starters, Buffett is remarkably self-reflective and self-deprecating, often calling purchases and decisions he made "dumb" and repeatedly stating that he was wrong, has "no magic plan," or struggles to understand something. He is also remarkably open to learning new models and changing his mind. In the late 1990s, Buffett publicly stated he'd never invest in technology stocks, yet he became one of Apple's largest shareholders in 2016. On missing the opportunity to invest in companies like Google and Amazon earlier on, Buffett admitted that he "had plenty of ways to ask questions, or anything of the sort, and educate myself, but I blew it."

Realizing a deeply held conviction was wrong is a new lease on life. It means you're still a student, still learning, and not done yet—and Warren Buffett is no exception. Most people at such a late stage in their career, with so much success behind them, would be more focused on celebrating their wins and reinforcing their legacy rather than lamenting on mistakes made and lessons learned. Not so for Buffett. By obsessing over what he's done wrong and being willing to change long-standing beliefs, he has the permeability and flexibility of someone just starting their career rather than someone nearing the finish.

Those I know who have met Buffett talk about his insatiable curiosity. He claims to have read between six hundred and one thousand pages a day of books on topics of interest at the beginning of his career, and he still spends 80 percent or so of each day reading. When someone visiting once asked him about his key to success, Buffett reportedly pointed to a stack of books on his desk and said, "Read five hundred pages like this every day. That's how knowledge works. It builds up, like compound interest. All of you can do it, but I guarantee not many of you will do it."

Such curiosity, self-scrutiny, and a willingness to change your convictions all share a common theme: the persistent desire to learn. Learning is an elixir of life, and Buffett drinks it daily.

You're either part of the living or the dying.

Our mortality is just about the only sure thing there is. At least that's one way to look at it. The other perspective is that we're living and will be for the foreseeable future. The perspective you apply impacts how you spend your time and your productivity.

Challenges will either depress or mobilize your efforts in new ways, but not both. If you see a challenge as the looming end, you'll likely lose faster. But if you focus on maximizing the moment at hand, it'll help you live even more.

My aunt, Arlis Aron, fought a battle with stage-four cancer that lasted fifteen years. Every time she received a death sentence from the dozens of doctors she met, the more she got into gardening, family, travel, and the relationships around her. Every time she was asked to accept her fate that she was dying, Arlis became more immersed in living. In her final month alive, Arlis was still talking about the flowers in her garden and how, at breakfast, she stares and gets lost in their patterns and colors.

For someone like me, who considers his mortality when suffering the common cold, Arlis was an incredible inspiration. More than anyone else I have known who has suffered a serious illness, Arlis chose to be a part of the living. She found something beautiful or funny in almost every moment and considered every additional day of consciousness an opportunity to do more of what she enjoyed. Whenever I found myself worrying about the trivialities of my job or getting frustrated with paperwork or getting our children ready for preschool, I'd remind myself that Arlis was living that day more than I was.

When she passed away, her legacy was one of courage and love for life. While every funeral is sad, especially for someone as young and vibrant as Arlis was, everyone spoke about being uplifted by her spirit and approach to life. I'm convinced that Arlis survived fifteen years—defying the odds given to her by every doctor she met—because she refused to spend her days dying.

Whatever challenge you're suffering from, you can use it to decide if you want to live less or live more. When you find yourself dwelling on the end of a journey, double down on the joys and curiosities of the day. Not only are they real, they offer a path to a richer life.

We are so willing to trade time for money when we are young, and money for time as we age.

We are so willing to trade time for money in the early days because so much of life is ahead of us, and money seems more finite than time. As my friends and I navigated our early careers with the burden of providing for our families and getting our lives situated, we spent inordinate amounts of time at the office, if only for marginal returns.

But as you age, time feels more scarce. Like most people who find themselves busier as the years pass, I have a dire want of more time. As a father, time is the only way to build relationships with my children. Resources can be enjoyed only by taking the time to have experiences with the people you love. As I look back in my earlier years, I'm surprised by how much time I squandered.

Should you live your life assuming it will be short or long? The former makes you relish every moment, while the latter encourages you to sacrifice near-term joy for long-term gain. What we assume impacts the decisions and trade-offs you're willing to make.

More than one mentor has told me that the ultimate achievement is being able to spend your time as you wish. But affording autonomy of your time is different from practicing autonomy. Allan Ash, the grandfather of my accountant and founder of his firm, repeated many adages to his clients. One of these was passed down the family tree and eventually stuck with me. According to his grandson, Neil Ash, Allan would say, "I can lose a thousand dollars and, as much as it bothers me, I can always make those lost funds back and break even. However, when I lose a day or a weekend, I can never do anything to get that time back. That is a true realized loss."

We lose time when we let others spend it for us. While you may know how you wish to spend it, if you're like me, you probably lack the guts or self-control to do so. You don't want to say no to friends, even if you'd rather spend the time somewhere else. You don't want to pass up on professional opportunities that are coveted by others, even if it doesn't quite feel like the right fit for you. You don't want to miss the action in your industry or favorite sports team, even if the people around you are more important to you. But if the things that people ask of you or your phone presents to you are not experiences you wish to remember, why spend time on something you'll likely—or want to—forget? The most actionable advice I once heard was, when you find yourself distracted by technology or some other preoccupation while with your children or loved ones, pretend you're forty years older and longing to have just one more moment with these people at this time in your life. It helps.

Some parts of life are resource intensive and you need to accept the investment of time they will take. Developing new things, whether they are products or children, brings inevitable friction that requires raw time to navigate. If you're leading a team and developing a new product vision, you'll need uninterrupted time to get each member of your team on board with your plan. Parenting is a huge chunk of time and energy over many years, and any attempts to economize time with your family carry consequences. The more you value your time, the more pressure you will feel to spend it wisely, and the more you'll struggle with these parts of life that have no shortcuts. Remind yourself that these parts of life are not meant to be sped through. For these time-intensive, friction-filled portions of life that you chose, consider the time you spend as an effort to permanently embed the experience in your memory. You see, life's frictions have another purpose aside from consuming your time: They make portions of your life more memorable. For an experience to be memorable, it must have friction. Just as all of life's beach vacations become somewhat indistinguishable from one another, experiences without friction are hard to remember.

The answer to the time equation is not as simple as saying yes to things you want to spend time on and no to things you don't. Some of the most important and memorable parts of life are the ones that have taken the longest. Instead, the test for time investments is whether or not the experience is something you want to remember. Looking back at the end of your life, do you want to remember toiling away on a particular project? Do you want to remember raising your children? Do you want to remember working on your relationship with your partner? Do you want to remember coaching people in their careers?

If it's something you just want to accomplish but don't wish to remember doing, consider saying no. However, if it is an experience that you wish to remember, then spend the time enduring the friction to create memories you'll never forget. Because the best parts of life have friction, and memories are all that we have.

To be done
is to die.

The notion of being "done" suggests that your interest has ceased. But for those who love what they do, this never happens. The creative pursuit never ends. Creativity is never finished.

Brad Smith, a New York–based serial entrepreneur of companies like Virb, Wayward Wild, and Simplecast, has cycled through his share of ventures. Looking back on his roller coaster of a journey, he's aware that there will be more peaks ahead.

"Four times over, with four ventures, I've always had an end goal in mind. But it is never, ever where I ended up. Not to say the endings weren't sweet or a proper close to a chapter: It only seems that, for me, the journey itself always changes the desired outcome. Every goddamn time. I've wrapped up and 'finished' projects before, yet all it really has ever meant is that I now have the time to start a project anew. The circle of entrepreneurial life continues. Ashes to ashes, spreadsheets to P&L. A project—a REAL project—isn't a project. It's a passion. Those don't die."

Ashes to ashes indeed. Projects and passionate pursuits may die, but only in the way that vegetation dies and becomes soil for new growth. The embers of every dying project become the energy that feeds the next. When you execute and ship your creations, you should celebrate—you deserve every accolade that is bestowed upon you. But then you need to kill the feeling of being done. Destroy it with something new.

In Hindu theology, there are three main gods that exist and function in unison with equal importance. Brahma is the creator, the source of new ideas and things. Vishnu is the preserver, there to maintain and nourish what already is. And Shiva is the destroyer, there to bring all things to an end. These gods don't work in a linear order, however—with Brahma creating, Vishnu preserving, and Shiva destroying—they all work at the same time, constantly feeding into one another. In this case, Shiva isn't known as the evil god. On the contrary, Shiva represents the power of regeneration and the importance of making room for new and better things. When you don't factor in the third and equally essential part of a holy trinity, the whole cycle breaks.

As your project comes full circle and you return to where you started, you'll need to regenerate. You'll need to stare down your past accomplishments. The companies, leaders, and designers I admire most find ways to make their greatest creations obsolete. Whether it's the iPhone cannibalizing the smashing success of the iPod or an artist's new style that makes her old work look antiquated, you should strive to make your last creation irrelevant. This is a healthy, grounding, and challenging way to approach a creative career. Roll up your sleeves and move on. The beauty of competing with yourself is that you're never done.

As you approach a major finish in your life, you'll need to return your mind-set to the "early innings," you'll need to summon up your dissatisfactions and curiosities, and you'll need to suppress the sensation of being done by adding more and more to your list. Italian novelist and philosopher Umberto Eco once suggested that "we like lists because we don't want to die." Lists keep us unfinished, and the sensation of having more to do is very much what keeps us learning and striving. Lists keep us alive. Be satisfied with your life, but not with what you've made. Strive to be more fulfilled by what you're doing than what you've done. Keep on doing.

The greatest end is a new beginning, and feeling done is your greatest obstacle. Your final mile needs to give rise to a new first mile experience in which you, once again, start something because you can't stop thinking about it, where you're naive enough to embrace all possibilities, and when you've become empathetic for people suffering a problem that either fascinates or frustrates you (one hopes both). You'll need to keep feeding your interests, stay permeable, and never assume that what worked before will work again.

The messy middle miles that you endure and optimize your way through don't get any easier and never repeat themselves, because they are the moat between vision and reality. The messy middle is a life's work, and when anyone crosses the finish line and pushes an extraordinary creation out to the world, we all benefit. In this sense, we're all in this together, learning the hard way, and sharing the insights garnered from our own journeys to help us all maximize our middles so that more great ideas see the light of day. The future is created by those who endured and optimized through the messy middle to create it. For you and for the rest of us, stick with it.

Acknowledgments

This book would have nothing but empty pages if it weren't for the founders and teams that have allowed me to participate in their businesses as a cofounder, investor, adviser, confidant, and student. To the hundreds of entrepreneurs and leaders I interviewed or surveyed for this book, and especially to those whom I have worked with over the years, thank you. The experiences you afforded me, and the wisdom you shared, inspired all of the content in this book, and I did my best to do you justice in hopes that others can benefit as much as I have. The same gratitude goes to the remarkable designers, engineers, and leaders at Adobe who welcomed my team and me into the company and empowered us to do some of the greatest work of our lives. I have come to love the company and its purpose in the creative world, and I feel so fortunate to work with all of you. I also want to recognize Matias Corea, Dave Stein, Chris Henry, Bryan Latten, Jackie Balzer, Zach Mc-Cullough, Clément Faydi, Alex Krug, and other early members of the Behance team with whom I traversed an especially volatile middle.

I am grateful to Georgia Frances King for her role as an editor throughout the first draft of the manuscript and for serving as a fantastic thought partner and occasional cheerleader when I felt perpetually stuck in the middle and wondered if this project would ever end. I also want to thank Leah Fessler for her help collecting and synthesizing research for parts of the book that required additional sources, and Raewyn Brandon for her help designing the graphics in the book and the cover—and for her support over the years on communication design of all kinds. I am extremely grateful to Stephanie Frerich, my editor at Penguin's Portfolio imprint, for seeking me out while all of these insights were still a disorganized collection of random notations and for encouraging me to commit to this project and helping bring it to the finish line. I would like to thank my longtime literary agent, Jim Levine, from Levine Greenberg Rostan Literary Agency, who took a chance on me about ten years ago with the idea for *Making Ideas Happen* and, once again, encouraged me to push this project to fruition. I'd also like to thank a few people who have been mentors or played an encouraging role for me in this project, whether they know it or not, including Itai Dinour, Michael Schwalbe, Mike Brown, Erin Brannan, Alex Shapses, Garrett Camp, Tim Ferriss, Yves Behar, Dave Morin, Jenn Hyman, Jocelyn Glei, Felecitas Yeske, Michael Meyer, the Benchmark team, Hunter Walk and Satya Patel at Homebrew, Fred Wilson, Joanne Wilson, Albert Wenger, the Founder Collective, JB Osborne, Emily Heyward, Becky Grossman, Ben Grossman, the Posternack family, Josh Elman, Semil Shah, Julio Vasconcellos, Andrew Barr, the Prefer team, my amazing product leadership team at Adobe, the sweetgreen guys, Mike from the music-now-cheese shop, Rabbi Elliot Cosgrove, James Higa, Elliot Zeisel, John Maeda, Simon Sinek, and Seth Godin. I am also especially grateful to Nina Bingham, my longtime executive assistant, whose judgment, commitment, and talent help me make the most of every day.

I want to thank my parents, Nancy and Mark, and my sisters, Julie and Gila, who have always been such cheerleaders and have spawned in me a sense of confidence that, no doubt, exceeds my own abilities. I also want to take this opportunity to thank my extended family that has been supportive throughout my career roller coaster, multiple cross-country moves, and the many creative projects along the way—Ellen and Alain Roizen, Andrew and Remy Weinstein, Alex Modell, Susan Kaplan, and Ahuvi Golden.

Most of all, I want to thank my wife, Erica, my daughter, Chloe, and my son, Miles, for supporting this project, tolerating the years of weekend writing blocks, writing retreats, and middle-of-the-night notations required to make this book happen. You made it possible while also challenging me to keep my priorities at the front and values at the center. I love you so much and can think of no better team with whom to endure and optimize—and enjoy—the middle.

skb

Notes

ENDURE

LEADING THROUGH THE ANGUISH AND THE UNKNOWN

SHORT-CIRCUIT YOUR REWARD SYSTEM.

26 **"With each success":** Monica Mehta, "Why Our Brains Like Short-term Goals," *Entrepreneur*, January 3, 2013, www.entrepreneur.com/article/225356.

26 **average life expectancy:** "Medicine and Health," *Stratford Hall*, accessed March 22, 2018, www.stratfordhall.org/educational-resources/teacher-resources/medicine-health.

26 **40 percent of people:** "Death in Early America," *Digital History*, December 30, 2010, https://web.archive.org/web/20101230203658/http://www.digitalhistory.uh.edu/historyonline/usdeath.cfm.

DON'T SEEK POSITIVE FEEDBACK OR CELEBRATE FAKE WINS AT THE EXPENSE OF HARD TRUTHS.

29 **"The truth about telling":** Ben Horowitz, "How to Tell the Truth," Andreessen Horowitz, accessed March 22, 2018, https://a16z.com/2017/07/27/how-to-tell-the-truth.

FRICTION BRINGS US CLOSER.

37 **the case for friction:** Hugo Macdonald, "Friction Builds Fires, Moves Mountains, and Makes Babies—And May Be the Key to Social Progress," *Quartz*, March 29, 2017, https://qz.com/944434/friction-builds-fires-moves-mountains-and-makes-babies-and-may-be-the-key-to-social-progress/.

38 **"When staying alive":** Richard F. Taflinger, "Taking ADvantage: Social Basis of Human Behavior," *Social Basis of Human Behavior*, May 28, 1996, https://public.wsu.edu/~taflinge/socself.html.

38 **"In ancient history":** E. O. Wilson, "Why Humans Hate," *Newsweek*, April 02, 2012, www.newsweek.com/biologist-eo-wilson-why-humans-ants-need-tribe-64005.

39 **"it actually paid":** Sarah Green Carmichael, "Sheryl Sandberg and Adam Grant on Resilience," *Harvard Business Review*, April 27, 2017, https://hbr.org/ideacast/2017/04/sheryl-sandberg-and-adam-grant-on-resilience.html.

39 **"I never would have gotten":** Ibid.

39 **"The impediment to action":** Eric Ravenscraft, "The Impediment to Action Advances Action," *LifeHacker*, October 9, 2016, https://lifehacker.com/the-impediment-to-action-advances-action-1788748064.

STRENGTHENING YOUR RESOLVE

NOBODY REMEMBERS, OR IS INSPIRED BY, ANYTHING THAT FITS IN.

58 **"Learn to say 'fuck you'":** Maria Popova, "Do: Sol LeWitt's Electrifying Letter of Advice on Self-Doubt, Overcoming Creative Block, and Being an Artist," *Brain Pickings*, accessed March 22, 2018, www.brainpickings.org/2016/09/09/do-sol-lewitt-eva-hesse-letter.

59 **In a 2015 study:** Tim Ramsay, Sarasa Togyama, Alexander Tuttle, et al, "Increasing placebo responses over time in U.S. clinical trials of neuropathic pain," *Pain* 156, no. 12 (December 2015): 2616–26, https://journals.lww.com/pain/pages/articleviewer.aspx?year=2015&issue=12000&article=00027&type=abstract.

ATTEMPT A NEW PERSPECTIVE OF IT BEFORE YOU QUIT IT.

62 **In 2016, she wrote:** Angela Duckworth, *Grit: The Power of Passion and Perseverance* (New York: Scribner, 2016).

62 **"Grit is having stamina":** Angela Duckworth, "Grit: The Power of Passion and Perseverance," filmed April 2013 in Vancouver, Canada, TED video, 6:09, www.ted.com/talks/angela_lee_duckworth_grit_the_power_of_passion_and_perseverance.

63 **"when you look at healthy":** Julie Scelfo, "Angela Duckworth on Passion, Grit and Success," *New York Times*, April 8, 2016, www
.nytimes.com/2016/04/10/education/edlife/passion-grit-success.html.

SOMETIMES A RESET IS THE ONLY WAY FORWARD.

73 **"I spent three weeks":** Jennifer Wang, "How 5 Successful Entrepreneurs Bounced Back After Failure," *Entrepreneur*, January 23,
2013, www.entrepreneur.com/article/225204.

73 **"I was blindsided":** Ibid.

73 **"It was painful":** Ibid.

73 **The Muse was accepted:** Kathryn Minshew, "The Muse's Successful Application to Y Combinator (W12)," The Muse, accessed
March 22, 2018, www.themuse.com/advice/the-muses-successful-application-to-y-combinator-w12.

73 **"My heroes, in real life":** Wang, "How 5 Successful Entrepreneurs Bounced Back."

73 **Anthropologie's "Woman of Character":** "Women of Character: Kathryn Minshew," Anthropologie, September 30, 2015, www
.youtube.com/watch?v=M32tPGYzCXs.

EMBRACING THE LONG GAME

PLAYING THE LONG GAME REQUIRES MOVES THAT DON'T MAP TO TRADITIONAL MEASURES OF PRODUCTIVITY.

79 **"Invention requires a long-term":** Derek Thompson, "The Amazon Mystery: What America's Strangest Tech Company Is Really
Up To," *The Atlantic*, November 2013, www.theatlantic.com/magazine/archive/2013/11/the-riddle-of-amazon/309523.

STRATEGY IS NOURISHED BY PATIENCE.

81 **"Because of our emphasis":** Jeffrey P. Bezos, "1997 Letter to Shareholders," *Amazon*, accessed March 22, 2018, www.amazon.com
/p/feature/z6o9g6sysxur57t.

82 **"If we have a good quarter":** Arjun Kharpal, "Amazon CEO Jeff Bezos Has a Pretty Good Idea of Quarterly Earnings 3 Years in
Advance," CNBC, May 8, 2017, www.cnbc.com/2017/05/08/amazon-ceo-jeff-bezos-long-term-thinking.html.

83 **"Startups win by":** Aaron Levie (@levie), "Startups win by being impatient over a long period of time," Twitter, January 12, 2013, 5:17
P.M., https://twitter.com/levie/status/290266267682758656.

83–84 **Netflix CEO Reed Hastings:** Marc Graser, "Epic Fail: How Blockbuster Could Have Owned Netflix," *Variety*, November 12, 2013,
http://variety.com/2013/biz/news/epic-fail-how-blockbuster-could-have-owned-netflix-1200823443.

84 **"a very small niche":** Ibid.

84 **Blockbuster went bankrupt:** Greg Satell, "A Look Back at Why Blockbuster Really Failed and Why It Didn't Have To," *Forbes*,
September 5, 2014, www.forbes.com/sites/gregsatell/2014/09/05/a-look-back-at-why-blockbuster-really-failed-and-why-it-didnt-have
-to/#223776561d64.

84 **a $150 billion:** Paul R. La Monica, "Netflix Is No House of Cards: It's Now Worth $70 Billion," *CNN Money*, May 30, 2017, https://
money.cnn.com/2017/05/30/investing/netflix-stock-house-of-cards/index.html.

84 **"Longevity of focus":** Alexandra Appolonia and Matthew Stuart, "*Wonder Woman* Director Patty Jenkins on the Biggest Challenge
She Faced Bringing the Hero to the Big Screen," *Business Insider*, May 30, 2017, www.businessinsider.com/wonder-woman-director
-patty-jenkins-biggest-challenge-faced-pressure-2017-5.

JUST STAY ALIVE LONG ENOUGH TO BECOME AN EXPERT.

90 **software company Basecamp:** Jason Fried (@jasonfried), "Outlasting is one of the best competitive moves you can ever make.
Requires a sound, sustainable business at the core which is why it's so hard for so many to do." Twitter, January 28, 2018, 5:25 P.M.,
https://twitter.com/jasonfried/status/957786841821802496.

DO THE WORK REGARDLESS OF WHOSE WORK IT IS.

92 **"The best way to complain":** James Murphy, "The Best Way to Complain Is to Make Things," *Startup Vitamins*, accessed March 22,
2018, http://startupquotes.startupvitamins.com/post/41941517470/the-best-way-to-complain-is-to-make-things-james.

OPTIMIZE

BUILDING, HIRING, AND FIRING

RESOURCEFULNESS > RESOURCES

101 **Their first satellite:** James Temple, "Everything You Need to Know About Skybox, Google's Big Satellite Play," *Recode*, June 11, 2014,
www.recode.net/2014/6/11/11627878/everything-you-need-to-know-about-skybox-googles-big-satellite-play.

102 **"I've seen many startups shift":** Jessica Livingston, "Subtle Mid-Stage Startup Pitfalls," *Founders at Work*, April 29, 2015, http://
foundersatwork.posthaven.com/subtle-mid-stage-pitfalls.

DIVERSITY DRIVES DIFFERENTIATION.

107 **"Where do new ideas":** Nicholas Negroponte, "Being Decimal," *Wired*, November 1, 1995, https://www.wired.com/1995/11/nicholas.

107 **"It's a simple idea":** John Maeda, "Did I Grow Up and Become the Yellow Hand?" *Medium*, January 25, 2016, https://medium.com
/tech-diversity-files/did-i-grow-up-and-become-the-yellow-hand-dea56464237c.

107   **A 2015 study by:** Peter Schulz, "Introducing *The Information*'s Future List," *The Information*, October 6, 2015, www.theinformation .com/articles/introducing-the-informations-future-list.

107   **She points out how:** Gabrielle Hogan-Brun, "People Who Speak Multiple Languages Make the Best Employees for One Big Reason," *Quartz*, March 9, 2017, https://qz.com/927660/people-who-speak-multiple-languages-make-the-best-employees-for-one-big-reason.

108   **"In the German mind":** Ibid.

108   **"If your strategy is":** Gabrielle Hogan-Brun, "Why Multilingualism Is Good for Economic Growth," *The Conversation*, February 3, 2017, http://theconversation.com/why-multilingualism-is-good-for-economic-growth-71851.

108   **According to research by Bern:** Simon Bradley, "Languages Generate One Tenth of Swiss GDP," *Swiss Info*, November 20, 2008, www.swissinfo.ch/eng/languages-generate-one-tenth-of-swiss-gdp/7050488.

108   **Hogan-Brun cites:** Hogan-Brun, "People Who Speak Multiple Languages."

108   **"The Bilingual Brain":** Angela Grant, "The Bilingual Brain: Why One Size Doesn't Fit All," *Aeon*, March 13, 2017, https://aeon.co /ideas/the-bilingual-brain-why-one-size-doesnt-fit-all.

GRAFTING TALENT IS JUST AS IMPORTANT AS RECRUITING TALENT.

122   **"a shared belief that":** Amy Edmondson, "Psychological Safety and Learning Behavior in Work Teams," *Administrative Science Quarterly* 44, no. 2 (June 1999), www.iacmr.org/Conferences/WS2011/Submission_XM/Participant/Readings/Lecture9B_Jing/Ed mondson,%20ASQ%201999.pdf.

122   **is "a sense of confidence that the":** Erica Dhawan, "The Secret Weapon for Collaboration," *Forbes*, April 14, 2016, www.forbes.com /sites/ericadhawan/2016/04/14/the-secret-weapon-to-collaboration/#54a66efa7b50.

122   **"What Project Aristotle":** Charles Duhigg, "What Google Learned from Its Quest to Build the Perfect Team," *New York Times*, February 25, 2016, www.nytimes.com/2016/02/28/magazine/what-google-learned-from-its-quest-to-build-the-perfect-team.html.

A STEADY STATE IS UNSUSTAINABLE; KEEP PEOPLE MOVING.

131   **"The more voluntary":** Tim Ferriss (@tferriss), "The more voluntary suffering you build into your life, the less involuntary suffering will affect your life," Twitter, January 15, 2017, 1:28 P.M., https://twitter.com/tferriss/status/820744508778246144.

CULTURE, TOOLS, AND SPACE

CULTURE IS CREATED THROUGH THE STORIES YOUR TEAM TELLS.

135   **"Culture is not something":** Ben Thompson, "The Curse of Culture," *Stratechery*, May 24, 2016, https://stratechery.com/2016 /the-curse-of-culture.

STRUCTURE AND COMMUNICATION

MERCHANDISE TO CAPTURE AND KEEP YOUR TEAM'S ATTENTION.

159   **"Year of the Driver":** Johana Bhuiyan, "Drivers Don't Trust Uber. This Is How It's Trying to Win Them Back," *Recode*, February 5, 2018, www.recode.net/2018/2/5/16777536/uber-travis-kalanick-recruit-drivers-tipping.

160   **"Of all the things that can":** Teresa Amabile and Steven J. Kramer, "The Power of Small Wins," *Harvard Business Review*, May 2011, https://hbr.org/2011/05/the-power-of-small-wins.

A MOCK-UP > ANY OTHER METHOD OF SHARING YOUR VISION

162   **"When evaluating a product":** Peep Laja, "8 Things That Grab and Hold Website Visitor's Attention," *Conversation XL*, May 8, 2017, https://conversionxl.com/blog/how-to-grab-and-hold-attention.

DELEGATE, ENTRUST, DEBRIEF, AND REPEAT.

167   **The problem is that, in the heat:** David Marquet, "The Counterintuitive Art of Leading by Letting Go," 99U, accessed March 23, 2018, https://99u.adobe.com/articles/43081/the-counter-intuitive-art-of-leading-by-letting-go.

KNOW HOW AND WHEN TO SAY IT.

171   **"The medium is the message":** Marshall McLuhan, *Understanding Media: The Extensions of Man*, (New York: McGraw-Hill, 1964).

172   **"means that our body":** Vanessa Van Edwards, "3 Tips for Women to Improve Their Body Language at Work," *Forbes*, May 21, 2013, www.forbes.com/sites/yec/2013/05/21/3-tips-for-women-to-improve-their-body-language-at-work/#7d8f65c98153.

CLEARING THE PATH TO SOLUTIONS

TACKLE "ORGANIZATIONAL DEBT."

178   **"all the compromises":** Scott Belsky, "Avoiding Organizational Debt," *Medium*, September 12, 2016, https://medium.com /positiveslope/avoiding-organizational-debt-3e47760803a0.

179   **"any employee who encounters a policy":** Aaron Dignan, "How to Eliminate Organizational Debt," *Medium*, June 30, 2016, https://medium.com/the-ready/how-to-eliminate-organizational-debt-8a949c06b61b.

A LOT OF BIG PROBLEMS DON'T GET SOLVED BECAUSE WE CAN SOLVE SMALL PROBLEMS FASTER.

180 **"the name we give":** Charles Duhigg, *Smarter Faster Better* (New York: Random House, 2016), Kindle location 80.

181 **"Chipping away at":** Jocelyn Glei, *Unsubscribe: How to Kill Email Anxiety, Avoid Distractions, and Get Real Work Done* (New York: Public Affairs, 2016), 11.

181 **"The problem is that while winnowing":** Ibid. 13.

CREATIVE BLOCK IS THE CONSEQUENCE OF AVOIDING THE TRUTH.

193 **"It's easier to tell Zuck":** Paul Graham (@paulg), "It's easier to tell Zuck that he's wrong than to tell the average noob founder. He's not threatened by it. If he's wrong, he wants to know," Twitter, May 8, 2017, 1:31 A.M., https://twitter.com/paulg/status/861498777160622080.

193 **"What distinguishes great":** Paul Graham (@paulg), "What distinguishes great founders is not their adherence to some vision, but their humility in the face of the truth," Twitter, May 8, 2017, https://twitter.com/paulg/status/861498048949735424.

VALUE THE MERITS OF SLOW COOKING.

196 **"Human beings are very":** Daniel Gilbert, "Humans Wired to Respond to Short-term Problems," NPR, July 3, 2006, www.npr.org/templates/story/story.php?storyId=5530483.

"ASK FOR FORGIVENESS, NOT PERMISSION."

200 **In May 1886:** Pauline de Tholozany, "Paris: Capital of the 19th Century," *Brown University Library Center for Digital Scholarship*, 2011, https://library.brown.edu/cds/paris/worldfairs.html.

201 **"We, writers, painters":** CBS Team, "Eiffel Tower—The Fascinating Structure," *CBS Forum*, January 14, 2013, www.cbsforum.com/cgi-bin/articles/partners/cbs/search.cgi?template=display&dbname=cbsarticles&key2=eiffel&action=searchdbdisplay.

201 **the French writer:** Phil Edwards, "The Eiffel Tower Debuted 126 Years Ago. It Nearly Tore Paris Apart," *Vox*, March 31, 2015, https://.vox.com/2015/3/31/8314115/when-the-eiffel-tower-opened-to-the-public.

201 **"hole-riddled suppository":** Ibid.

201 **opening on March:** Oliver Smith, "Eiffel Tower: 40 Fascinating Facts," *Telegraph*, March 31, 2014, www.telegraph.co.uk/travel/destinations/europe/france/paris/articles/Eiffel-Tower-facts.

201 **tallest structure in the world:** Ibid.

201 **During the Exposition:** CBS Team, "Eiffel Tower."

201 **The Louvre Pyramid, designed as:** Paul Goldberger, "Pei Pyramid and New Louvre Open Today," *New York Times*, March 29, 1989, www.nytimes.com/1989/03/29/arts/pei-pyramid-and-new-louvre-open-today.html.

201 **pyramid sparked hatred:** Elizabeth Evitts Dickinson, "Louvre Pyramid: The Folly That Became a Triumph," *Architect*, www.architectmagazine.com/awards/aia-honor-awards/louvre-pyramid-the-folly-that-became-a-triumph_o.

201 **François Mitterrand, then president:** Richard Bernstein, "I. M. Pei's Pyramid: A Provocative Plan for the Louvre," *New York Times*, November 24, 1985, www.nytimes.com/1985/11/24/magazine/im-pei-s-pyramid-a-provative-plan-for-the-louvre.html.

201 **"As soon as the project":** "The Louvre Pyramid: History, Architecture, and Legend," Paris City Vision, accessed March 23, 2018, www.pariscityvision.com/en/paris/museums/louvre-museum/the-louvre-pyramid-history-architecture-legend.

201 **90 percent of Parisians:** Dickinson, "Louvre Pyramid."

201 **In 1983, Andre:** "Life of Pei: Creator of Famous Louvre Pyramid Survived the Critics, and Today He Turns 100," *South China Morning Post*, April 26, 2017, www.scmp.com/news/world/europe/article/2090450/life-pei-creator-famous-louvre-pyramid-paris-was-savaged-then.

201 **"I received many angry":** Ibid.

CONVICTION > CONSENSUS

203 **"A committee is a group":** M. P. Singh, *Quote Unquote* (Detroit: Lotus Press, 2005), 85.

204 **"The vast majority of human":** Charalampos Konstantopoulos and Grammati Pantziou, eds., *Modeling, Computing and Data Handling Methodologies for Maritime Transportation* (New York: Springer, 2017), 2.

204 **"No answers are obvious":** Mark Suster, "My Number One Advice for Startups or VCs: Conviction > Consensus," *Both Sides of the Table*, May 3, 2015, https://bothsidesofthetable.com/my-number-one-advice-for-startups-or-vcs-conviction-consensus-7a73d7d8b45b.

SIMPLIFYING AND ITERATING

KILL YOUR DARLINGS.

220 **"In writing, you must":** Forrest Wickman, "Who Really Said You Should 'Kill Your Darlings'?" *Slate*, October 18, 2013, www.slate.com/blogs/browbeat/2013/10/18/_kill_your_darlings_writing_advice_what_writer_really_said_to_murder_your.html.

220 **"Kill your darlings, kill your darlings":** Ibid.

220 **"If you here require":** Ibid.

222 **In my first book:** Scott Belsky, *Making Ideas Happen* (New York: Portfolio, 2010), 75.

IF YOU DON'T THINK IT'S AWESOME, STOP MAKING IT.

224 **As Aaron Levi, founder and CEO:** Aaron Levie (@levie), "To make everyone happy with the decision, you'll make no one happy with the outcome." Twitter, April 23, 2013, 5:06 A.M., https://tweetgrazer.com/levie/tweets/6.

224 **"Some decisions are consequential":** Jeffrey P. Bezos, "2016 Letter to Shareholders," SEC, accessed March 23, 2018, www.sec.gov/Archives/edgar/data/1018724/000119312516530910/d168744dex991.htm.

TOO MUCH SCRUTINY CREATES FLAWS.

228 **"If the ability":** Becky Kane, "The Science of Analysis Paralysis: How Overthinking Kills Your Productivity & What You Can Do About It," *Todoist*, July 8, 2015, https://blog.todoist.com/2015/07/08/analysis-paralysis-and-your-productivity.

229 **studies conducted at Swarthmore:** Barry Schwartz, "The Tyranny of Choice," *Scientific American*, December 2004, www.scientific american.com/article/the-tyranny-of-choice.

229 **economist Herbert Simon coined:** "Herbert Simon," *Economist*, March 20, 2009, economist.com/node/13350892.

229 **as journalist Becky:** Kane, "The Science of Analysis Paralysis."

EFFECTIVE DESIGN IS INVISIBLE.

230 **"Good design is as little":** Muriel Domingo, "Dieter Rams: 10 Timeless Commandments for Good Design," *Interaction Design Foundation*, March 9, 2018, www.interaction-design.org/literature/article/dieter-rams-10-timeless-commandments-for-good-design.

ANCHORING TO YOUR CUSTOMERS

EMPATHY AND HUMILITY BEFORE PASSION.

250 **"It's very important to know":** Daniel McGinn, "Life's Work: An Interview with Jerry Seinfeld," *Harvard Business Review*, January–February 2017, https://hbr.org/2017/01/lifes-work-jerry-seinfeld.

THE LEADERS OF THRIVING COMMUNITIES (ONLINE AND OFF-) ACT AS STEWARDS, NOT OWNERS.

259 **"It's not just how":** Austin Carr, "I Found Out My Secret Internal Tinder Rating and Now I Wish I Hadn't," *Fast Company*, January 11, 2016, www.fastcompany.com/3054871/whats-your-tinder-score-inside-the-apps-internal-ranking-system.

260 **"I used to play":** Ibid.

260 **"It's a vague":** Ibid.

260 **"You can't really manage":** Bo Burlingham, "Jim Collins: Be Great Now," *Inc.*, May 29, 2012, www.inc.com/magazine/201206/bo-burlingham/jim-collins-exclusive-interview-be-great-now.html.

MYSTERY IS THE MAGIC OF ENGAGEMENT.

271 **"I have no special":** Alice Calaprice and Trevor Lipscombe, *Albert Einstein: A Biography* (Westport, CT: Greenwood, 2005), 2.

272 **The leading psychological:** Russell Golman and George Loewenstein, "An Information-Gap Theory of Feelings About Uncertainty," Carnegie Mellon University, January 2, 2016, www.cmu.edu/dietrich/sds/docs/golman/Information-Gap%20Theory %202016.pdf.

272 **"Such information gaps":** George Loewenstein, "The Psychology of Curiosity: A Review and Reinterpretation," *Psychological Bulletin*, 116, no. 1 (July 1994): 75–98, https://pdfs.semanticscholar.org/f946/7adac17f3ef6d65cdcf38b46afb974abfa55.pdf.

272 **"Its onset, like hunger":** Eric Jaffe, "Upworthy's Headlines Are Insufferable. Here's Why You Click Anyway," *Fast Company*, www .fastcodesign.com/3028193/upworthys-headlines-are-insufferable-heres-why-you-click-anyway.

272 **"test participants had":** Ibid.

272 **"The lesson is that":** Jonah Lehrer, "The Itch of Curiosity," *Wired*, August 3, 2010, www.wired.com/2010/08/the-itch-of-curiosity.

272 **"The [Caltech] researchers":** Jaffe, "Upworthy's Headlines Are Insufferable."

272 **"The fact that curiosity":** Lehrer, "The Itch of Curiosity."

273 **2017 Super Bowl:** 84 Lumber, "84 Lumber Super Bowl Commercial—The Entire Journey," February 5, 2017, YouTube video, 5:44, www.youtube.com/watch?v=nPo2B-vjZ28.

273 **features like "ludicrous speed":** Victor Luckerson, "Tesla's New 'Ludicrous Speed' Might Make Your Brain Explode," *Time*, July 17, 2015, http://time.com/3963205/tesla-ludicrous-speed.

PLANNING AND MAKING DECISIONS

MAKE A PLAN BUT DON'T PLAN ON STICKING TO IT.

280 **"In preparing for battle":** Tom Kendrick, *Identifying and Managing Project Risk: Essential Tools for Failure-Proofing* (New York: AMACOM, 2015), 335.

SUCCESS FAILS TO SCALE WHEN WE FAIL TO FOCUS.

284 **In his revered:** Barry Schwartz, *The Paradox of Choice: Why More Is Less* (New York: Ecco, 2004).

284 **"Maximizers need to be":** Ibid.

285 **"For decades, books":** Gerd Gigerenzer, *Gut Feelings: The Intelligence of the Unconscious* (New York: Viking, 2007), 5.

IN ALMOST ALL CASES, BEST TO IGNORE SUNK COSTS.

291 **"If I didn't have this":** Tom Stafford, "Why We Love to Hoard . . . and How You Can Overcome It," BBC, July 17, 2012, www.bbc.com /future/story/20120717-why-we-love-to-hoard.

292 **Jeff Bezos once remarked:** Jason Fried, "Some Advice from Jeff Bezos," *Signal v. Noise*, October 19, 2012, https://signalvnoise.com /posts/3289-some-advice-from-jeff-bezos.

CRAFTING BUSINESS INSTINCTS

MINE CONTRADICTORY ADVICE AND DOUBT TO DEVELOP YOUR OWN INTUITION.

295 **"Look for investors"**: Joe Fernandez (@JoeFernandez), "Look for investors that respect the fact you're not always going to follow their advice," Twitter, May 20, 2016, 7:03 A.M., https://twitter.com/JoeFernandez/status/733659372535091200.

295 **"another one of Apple's"**: Macworld Staff, "What They Said About the iPod: 'Another One of Apple's Failures Just Like the Newton,'" *Macworld*, October 23, 2006, www.macworld.com/article/1053500/consumer-electronics/ipodreax.html.

295 **"No wireless. Less space"**: Ibid.

DON'T BLINDLY OPTIMIZE, KEEP AUDITING YOUR MEASURES.

297 **"Sometimes, the thing"**: Seth Godin, "Measure What You Care About (Re: The Big Sign over Your Desk)," sethgodin.typepad .com, February 14, 2015, http://sethgodin.typepad.com/seths_blog/2015/02/measure-what-you-care-about-avoiding-the-siren-of-the -stand-in.html.

DATA IS ONLY AS GOOD AS ITS SOURCE, AND DOESN'T REPLACE INTUITION.

301 **Here's the chart:** superpaow, "My eyes hurt," Reddit, August 2017, www.reddit.com/user/superpaow.

301 **As *Quartz* reported:** Nikhil Sonnad, "The Misleading Chart Showing Google Searches for 'My Eyes Hurt' After the Eclipse," *Quartz*, August 23, 2017, https://qz.com/1060484/solar-eclipse-2017-solar-eclipse-2017-google-search-data-for-my-eyes-hurt-didnt-really -spike-after-the-solar-eclipse.

302 **25 percent of Muslims:** "Poll of U.S. Muslims Reveals Ominous Levels of Support for Islamic Supremacists' Doctrine of Shariah, Jihad," Center for Security Policy, June 23, 2015, www.centerforsecuritypolicy.org/2015/06/23/nationwide-poll-of-us-muslims-shows -thousands-support-shariah-jihad.

303 **opt-in online survey:** Lauren Carroll and Louis Jacobson, "Trump Cites Shaky Survey in Call to Ban Muslims from Entering US," PolitiFact, December 9, 2015, www.politifact.com/truth-o-meter/statements/2015/dec/09/donald-trump/trump-cites-shaky-survey -call-ban-muslims-entering.

STRESS-TEST YOUR OPINIONS WITH RADICAL TRUTHFULNESS.

305 **"I wanted to make"**: Ray Dalio, "How to Build a Company Where the Best Ideas Win," TED talk, April 2017, www.ted.com/talks/ray _dalio_how_to_build_a_company_where_the_best_ideas_win/transcript?language=en.

306 **"Rules for Bridgewater's"**: Rob Copeland and Bradley Hope, "The World's Largest Hedge Fund Is Building an Algorhythmic Model from Its Employees' Brains," *Wall Street Journal*, December 22, 2016, www.wsj.com/articles/the-worlds-largest-hedge-fund-is -building-an-algorithmic-model-of-its-founders-brain-1482423694.

307 **"Bridgewater says about"**: Ibid.

307 **"Understand that the ability"**: Ray Dalio, "Full Text of 'Bridgewater Ray Dalio Principles,'" archive.org, 2011, https://archive.org /stream/BridgewaterRayDalioPrinciples/Bridgewater%20-%20Ray%20Dalio%20-%20Principles_djvu.txt.

WITH NAIVETY COMES OPENNESS.

308 **"Knowing when to ignore"**: John Maeda (@johnmaeda), "Knowing *when* to ignore your experience is a true sign of experience," Twitter, May 1, 2016, 8:32 P.M., https://twitter.com/johnmaeda/status/726977556008701952.

SHARPENING YOUR EDGE

LEAVE SOME MARGIN TO MINE THE CIRCUMSTANTIAL.

324 **"mistakes or tricks"**: Behance Team, "Seek Stimulation from Randomness," 99U, accessed March 23, 2018, http://99u.adobe.com /articles/5693/seek-stimulation-from-randomness.

WHEN YOU FAIL TO DISCONNECT, YOUR IMAGINATION PAYS THE PRICE.

327 **a movement called the "Sabbath Manifesto"**: "Sabbath Manifesto," www.sabbathmanifesto.org, 2010, www.sabbathmanifesto .org.

327 **called the "Unplug Challenge"**: "Join Our Unplugging Movement," sabbathmanifesto.org, 2010, www.sabbathmanifesto.org /unplug_challenge.

328 **"National Day of Unplugging"**: "National Day of Unplugging," accessed March 23, 2018, www.nationaldayofunplugging.com.

328 **The manifesto included ten principles:** "Sabbath Manifesto."

STAYING PERMEABLE AND RELATABLE

REMOVE YOURSELF TO ALLOW OTHERS' IDEAS TO TAKE HOLD.

333 **"I really appreciate the power"**: Hrishikesh Hirway, "Episode 70: Weezer," *Song Exploder*, April 18, 2016, https://songexploder.net /weezer.

THE FINAL MILE

APPROACHING THE FINISH LINE

STAY IN THE EARLY INNINGS.
350 **$19** *billion* **seemed:** Josh Constine, "A Year Later, $19 Billion for WhatsApp Doesn't Sound So Crazy," *TechCrunch*, February 19, 2015, https://techcrunch.com/2015/02/19/crazy-like-a-facebook-fox.

350 **in February 2018, WhatsApp:** Rani Molla, "WhatsApp Is Now Facebook's Second-biggest Property, Followed by Messenger and Instagram," *Recode*, February 1, 2018, www.recode.net/2018/2/1/16959804/whatsapp-facebook-biggest-messenger-instagram -users.

PASSING THE BATON

YOU ARE NOT YOUR WORK.
360 **"I am not my Twitter":** Rohan Gunatillake, "You Are Not Your Work," 99U, 2015, 99u.adobe.com/videos/51943/rohan-gunatillake -you-are-not-your-work#.

ASPIRE TO FINISH ON YOUR OWN TERMS.
362 **a documentary was filmed:** Isuzu Sakurada, *Sakurada: Zen Chef*, directed by Hirokazu Kishida, Seattle, 2016, http://zenchef.strik ingly.com.

NEVER BEING FINISHED

CONTINUING TO LEARN IS AN ELIXIR TO LIFE.
366 **holds more than $600 billion:** "Warren Buffett: Latest Portfolio," Warren Buffett Stock Portfolio, February 14, 2018, http://warren buffettstockportfolio.com.

366 **Buffett publicly stated:** Henry Blodget, "Here's the Real Reason Warren Buffett Doesn't Invest in Technology—Or Bitcoin," *Business Insider*, March 26, 2014, www.businessinsider.com/why-buffett-doesnt-invest-in-technology-2014-3.

366 **one of Apple's largest:** Chuck Jones, "Apple Is Now Warren Buffett's Largest Investment," *Forbes*, February 15, 2018, www.forbes .com/sites/chuckjones/2018/02/15/apple-is-now-warren-buffetts-largest-investment/#35e572fb4313.

367 **"had plenty of ways":** Jen Wieczner, "Not Buying Google Is Berkshire Hathaway's Biggest Mistake," *Fortune*, May 6, 2017, http:// fortune.com/2017/05/06/warren-buffett-berkshire-hathaway-apple-google-stock.

367 **between six hundred and one thousand:** Andrew Merle, "If You Want to Be Like Warren Buffett and Bill Gates, Adopt Their Voracious Reading Habits," *Quartz*, April 23, 2016, https://qz.com/668514/if-you-want-to-be-like-warren-buffett-and-bill-gates-adopt -their-voracious-reading-habits.

367 **"Read five hundred pages":** Steve Jordon, "Investors Earn Handsome Paychecks by Handling Buffett's Business," *Omaha World-Herald*, April 28, 2013, www.omaha.com/money/investors-earn-handsome-paychecks-by-handling-buffett-s-business/article _bh1fc40f-e6f9-549d-be2f-be1cf4c0da03.html.

TO BE DONE IS TO DIE.
374 **"we like lists":** Susanne Beyer and Lothar Gorris, "We Like Lists Because We Don't Want to Die," *Spiegel*, November 11, 2009, www .spiegel.de/international/zeitgeist/spiegel-interview-with-umberto-eco-we-like-lists-because-we-don-t-want-to-die-a-659577.html.

Index

progress (cont.)
  process and, 154
progress bars, 181
prototypes and mock-ups, 161–63
Psychological Bulletin, 272
psychological safety, 122
Psychological Science, 272–73
psychology, 316, 317

Quartz, 37–38, 108, 301
questions, 69–71, 183–84, 321
Quiller-Couch, Arthur, 220
Quinn, Megan, 303–4
quitting, perspective and, 62–64
Quora, 138, 167

Rad, Sean, 259
Radcliffe, Jack, 197
Rams, Dieter, 230
reactionary workflow, 327, 328
Ready, The, 179
reality-distortion field, 41
Reboot, 327
Reddit, 261, 300, 302
rejection, 58
relatability, 57
relationships:
  commitments and, 283–84
  and how others perceive you, 316–17
  negotiation and, 286–87
REMIX, 165
resets, 63–64, 72–75
resistance, fighting, 35–36
resourcefulness, and resources, 100–102
reward system, short-circuiting, 24–27
Rhode Island School of Design, 186, 354
rhythm of making, 16
Ries, Eric, 194
risk, 122, 316, 337
ritual, 328
rock gardens, 67–68
routines, 323
ruckus, making, 337–38

Saatchi Online, 89
Sabbath Manifesto, 327–28
safety, psychological, 122
Sakurada, Isuzu, 361–62
salaries, 141–42
sales, salespeople, 262–63
Salesforce, 159, 204
Sandberg, Sheryl, 39

Santa Fe, USS, 167
satisficers, 229, 284–85
scalability, 242
Schouwenburg, Kegan, 50–51
Schwartz, Barry, 284–85
science vs. art of business, 310–13
Seinfeld, Jerry, 250
self, optimizing, 8, 17, 277–338
  crafting business instincts, 293–313
    auditing measures instead of blindly optimizing,
      297–99
    data vs. intuition in, 300–304
    mining contradictory advice and developing
      intuition, 294–96
    naivety and openness in, 308–9
    science vs. art of business, 310–13
    stress-testing opinions with truthfulness, 305–7
  planning and making decisions, 279–92
    focus and choice, 282–85
    making a plan vs. sticking to it, 280–81
    negotiation in, 286–87
    sunk costs and, 291–92
    timing and, 288–90
  sharpening your edge, 315–28
    building a network and increasing signal, 320–21
    commitments and, 318–19
    disconnecting, 326–28
    and how you appear to others, 316–17
    leaving margins for the unexpected, 324–25
    values and time use, 322–23
  staying permeable and relatable, 329–38
    attention and, 335–36
    credit-seeking and, 330–32
    and making a ruckus, 337–38
    removing yourself to allow for others' ideas, 333–34
self-awareness, 54–56, 305–7
selfishness, laziness, and vanity, 235–37
setbacks, 41
70/20/10 model for leadership development, 125
Shapeways, 50
Shiva, 374
shortcuts, 85
signal and noise, 320–21
Silberman, Ben, 86–87, 94, 112, 165, 319
Silicon Valley, 86
Simon, Herbert, 229, 284
SimpleGeo, 267
Sinclair, Jake, 334
skills, and choosing commitments, 283–84
Skybox, 101
sky decks, 117
Slack, 139, 210, 241

About the Author

Scott Belsky has spent more than a decade leading in the worlds of technology, design, and start-ups—as an entrepreneur, venture investor, and executive. In 2005, Scott founded Behance, the world's leading creative network used by more than twelve million professionals to showcase and discover creative work. Scott is also the founder of 99U—a conference and think tank devoted to productivity in the creative world—and is the author of the national bestselling book *Making Ideas Happen*. Upon Adobe's acquisition of Behance in late 2012, Scott took on additional responsibilities, including rebooting the company's mobile product and Creative Cloud service offerings. After some time off, spent as a full-time investor and working on this book, Scott returned to Adobe in early 2018 as the company's chief product officer overseeing the company's creative products. Scott also serves as an adviser and early-stage investor in fast-growing companies such as Pinterest, Uber, sweetgreen, and Periscope (now a part of Twitter). He is also a Venture Partner with Benchmark, a Silicon Valley venture capital firm, and is the cofounder of Prefer, a referral network for independent service professionals. Scott is deeply passionate about building and iterating products, managing and growing teams, and empowering the careers of creative people.